VOLUME 4

THE
Afterlife
SERIES

Heaven

THE FINAL DESTINATION
FOR BELIEVERS

Don Stewart

Heaven:
The Final Destination For Believers
© 2016 By Don Stewart

Published by Educating Our World
www.educatingourworld.com
All rights reserved

English Versions Cited

The various English versions which we cite in this course, apart from the King James Version, all have copyrights. They are listed as follows.

TABLE OF CONTENTS

Heaven: The Final Destination For Believers
(Volume 4 of 5)

We now arrive at our fourth book in the series on the afterlife. In our first book, we looked at the subjects of death and dying, and then how we should live in the light of eternity.

In our second volume, we considered what happens one second after we die. We saw what the Bible has to say about the condition of people immediately after death.

Our third volume covered the subjects of the resurrection of the dead and the coming biblical judgments.

In this book, we will look at the subject of the final destination of those who believe in the God of the Bible. Scripture says that when believers die in Jesus Christ they go to be with the Lord in a place called heaven.

There are so many questions that arise about heaven. Where is it? What will people do in heaven? Will we recognize our loved ones?

This book deals with these and other questions about the future home of believers.

QUESTION 1

Does Heaven Actually Exist?

It has been said that everyone thinks about heaven, even if only to deny that such a place exists. We all want to know if this life is all that there is or if there is something that awaits us in the hereafter.

In fact, the Bible records the question that a man named Job asked some 3,500 years ago.

> If a person dies, will he go on living? (Job 14:14 God's Word).

People are still asking this question today. Indeed, we have so many questions about the afterlife.

Is there some place of happiness on the "other side?" Does heaven really exist? If so, then what can we know about it?

THE BIBLE HAS THE ANSWER

Fortunately, we do have an authoritative source that provides us the answer, the Bible. It has much to say on this matter.

Indeed, the Scripture teaches that death is not the cessation of our existence. In fact, the Living God has made humans to exist for all eternity; though not in this present body. Those who follow God's provision and trust Jesus Christ as their Savior will spend eternity in

His Holy presence. This will be their final state.

Therefore, the realistic hope of the believer is to be with God in a place called, "heaven." This being the case, we should learn as much as we can about our final destination.

HEAVEN CAN MEAN EITHER THE SKY ABOVE US OR THE RESIDENCE OF THE CREATOR

The primary meaning of the word translated "heaven" is the sky overhead. This is the meaning of the Hebrew *shamaim*. It from the word *shami* which means, "the high." The word came to mean not only the vast space overhead, but also the unseen mysterious world where the Creator resides.

The Greek word *ouranos* has the same idea. Sometimes *ouranos* is used in the singular, other times in the plural. However, there does not seem to be any real difference between the singular and plural usage of this term.

THE WORD HEAVEN IS USED IN A NUMBER OF WAYS IN THE BIBLE

The Hebrew and Greek words which are translated "heaven" in Scripture are used in a number of different ways. They include the following.

1. THE PHRASE "HEAVEN AND EARTH" MEANS THE ENTIRE UNIVERSE

The word heaven is used with the word "earth" to mean the universe. The first verse of the Bible reads in this manner.

> In the beginning God created the heaven and the earth (Genesis 1:1 KJV).

Thus, in the beginning, God created the universe. Since the Hebrews did not have a specific word for the entire universe, when they wanted to express this concept they said "heaven and earth." The technical term for this figure of speech is "merism."

2. HEAVEN CAN BE SYNONYMOUS FOR GOD HIMSELF

Heaven is sometimes used as a synonym for God. Before Jesus fed the five thousand, the Bible says the following.

> Jesus took the five loaves and the two fish. He looked up to heaven and gave thanks. He broke them into pieces. Then he gave them to the disciples to set in front of the people (Luke 9:16 NIV).

In this case, the phrase "looking up to heaven" is the same as saying "looking up to God."

In another example, we find the wayward son saying.

> I'll get up, go to my father, and say to him, Father, I have sinned against heaven and in your sight (Luke 15:18 HCSB).

Sinning against heaven means to sin against God. Thus, heaven is used as a synonym for God in the Scripture.

3. HEAVEN CAN REFER TO AN ACTUAL PLACE

The term heaven is also used in Scripture of an actual place. Indeed, it is more than just a state a mind. Jesus spoke of the rooms that He has prepared in this place.

> My Father's house has many rooms. If that were not true, would I have told you that I'm going to prepare a place for you (John 14:2 God's Word).

The Lord Jesus is preparing an actual place for those people who belong to Him. Notice that He called this place, "My Father's house."

In addition, when He left the earth, the Bible says that Jesus ascended to a genuine place. We read about this in the Book of Acts.

> After Jesus said this, he was taken up to heaven. They watched until a cloud hid him from their sight. While he

was going up, they kept on looking at the sky. Suddenly two men dressed in white clothing stood beside them. "Men of Galilee," they said, "why do you stand here looking at the sky? Jesus has been taken away from you into heaven. But he will come back in the same way you saw him go" (Acts 1:9-11 NIV).

Jesus obviously went somewhere when He ascended upward. The Scripture says that He went to heaven.

Peter would later write that Jesus went to a place of honor. He put it this way.

Now Christ has gone to heaven. He is seated in the place of honor next to God, and all the angels and authorities and powers are bowing before him (1 Peter 3:22 NLT).

The place of honor was next to God the Father. As God the Son, this position was rightfully His.

4. HEAVEN SOMETIMES REFERS TO THE ACTUAL PRESENCE OF GOD

Although heaven is an actual place, the term can also refer to being in the presence of God. Jesus said.

What about someone who says in front of others that he knows me? I will also say in front of my Father who is in heaven that I know him. But what about someone who says in front of others that he doesn't know me? I will say in front of my Father who is in heaven that I don't know him (Matthew 10:32-33 NIV).

The actual presence of the Lord is termed "heaven."

In the Book of Revelation, John spoke of the time when God Himself would live among His people. Heaven, in this case, equals the presence of God who is dwelling among His people.

I heard a loud voice from the throne say, "God lives with humans! God will make his home with them, and they will be his people. God himself will be with them and be their God" (Revelation 21:3 God's Word).

The good news is that believers will one day live in the presence of the Living God. This truly will be heaven!

5. HEAVEN IS THE PLACE OF BELIEVER'S CITIZENSHIP

The Bible also says that heaven is a place where believers have their true or genuine citizenship. Paul wrote to the Philippians.

But we are citizens of heaven. And we can hardly wait for a Savior from there. He is the Lord Jesus Christ. He has the power to bring everything under his control. By his power he will change our earthly bodies. They will become like his glorious body (Philippians 3:20-21 NIV).

One can only have citizenship in a real place! Therefore, heaven must truly exist.

All of these facts from Scripture make it clear that heaven is indeed a genuine place.

SUMMARY TO QUESTION 1
DOES HEAVEN ACTUALLY EXIST?

While many people think heaven is only a state of mind, or a mythological place, Scripture makes it clear that heaven is an actual place that exists. From the Bible, the Word of God, we discover the following about heaven.

For one thing, we find that the word translated heaven in the Bible has a number of different meanings. The Hebrew and Greek words can mean either the sky above or the place where God resides in a special way.

When the terms "heaven and earth" are used together it means the entire universe.

In Scripture, the term heaven is often synonymous for God Himself. Praying to heaven has the idea of praying to God. Looking up to heaven means looking up to God, etc.

However, there is an actual place called heaven. Jesus ascended to a definite place when He left this world. He called it "My Father's house."

At times, the word heaven is used for the idea of being in God's presence. In fact, in eternity, when the Lord creates a new heaven and a new earth, God will dwell among His people. In this sense, heaven, is where the presence of God is.

We are also told that heaven is the place of citizenship for the believer. Since you cannot be a citizen of some place which does not exist, this is another indication of the reality of heaven.

In sum, from the totality of Scripture, we can easily see that heaven is a place which actually does exist.

What Is Heaven Like? (Does It Actually Have Streets Of Gold And Pearly Gates?)

Do we have any idea of what heaven is really like? Do we know what it looks like? What goes on in God's presence? Does it actually have golden streets and pearly gates? Does the Bible tell us anything about it?

Happily, the Bible, in both testaments, gives us a good idea of what heaven is all about.

THE OLD TESTAMENT TEACHING ABOUT HEAVEN

In the Old Testament, we are told a number of things about the future home of believers. This includes the following teaching about heaven.

1. IT IS THE SEAT OF GOD'S THRONE

To begin with, heaven is the seat of God's throne. The psalmist wrote the following.

> The LORD has established His throne in heaven, and His kingdom rules over all (Psalm 103:19 HCSB).

Therefore, we find that the throne of God is in heaven.

2. IT IS WHERE GOD RULES

God rules in both heaven and the earth from His place in heaven. We read in Joshua the testimony of Rahab the harlot. She testified that the citizens of Jericho realized that the God of Israel, Yahweh or Jehovah, ruled in both heaven and on the earth. She said.

> And as soon as we heard it, our hearts melted, and there was no spirit left in any man because of you, for the LORD your God, he is God in the heavens above and on the earth beneath (Joshua 2:11 ESV).

The Lord rules from heaven above and has authority as well over the earth below.

3. IT IS WHERE GOD SPEAKS TO HIS PEOPLE

We also find from Scripture that heaven is a place from where God speaks to His people. Moses told the people of Israel about this. He wrote.

> From heaven he made you hear his voice. He wanted to teach you. On earth he showed you his great fire. You heard his words coming out of the fire (Deuteronomy 4:36 NIV).

Here heaven is referring to the place where the Lord speaks to His special people.

4. HE IS SURROUNDED BY SPIRITUAL BEINGS IN HEAVEN

We are also informed that in heaven God is surrounded by a great number of spiritual beings. We read the following account in the Book of First Kings.

> Micaiah continued, "Listen to the LORD's message. I saw the LORD sitting on his throne. Some of the angels of heaven were standing at his right side. The others were standing at his left side. So all of them were standing around him" (1 Kings 22:19 NIV).

Heaven is a place where spiritual beings exist. Not only is the God of the Bible there, He has innumerable spiritual beings with Him.

5. IT IS WHERE THE SINS FROM EARTH REACH

The sins and injustices from the people on the earth make it all the way into heaven. Scripture talks about the anger of God because the sin of Samaria had reached to heaven.

We read the following account in Second Chronicles.

> A prophet of the LORD named Oded was there. He went out to meet the army that came to Samaria and said to them, "Look, the LORD God of your ancestors handed them over to you because of His wrath against Judah, but you slaughtered them in a rage that has reached heaven" (2 Chronicles 28:9 HCSB).

The sins of these people reached high into heaven. In other words, it was so great that reached all the way to the presence of the Lord. This is a figurative way of explaining the horrible nature of the sin.

This sums up some of the things which the Old Testament has to say about heaven.

THE NEW TESTAMENT TEACHING ABOUT HEAVEN

The New Testament adds to our knowledge about the subject of heaven. From it, we learn the following truths.

1. THE NAMES OF BELIEVERS ARE WRITTEN IN HEAVEN

Heaven is a place where the names of believers are written. Jesus said.

> But don't rejoice just because evil spirits obey you; rejoice because your names are registered as citizens of heaven (Luke 10:20 NLT).

The believers have been registered with the Lord! Indeed, He knows the ones who are His. Indeed, their names are safe with Him in heaven.

2. THE TREASURE OF BELIEVERS RESIDES IN HEAVEN

Heaven is also the place where the believers in Jesus Christ have their real treasure. In the Sermon on the Mount, Jesus said.

> But lay up for yourselves treasures in heaven, where neither moth nor rust destroys and where thieves do not break in and steal (Matthew 6:20 NKJV).

Our treasures should be laid up in heaven, not here upon the earth.

To the rich young ruler, Jesus told him what he must do to have treasure in heaven.

> Then, looking at him, Jesus loved him and said to him, "You lack one thing: Go, sell all you have and give to the poor, and you will have treasure in heaven. Then come, follow Me" (Mark 10:21 HCSB).

The true treasures of believers are in heaven. This is something we should never forget. Indeed, in this instance, we find the Lord Jesus emphasizing this truth.

3. IT IS THE DIRECTION OF PRAYER

Heaven is where believers direct our prayers. On the night He was betrayed, we read of Jesus looking up into heaven and praying. The Bible says.

> After Jesus said this, he looked toward heaven and prayed. He said, "Father, the time has come. Bring glory to your Son. Then your Son will bring glory to you" (John 17:1 NIV).

He looked up toward the direction of His Father. We should do likewise when we address God the Father.

4. IT IS THE PRESENCE OF GOD

Heaven is where the presence of the God of the Bible resides in a unique way. John wrote of the Holy City, the future New Jerusalem, in the Book of Revelation. He said.

> But I saw no temple in it, for the Lord God Almighty and the Lamb are its temple (Revelation 21:22 NKJV).

No temple will be necessary in the future because the Lord God Almighty Himself, and the Lamb, God the Son, Jesus Christ, are that temple. Indeed, there is no need for any type of representation of His presence since the Lord Himself will dwell with us!

THE GOLDEN STREETS AND GATES OF PEARLS ARE IN THE NEW JERUSALEM

Finally, the golden streets and pearly gates do not portray heaven, the present abode of God, but rather the New Jerusalem which comes down out of heaven, the sky, as part of a new heaven and new earth. It is described in this manner.

> I saw a new heaven and a new earth. The first heaven and the first earth had disappeared, and so had the sea. Then I saw New Jerusalem, that holy city, coming down from God in heaven. It was like a bride dressed in her wedding gown and ready to meet her husband . . . Each of the twelve gates was a solid pearl. The streets of the city were made of pure gold, clear as crystal (Revelation 21:1,2,21 CEV).

The streets of the New Jerusalem. are paved with gold and the gates are made of pearls. It is part of the new heaven and new earth which are created after the old heaven and old earth disappear.

These are some of the things which the Bible has to say about heaven and what it is actually like. It will indeed be a wonderful place!

SUMMARY TO QUESTION 2
WHAT IS HEAVEN LIKE? (DOES IT ACTUALLY HAVE STREETS OF GOLD AND PEARLY GATES?)

From the biblical descriptions, we discover many things about the place the Bible calls heaven.

For one thing, the Old Testament says that heaven is the seat of God's throne. Indeed, it is the place where God's presence resides in a unique way. In fact, the Old Testament says that the Lord rules and reigns from this place called heaven.

In heaven, the Lord is surrounded by a large number of spiritual beings. They are there to do His bidding.

The Bible, in the Old Testament, says that heaven is where certain sins of the earth may eventually reach. In other words, the sins are so terrible they reach all the way to God's very presence.

The New Testament also has a number of things to say about heaven. For one thing, it tells us that the names of believers are written or registered in heaven. Those of us who belong to the Lord have our names inscribed in God's presence.

It is also the place where the treasures of believers are kept. This is a key point. We cannot lose these heavenly treasures because they are kept safe in the presence of the Lord.

Heaven is the direction in which believers pray. This makes sense because the place of God's unique presence is always described as somewhere above, never below.

The New Testament, like the Old Testament, describes heaven as the place where God's presence resides in a unique way. In some sense, He dwells there. Though certainly He is not limited to one particular place.

The famous streets of gold and the gates of pearls are part of the new heaven and new earth, the New Jerusalem. This new order will appear only after the old heaven and the old earth disappear.

However, the focus in this new heaven will not be so much on its beauty as it will be on the One which this new heaven glorifies, the living God.

This sums up a few of the many things we learn about heaven from the Scripture.

What Are The Various Ways In Which Heaven Is Described In The Bible?

Heaven, the everlasting home of believers, is depicted in a variety of ways in the Bible. These descriptions give us a better understand of this actual place where the God of the Bible resides in a unique way. We can make the following observations about heaven.

1. MY FATHER'S HOUSE

Jesus called the future home of believers "My Father's House." When speaking to His disciples on the night of His betrayal, He put it this way.

> Do not let your hearts be troubled. Trust in God; trust also in me. In my Father's house are many rooms; if it were not so, I would have told you. I am going there to prepare a place for you. And if I go and prepare a place for you, I will come back and take you to be with me that you also may be where I am (John 14:1-3 NIV).

This is a wonderful truth! God the Father is also our Father. Therefore, we are going home to the house of our loving Father when we die. He has a room that is being prepared for each of us. We have a home in heaven.

2. THE PLACE OF EVERLASTING INHERITANCE

Heaven is also called the place of everlasting, or eternal, inheritance of those who have believed. Indeed, it is an inheritance that will last forever. We read of this in Hebrews. It says,

Because Christ offered himself to God, he is able to bring a new promise from God. Through his death he paid the price to set people free from the sins they committed under the first promise. He did this so that those who are called can be guaranteed an inheritance that will last forever (Hebrews 9:15 God's Word).

Heaven is the forever inheritance of the believer.

The Apostle Paul added more. He said that, as co-heirs of Jesus Christ, believers receive everything that He receives. He wrote.

Now if we are children, then we are heirs—heirs of God and co-heirs with Christ, if indeed we share in his sufferings in order that we may also share in his glory (Romans 8:17 NIV).

The New Living Translation puts it this way.

And since we are his children, we will share his treasures— for everything God gives to his Son, Christ, is ours, too. But if we are to share his glory, we must also share his suffering (Romans 8:17 NLT).

We share His treasures as co-heirs. Indeed, all the benefits of heaven are ours because of Jesus.

3. A TEMPLE

Heaven is also symbolically referred to as a temple. We find this reference by King David in the Old Testament book of Second Samuel. As he was fleeing from his enemies, as well as King Saul, David acknowledged that God heard his cries for help. He actually sang these words.

I called on the Lord in my distress. I called to my God for help. He heard my voice from his temple, and my cry for help reached his ears (2 Samuel 22:7 God's Word).

In this instance, His temple refers to heaven or God's presence. It was not referring to any earthly temple because no temple existed at that time.

4. A CITY, A COUNTRY, AND A HEAVENLY HOMELAND

Heaven is also compared to a country, a city, as well as our heavenly homeland. We read about all of this in one passage in the letter to the Hebrews. It says.

> And obviously people who talk like that are looking forward to a country they can call their own. If they had meant the country they came from, they would have found a way to go back. But they were looking for a better place, a heavenly homeland. That is why God is not ashamed to be called their God, for he has prepared a heavenly city for them (Hebrews 11:14-16 NLT).

In this heavenly country, the writer to the Hebrews says that God has prepared a heavenly city for His people. This heavenly city will be our home!

5. THE CITY OF THE LIVING GOD, MT. ZION, THE HEAVENLY JERUSALEM

In one verse in the Book of Hebrews, we have three different names given for heaven. They are as the city of the living God, Mt. Zion, and the heavenly Jerusalem. The writer to these Hebrews Christians put it this way.

> But you have come to Mount Zion, to the heavenly Jerusalem, the city of the living God. You have come to thousands upon thousands of angels in joyful assembly (Hebrews 12:22 NIV).

These are further descriptive terms of our heavenly home.

6. THE HOLY CITY

In the Book of Revelation, we find that the old heaven and earth will pass away and that there will be a new heaven and a new earth. In the new heaven, there is a "New Jerusalem." It is called the "Holy City." John wrote.

> I saw the Holy City, the new Jerusalem, coming down out of heaven from God, prepared as a bride beautifully dressed for her husband (Revelation 21:2 NIV).

The Holy City is indeed an appropriate name for our heavenly home. Everything has been made new!

GOD'S KINGDOM IS MORE THAN HEAVEN

Believers will spend eternity in God's presence but we will not be limited to heaven. Not only will heaven be the home of believers, so will the new earth. God's kingdom involves everything there is, the heavens and the earth. In other words, it is the entire universe.

SUMMARY TO QUESTION 3
WHAT ARE THE VARIOUS WAYS HEAVEN IS DESCRIBED IN THE BIBLE?

Heaven is a real place. There is no doubt about this. It is described in a number of ways in Scripture. They can be summarized as follows.

Jesus called heaven "My Father's house." According to Jesus, God the Father is preparing a room for each of us who believe.

We are also told that heaven is a place of everlasting inheritance for the believer. It is in heaven where we receive our inheritance because we are fellow-heirs with Jesus. In other words, we receive these things because of Him.

Heaven is also compared to a temple. The temple on earth represented the presence of the Lord. Heaven is where the presence of the Lord dwells in a special way. Therefore, there will be no need for an actual temple in heaven because God the Father, and God the Son, Jesus Christ, will be the temple.

Heaven is also called home. Our heavenly home is also called a heavenly city and a better country. Even the richest person in this world has nothing in comparison to the better country to which believers are going.

We also find it called the city of the living God. It is the place where God Himself will personally dwell with His people.

Finally, when the Lord creates a new heaven He will also create a heavenly city called the "New Jerusalem." It is called the "Holy City." This emphasizes that people in heaven are holy or set apart from all the evil in the previous world.

In sum, heaven is the place where all those who have trusted the promises of God can look forward to spending eternity.

Yet, the Bible also says God's kingdom involves more than what we call heaven. Indeed, it also includes the entire universe. Everything in the universe is His and because we belong to Him we will share these things also. Heaven is indeed described as something wonderful!

QUESTION 4

What Is Paradise?
Is It The Same As Heaven?

Three times in the New Testament we are told of a place called "paradise." What is paradise? Where is it? Is it another term for heaven or is it a separate place?

The evidence will show that it is indeed a synonym for heaven.

THE BIBLICAL REFERENCES TO PARADISE

We find the following references to paradise in Scripture.

1. THE REPENTANT CRIMINAL NEXT TO JESUS ON THE CROSS WAS PROMISED PARADISE

As He was being crucified, Jesus told the repentant criminal, that was dying next to Him on the cross, that he would be with the Lord in paradise. Luke records the promise which Jesus gave to this individual.

> And Jesus said to him, "Assuredly, I say to you, today you will be with Me in Paradise" (Luke 23:43 NKJV).

He was promised that he would be immediately with Jesus in God's presence. Indeed, the man would be in a place called paradise.

2. PAUL SAID THAT THE THIRD HEAVEN IS PARADISE

Paul told the Corinthians that he had once been caught up to the third heaven, which he defines as paradise. He described this experience in the following manner.

> I was caught up into the third heaven fourteen years ago. Whether my body was there or just my spirit, I don't know; only God knows. But I do know that I was caught up into paradise and heard things so astounding that they cannot be told (2 Corinthians 12:2-4 NLT).

The "third heaven" is another way of describing the presence of the Lord. Therefore, we find that paradise means heaven; the special habitation of God.

3. PARADISE HAS BEEN LOST BUT IT WILL BE REGAINED

The Book of Revelation also speaks of paradise. John recorded Jesus saying the following to the churches.

> He who has an ear, let him hear what the Spirit says to the churches. To the one who conquers I will grant to eat of the tree of life, which is in the paradise of God (Revelation 2:7 ESV).

Later in the Book of Revelation we are told about this tree of life which will be in the Holy City, the New Jerusalem. Believers will be able to eat of this tree in paradise.

The reference to the tree of life in the Book of Revelation speaks of the paradise that was originally lost in the Garden of Eden. It has been regained through the sacrifice of Jesus Christ on the cross at Calvary. This is the great message of Scripture. Paradise lost will be paradise regained.

IT IS A REFERENCE TO HEAVEN

From Scripture we find that paradise and heaven are different descriptions of the same place.

SUMMARY TO QUESTION 4
WHAT IS PARADISE? IS IT THE SAME AS HEAVEN?

One of the words used in Scripture to describe the next life is paradise. The word paradise is used in the Bible as a synonym for the presence of the Lord, heaven. It is employed three times in the New Testament. The three times all refer to the place where the God of the Bible dwells, heaven.

In one instance, Jesus promised the repentant criminal who was crucified next to Him would be immediately in paradise. This would be understood by the man to refer to God's presence. Paradise is where God is.

The Apostle Paul told the church at Corinth that he had been previously caught up in the "third heaven." Paul defined the third heaven as paradise. The third heaven is the place where God dwells in a unique way. Again, paradise is equal to God's presence.

Furthermore, since Jesus promised the criminal next to him that he would be immediately in paradise, and since we are told paradise is the "third heaven" the abode of God, then the criminal went immediately to heaven upon his death.

The Book of Revelation speaks of the tree of life in the paradise of God. This passage refers to the New Jerusalem, the Holy City, which comes down from heaven after the Last Judgment. It is another reference to the presence of the Lord. The paradise which was lost in the Garden of Eden will be regained in eternity.

Simply put, paradise is another way of saying "heaven."

What Is Abraham's Bosom?(Abraham's Lap, Or Side) Is It A Description Of Heaven?

The Scripture speaks of a place for the dead that is called "Abraham's bosom" or "Abraham's lap, or side." We read of this place in a story told by Jesus and recorded in Luke's gospel. The reference is as follows.

> So it was that the beggar died, and was carried by the angels to Abraham's bosom. The rich man also died and was buried. "And being in torments in Hades, he lifted up his eyes and saw Abraham afar off, and Lazarus in his bosom" (Luke 16:22,23 NKJV).

The rich man was brought to a place called "Abraham's bosom." The New Living Translation renders the verses in this manner.

> Finally, the beggar died and was carried by the angels to be with Abraham. The rich man also died and was buried, and his soul went to the place of the dead. There, in torment, he saw Lazarus in the far distance with Abraham (Luke 16:22,23 NLT).

This version translates it "to be with Abraham." Other translations use the phrase "Abraham's side."

What exactly does this mean? Is it, like paradise, another term for heaven? As we examine the Scripture we will discover that it is indeed another way the Bible describes heaven.

From Scripture, we learn the following.

1. IT IS THE PLACE OF HONOR

In this story which Jesus gave, we are told that Lazarus reclined at Abraham's side. This was a position for the guest of honor at a banquet.

We read in the gospels that the Apostle John, the disciple that Jesus loved, had that honored position next to Christ.

> One of them, the disciple whom Jesus loved, was reclining next to him (John 13:23 NIV).

The Contemporary English Version puts it this way.

> Jesus' favorite disciple was sitting next to him at the meal (John 13:23 CEV).

Therefore, this place, which is next to the host of the banquet, is one of honor.

In fact, we find the Contemporary English Version rendering the verse in Luke in this manner.

> The poor man died, and angels took him to the place of honor next to Abraham. The rich man also died and was buried (Luke 16:22 CEV).

The image, therefore, indicates a place of high honor where the person is warm and secure.

2. GOD PROMISED BELIEVERS THEY WOULD BE UNITED WITH ABRAHAM

Jesus also taught that those who trusted in God's Word were promised to be with Abraham in God's kingdom. Christ said the following about the inhabitants of heaven.

I can guarantee that many will come from all over the world. They will eat with Abraham, Isaac, and Jacob in the kingdom of heaven (Matthew 8:11 God's Word).

Here Abraham is said to be with Isaac and Jacob in the kingdom of heaven. Therefore, the beggar Lazarus in Jesus' story was brought to a place of high honor with these patriarchs.

WHAT DOES THE TERM ABRAHAM'S SIDE MEAN?

What is this place that is called Abraham's bosom, or Abraham's side? There are a number of views that Bible students hold. They include the following.

OPTION 1: IT IS SYNONYMOUS WITH DEATH

Abraham's side, or bosom, is seen by some Bible students as a term that is synonymous with death. Those who are in Abraham's bosom are those who have died. Therefore, it is a symbolic way of describing the dead. Hence, both believer and unbeliever would be with Abraham when they died. Thus, it is a neutral term.

RESPONSE

This term is not neutral. Indeed, it is used for a place of high honor. Those who have died in unbelief certainly would not go to such a place. In fact, in His response to the great faith showed by a Roman centurion, Jesus said the following.

> When Jesus heard this he was amazed and said to those who followed him, "I tell you the truth, I have not found such faith in anyone in Israel! I tell you, many will come from the east and west to share the banquet with Abraham, Isaac, and Jacob in the kingdom of heaven, but the sons of the kingdom will be thrown out into the outer darkness, where there will be weeping and gnashing of teeth (Matthew 8:10-12 NET).

Note that these unbelieving Jews, the "sons of the kingdom" would not be with Abraham in the next world. This is further evidence that "Abraham's side" was only reserved for the righteous.

OPTION 2: IT IS HADES OR SHEOL

There is also the view that Abraham's bosom is another way of describing the unseen realm of the dead. This is known as Hades in the New Testament or Sheol in the Old Testament. Those in Abraham's bosom are in a specific place; the realm of the dead. This understanding would also have this to be a neutral term. It describes the place where all the dead gather.

RESPONSE

The problem with this view is that Jesus makes the distinction between Hades, where the dead rich man was, and Abraham's side, the place of honor. Furthermore, the Lord said that there was a great gulf, or wide area, between the two. In His story, the Lord has Abraham saying the following words to the rich man.

> Besides, a wide area separates us. People couldn't cross it in either direction even if they wanted to (Luke 16:26 God's Word).

Therefore, we are looking at two distinct places.

OPTION 3: IT WAS THE TEMPORARY PLACE OF RIGHTEOUS DEAD

There is a third option that limits Abraham's side to the righteous or believers. Abraham's side, or bosom, is also thought to be the specific place where only the righteous dead were gathered. It is not to be equated with the general idea of death or the general realm of the dead, Hades or Sheol.

Therefore, when someone was in Abraham's bosom, they were with the righteous dead, not in the general population of the dead. It is argued that Hades is only connected with the rich man while Lazarus is afar off in another place; a compartment in the unseen realm for the righteous.

Those who hold this view usually see Abraham's bosom as a temporary place of waiting for the righteous dead. In other words, it only existed until Christ came.

When the Messiah, Jesus Christ, came as promised, He emptied Abraham's bosom and brought the inhabitants with Him to heaven. It is usually thought that this occurred at His resurrection from the dead or at His ascension into heaven.

Thus, upon Jesus' resurrection from the dead or His ascension into heaven, those who had previously been in a place of waiting, usually thought to be somewhere underneath the earth, were now able to enter into God's presence. If this is the case, then Abraham's bosom no longer exists.

RESPONSE

There is nothing in the text that indicates that Lazarus was in some compartment underneath the earth. Every indication from Scripture is that the righteous dead were brought immediately to the presence of the Lord in heaven.

OPTION 4: IT IS HEAVEN

The best answer is that Abraham's bosom was simply another description of heaven. It has nothing to do with the unseen realm of the dead or some temporary place for deceased believers. It is merely one of a number of terms, like paradise, which the Bible uses for being in God's presence. Indeed, Scripture indicates that every righteous person who has died goes immediately into the presence of the Lord.

PARADISE, THE THIRD HEAVEN, AND ABRAHAM'S BOSOM ARE SYNONYMOUS

We know Abraham's bosom is the same as heaven for the following reasons.

First, the Apostle Paul was taken to the third heaven, the special abode of God. He also called this place paradise. We read about this in 2 Corinthians.

> I know a man in Christ who fourteen years ago (whether in the body or out of the body I do not know, God knows) was caught up to the third heaven. And I know that this man (whether in the body or apart from the body I do not know, God knows) was caught up into paradise and heard things too sacred to be put into words, things that a person is not permitted to speak (2 Corinthians 12:2-4 NET).

Therefore, these two terms, the third heaven and paradise are synonymous.

Furthermore, we know that the criminal who died next to Jesus on the cross was promised that he would be in paradise, or heaven that day. This indicates that those who died before Christ came into the world went immediately to heaven upon their death.

If this is the case, then Lazarus, in this story of Jesus, must have been where all the other Old Testament believers gathered after their death, heaven. Since the place he was in is also called "Abraham's bosom" we can conclude that this is simply another name for heaven.

Therefore, the phrase Abraham's bosom or Abraham's side refers to heaven itself.

SUMMARY TO QUESTION 5
WHAT IS ABRAHAM'S BOSOM? (ABRAHAM'S LAP, OR SIDE) IS IT A DESCRIPTION OF HEAVEN?

In a story which Jesus gave of two people who had died and went to the unseen world of the dead, He spoke of the beggar Lazarus being in "Abraham's bosom" upon death while the rich man who had died was in "Hades." The phrase "Abraham's bosom" or "Abraham's side" is not explained for the reader.

The image of reclining in the lap, or at the side, of a person refers to a place of honor at a banquet. The guest would recline next to the host of the banquet and would place his head near or touching the host. Therefore, in this case, Lazarus was brought to a place of high honor upon his death since he was brought next to Abraham, the father of the Hebrew race.

There are four possible ways in which the phrase "Abraham's side" has been interpreted. They are as follows.

It has been used for a general term for being dead. Those who are in Abraham's bosom are the conscious dead. This would make it a neutral term which describes the place where anyone who had died would be gathered.

The problem with this view is that the term is one of honor. The unrighteous dead would actually be sent away from Abraham, Isaac, and Jacob as well as the other believers in the afterlife.

It is also argued that this is a specific reference to Sheol or Hades, the unseen realm of the dead. This is the temporary place where the dead now reside. If this is what the term meant, then it is neutral. It would not have any special meaning for the saved as opposed to the lost.

Again, we have the same problem with this view as the previous one. It is not a neutral term. In fact, Jesus taught that there was a "great gap" between the righteous and the unrighteous in the next world.

There is a third option which sees this term as having a special meaning for people who read or heard this passage being read. This perspective sees Abraham's bosom to be a specific term referring to the place of the righteous dead. In other words, this is the place where the living should want to go after their death. It is not the place where all the dead gather together. The location is usually assumed to be somewhere in the center of the earth.

According to Jesus, the righteous dead are separated from the unbelieving dead in the unseen realm. Abraham's bosom was the place where the righteous dead gathered before the coming of Christ, or the Messiah.

Once Jesus died for the sins of the world and then rose from the dead, He emptied Abraham's bosom and brought these people up from the earth directly into the presence of the Lord. This would make it only a temporary place for the righteous dead. It is no longer occupied.

The main problem with this view is that Scripture consistently teaches that the righteous dead go immediately to heaven, not to some waiting place deep in the earth.

Finally, a fourth option says that Abraham's bosom, or Abraham's side, is another term for heaven. Those who go to Abraham's bosom are going to what we know as heaven or the presence of the Lord. It did not refer to any temporary place of waiting. Those who died in the Old Testament period went to be immediately with the Lord.

In fact, we know that the criminal who died next to Jesus on the cross went immediately to heaven. Jesus said that he would be in paradise that very day.

In Second Corinthians, Paul equated the presence of the Lord, the third heaven, with paradise. Therefore, all Old Testament saints would have gone to heaven. Consequently, Abraham's bosom is another name for heaven.

Lazarus, therefore, like all believers who died in the period before Christ, went immediately into the presence of the Lord.

QUESTION 6

Did The Old Testament Believers
Go Immediately To Heaven When They Died?

What happened to the Old Testament believers when they died? Did they go to heaven or some other place? When Christ ascended into heaven did He take the Old Testament saints with Him or were they already there? What does the Bible have to say about these matters?

IS THERE A PLACE OF WAITING?

Some people feel the Old Testament saints went to a place specially created by God. Until Jesus Christ sacrificed Himself on the cross of Calvary, heaven was not open to them. Their sins were atoned for, or covered up, but they were not taken away. The death of Christ is what took away sin and allowed these saints to go to heaven.

At His Ascension, Jesus brought them to where they could not go before; heaven. Paul's statement to the Ephesians is said to be speaking of this event.

> For it says: When He ascended on high, He took prisoners into captivity; He gave gifts to people. But what does "He ascended" mean except that He descended to the lower parts of the earth? The One who descended is the same as the One who ascended far above all the heavens, that He might fill all things (Ephesians 4:8-10 HCSB).

This passage has been used to argue for a place of waiting for the Old Testament saints. It was not until Jesus ascended into heaven once and for all that these believers could also enter God's presence. Until their sins were taken away, they had to be in this place of waiting.

THIS IS NOT WHAT THE PASSAGE TEACHES

However, this passage does not teach this. In fact, there is nothing in the context that would indicate it is referring to Christ taking believers with Him to heaven after His resurrection from the dead.

Indeed, there are several possible ways of understanding Paul's statement without assuming that He was speaking of Christ bringing the Old Testament believers into heaven with Him upon His ascension.

There are a number of points we should make about the immediate fate of the Old Testament saints.

WE HAVE LITTLE INFORMATION IN THE OLD TESTAMENT ABOUT THE FATE OF THE DEAD

First of all, the Old Testament provides us with very little information on this issue. Yet there are a number of passages that indicate the belief that the dead would be with God in heaven. This can be seen as follows.

1. ENOCH AND ELIJAH WENT SOMEWHERE AFTER THEY LEFT THIS WORLD

We know that two Old Testament characters, Enoch and Elijah, did not die but were taken into the presence of God. When the prophet Elijah arrived in heaven he certainly found others apart from God and Enoch!

We also find Elijah appearing with Moses at Jesus' Transfiguration. Obviously, he was somewhere in the next world in a conscious state.

2. THERE WILL BE A GENERAL RESURRECTION OF THE DEAD

We also find the idea of a general resurrection of the dead was taught in the Old Testament. The prophet Daniel wrote about the day in which the dead would be raised.

> Many of those who sleep in the dust of the earth will awake, some to eternal life, and some to shame and eternal contempt (Daniel 12:2 HCSB).

Yet this hope was always something in the future. It did not speak of the current status of the righteous dead during the Old Testament period.

3. THE RIGHTEOUS WERE ALREADY WITH GOD IN HEAVEN

There are, however, passages that seem to speak of the righteous entering the presence of the Lord. David wrote about his desire to dwell in God's house forever. In the famous 23rd Psalm we read the following words.

> Surely goodness and mercy shall follow me all the days of my life; and I will dwell in the house of the Lord forever (Psalm 23:6 NKJV).

The house of the Lord may be a reference to heaven.

4. THE PSALMIST BELIEVED THAT HE WOULD BE WITH GOD

The psalmist believed his spirit, his real self, would be with God in the next world. He had the following hope.

> You guide me with your counsel, and afterward you will receive me to glory. Whom have I in heaven but you? And there is nothing on earth that I desire besides you (Psalm 73:24,25 ESV).

He had the belief that he would be with the Lord. There does not seem to be any idea of a waiting place between his death and the time he would be with Him.

5. ABRAHAM WAS ALIVE IN THE NEXT WORLD

In the story of the rich man and Lazarus, we find that Abraham was alive and content in the next world. Jesus said.

> The poor man died, and angels took him to the place of honor next to Abraham. The rich man also died and was buried (Luke 16:22 CEV).

Abraham was in an actual place in the unseen realm.

The Book of Hebrews indicates that Abraham went to heaven. We read the following.

> For he was looking forward to the city that has foundations, whose architect and builder is God (Hebrews 11:10 HCSB).

Abraham was certainly not by himself in the next world! Thus, the inference is that he would be with the Lord in heaven.

6. THE HEROES OF FAITH ARE IN HEAVEN

According to the writer to the Hebrews, all the heroes of faith were looking for that heavenly country. We read the following.

> All these faithful ones died without receiving what God had promised them, but they saw it all from a distance and welcomed the promises of God. They agreed that they were no more than foreigners and nomads here on earth. And obviously people who talk like that are looking forward to a country they can call their own. If they had meant the country they came from, they would have found a way to

go back. But they were looking for a better place, a heavenly homeland. That is why God is not ashamed to be called their God, for he has prepared a heavenly city for them (Hebrews 11:13-16 NLT).

These people are now in heaven.

We also read in Hebrews.

You have come to tens of thousands of angels joyfully gathered together and to the assembly of God's firstborn children (whose names are written in heaven). You have come to a judge (the God of all people) and to the spirits of people who have God's approval and have gained eternal life (Hebrews 12:22,23 God's Word).

The spirits of these people have been made perfect. Consequently, they are allowed to be in God's presence. They are in heaven.

ONE OTHER LINE OF EVIDENCE: THE CRIMINAL THAT DIED NEXT TO JESUS ON THE CROSS

There is one final thing we should mention. As we have seen, the criminal that died next to Jesus on the cross was promised that he would be immediately in paradise

Jesus answered him, "Truly I tell you, today you will be with me in paradise" (Luke 23:43 NIV).

We have also seen that paradise is defined as the "third heaven," the actual presence of the Lord.

I know a man in Christ who fourteen years ago was caught up to the third heaven . . . was caught up to paradise and heard inexpressible things, things that no one is permitted to tell (2 Corinthians 12:2,4 NIV).

From these verses we can make the following conclusion. The criminal was promised instant access to paradise. Since paradise is defined in 2 Corinthians 12 as the third heaven, the presence of the Lord, we can conclude that this man, who died before Jesus rose from the dead, was promised immediate access to the presence of the Lord, heaven.

This is another indication that all those who died during the Old Testament period went immediately to heaven.

SUMMARY TO QUESTION 6
DID OLD TESTAMENT BELIEVERS IMMEDIATELY GO TO HEAVEN WHEN THEY DIED?

The righteous individuals who died before the coming of Jesus Christ are now in God's presence. The biblical evidence indicates that this has always been true.

There are some Bible students who think that these Old Testament believers were in a temporary waiting place before the coming of Jesus Christ. This is usually linked to Paul's statement in Ephesians that Christ, upon His resurrection or ascension, brought those Old Testament saints into the presence of the Lord.

However, in context, this reference in Ephesians is not dealing with the fate of those who died before Christ came. In fact, there is nothing in the context that indicates this. Furthermore, there are a number of other ways to understand Paul's statement in this context and none of them have anything to do with the destiny of the Old Testament believers.

Add to this, we do know that the Old Testament believers went somewhere. Enoch and Elijah did not die but were translated or removed from the earth to heaven while they were still alive.

We know that Elijah appeared at Jesus' Transfiguration. This is further evidence that he was conscious in the realm of the dead.

In certain of the psalms there is the belief that the righteous would be in God's presence immediately upon their death. Nothing is said about some place of waiting.

We know that Abraham was alive in the next world after his death. In Jesus' story of the rich man and Lazarus, Abraham is seen as comforting Lazarus in the afterlife.

In the Book of Hebrews we are told that the heroes of the faith are now in heaven.

Finally, the criminal that died next to Jesus on the cross provides us with an example of what happened to Old Testament believers. Jesus promised him that he would be in paradise that day. Paradise is later defined by Paul as the "third heaven," the presence of the Lord. Thus, this man, who died before Jesus' resurrection and ascension went immediately to heaven.

Consequently, there is every indication that the Old Testament believer, upon their death, went to be immediately with the Lord in heaven.

QUESTION 7

What Are The
Three Heavens?

We have seen that the term heaven is used in a number of ways in Scripture. In addition, we have also noted that terms like "paradise" and "Abraham's side" are also references to heaven, the presence of the Lord.

Furthermore, we encounter the term "the third heaven" in Scripture. What exactly is it referring to?

We will discover that when the term "heaven" is not used symbolically in Scripture, it usually refers to one of three realms. The idea of more than one 'heaven" can be seen as follows.

JESUS PASSED THROUGH THE HEAVENS

The fact that Jesus "passed through the heavens" seems to give evidence there is more than one heaven. The writer to the Hebrews said.

> Therefore since we have a great high priest who has passed through the heavens—Jesus the Son of God—let us hold fast to the confession (Hebrews 4:14 HCSB).

Another translation puts it this way.

> We need to hold on to our declaration of faith: We have a superior chief priest who has gone through the heavens. That person is Jesus, the Son of God (Hebrews 4:14 God's Word).

Consequently, the reference to plural "heavens," seems to refer to more than one "heaven."

THERE IS A THIRD HEAVEN

Furthermore, the Bible specifically refers to the "third heaven." Paul wrote about this to the Corinthians. He stated is as follows.

> I know about one of Christ's followers who was taken up into the third heaven fourteen years ago. I don't know if the man was still in his body when it happened, but God certainly knows (2 Corinthians 12:2 CEV).

The third heaven is another term for the dwelling place of God. If there is a third heaven, it seems there must also be a first and second heaven! The Bible, however, does not mention a first and second heaven.

THE THREE HEAVENS EXPLAINED

Usually, the three heavens are divided as follows.

1. OUR IMMEDIATE ATMOSPHERE

2. OUTER SPACE (THE SUN, MOON, AND STARS)

3. THE HOME OF GOD

The biblical evidence for the three heavens is as follows.

THE ATMOSPHERIC HEAVEN-THE FIRST HEAVEN

The first heaven is linked to what we call the "atmospheric heaven." The atmospheric heaven includes the air that we breathe as well as the space that immediately surrounds the earth. The technical term for this is the "troposphere." It extends about twenty miles above the earth. The space above this is called the "stratosphere."

The Scripture uses the term heaven to describe this area.

Then the Lord said, "I will wipe off from the face of the earth mankind, whom I created, together with the animals, creatures that crawl, and birds of the sky — for I regret that I made them (Genesis 6:7 HCSB).

In this passage, the "birds of the sky" are the "birds of heaven." The Hebrew word used here is the same word, in other contexts, used of the presence of God, heaven.

Jesus also spoke of the "birds of the sky" or the "birds of the air." In the Sermon on the Mount the following words of Jesus are recorded.

Look at the birds of the air, for they neither sow nor reap nor gather into barns; yet your heavenly Father feeds them. Are you not of more value than they (Matthew 6:26 NKJV).

The word translated "air" is *ouranos*, the same Greek word that is elsewhere translated "heaven." Thus, the word can mean heaven, sky, or air. It all depends upon the context.

We have another example of this use of the term in the book of James. James wrote.

And he prayed again, and the heaven gave rain, and the earth produced its fruit (James 5:18 NKJV).

Here we are told the "heaven gave rain." Another translation puts it this way.

Then he prayed again, and the sky gave rain and the land produced its fruit (James 1:18 HCSB).

It is the sky which gave rain, the first heaven. Therefore, Scripture often uses the term heaven in the same way as we would use the word "sky."

2. THE CELESTIAL HEAVEN-THE SECOND HEAVEN

The term heaven is also used of what we call the celestial heaven. This is what is known as the "second heaven." This use of the term heaven refers to outer space or the stellar heaven. It includes the sun, moon, and stars. We find this use of the term in the words of Jesus when He describes coming events. He said.

> Immediately after those horrible days end, the sun will be darkened, the moon will not give light, the stars will fall from the sky, and the powers of heaven will be shaken (Matthew 24:29 NLT).

The stars are said to be "in heaven" or in "the sky."

The Scripture also speaks of heavenly spheres which beyond that which is visible from the earth. It is called the "heaven of heavens."

> Remember that the sky, the highest heaven, the earth and everything it contains belong to the Lord your God (Deuteronomy 10:14 God's Word).

The psalmist also wrote about this heaven of heavens. He said.

> Praise him, you highest heavens, and you waters above the heavens (Psalm 148:4 ESV).

Therefore, there seems to be a second heaven, a celestial heaven.

3. HEAVEN AS THE HOME OF GOD-THE THIRD HEAVEN

The Bible is clear that God cannot be limited to any one geographical place. At the dedication of the first temple in the city of Jerusalem, King Solomon asked the following question when praying to the Lord.

> But will God indeed live on earth? Even heaven, the highest heaven, cannot contain You, much less this temple I have built? (1 Kings 8:27 HCSB).

He realized that the Lord was not limited to that one particular place.

Indeed, the entire universe cannot contain Him.

Yet Scripture also teaches us that there is a certain geographical place where God's presence resides in some unique sense. It is also designated heaven. The writer to the Hebrews said.

> The main point we want to make is this: We do have this kind of chief priest. This chief priest has received the highest position, the throne of majesty in heaven (Hebrews 8:1 God's Word).

God's throne is spoken of as residing somewhere. Indeed, it in heaven.

A. THE MARTYR STEPHEN KNEW HE WOULD BE IN GOD'S PRESENCE

Stephen knew that upon his death he was going a specific place. This would be into the presence of the Lord.

> But he, being full of the Holy Spirit, gazed into heaven and saw the glory of God, and Jesus standing at the right hand of God (Acts 7:55 NKJV).

While God does not reside in one particular area, there is a place where His presence dwells in a unique way. Stephen, was allowed to see that place as he was nearing death.

B. HEAVEN IS GOD'S PRESENCE

Heaven is called the presence of God. We read in Hebrews.

> For Christ has entered into heaven itself to appear now before God as our Advocate. He did not go into the earthly place of worship, for that was merely a copy of the real Temple in heaven (Hebrews 9:24 NLT).

The exact location of the abode of God is not revealed in Scripture. It is merely spoken of as being above the first and second heavens.

IT IS AN ACTUAL PLACE

We can conclude that there is such a specific place as the third heaven. It is always spoken of as being above the first and second heaven. In addition, since these first two heavens are actual places we should also conclude that the third heaven is a real place also. There is no reason to assume it is symbolic especially since the first two heavens are speaking of known realities.

While the Lord is not limited to this third heaven, in some special way He has a place there. This is the clear teaching of the Bible on the subject.

SUMMARY TO QUESTION 7
WHAT ARE THE THREE HEAVENS?

Sometimes the word heaven is used symbolically in the Scripture. When used of an actual place, Scripture speaks of three distinct heavens. The Apostle Paul spoke of being transported to the "third heaven." What exactly is meant by these three heavens? What is the first and second heaven?

The first heaven is the immediate atmosphere above us. It is the sky; the place where birds fly. The technical term is the troposphere. The same Hebrew and Greek word translated as heaven is translated as "sky" in contexts which refer to the first heaven.

The second heaven is the stellar heaven. It is the place where the sun, moon, and stars exist. This is the stratosphere. Again, the same Hebrew and Greek words are used for this heaven as they are for the third heaven.

The third heaven is the special place where the God of the Bible resides in a unique way. It is always spoken of as being above the other two regions.

While God has some type of residence in the third heaven the biblical writers never assume that He is limited to that one area. Indeed, as King Solomon prayed at the dedication of the temple "even the heaven of heavens could not contain Him."

There are a couple of things we must take note of with respect to these three heavens. Since the first two regions are actual places, there is every reason to believe that the third region, or the third heaven, is also an actual place.

Yet, as we have emphasized, God is certainly not limited to one geographical place. His presence is everywhere in the universe.

What Is The New Heaven And New Earth?

The story of the Bible is one of paradise lost and then paradise regained. God originally created a perfect world that became imperfect when sin entered. The good news is that there will be a new heaven and a new earth one day. We can summarize what the Bible says as follows.

1. THE PRESENT EARTH HAS BEEN CURSED BECAUSE OF SIN

When humanity sinned against God, the earth was cursed. The Bible speaks of this in the Book of Genesis. It says.

> To Adam he said, "Because you listened to your wife and ate from the tree about which I commanded you, 'You must not eat of it,' "Cursed is the ground because of you; through painful toil you will eat of it all the days of your life. It will produce thorns and thistles for you, and you will eat the plants of the field" (Genesis 3:17,18 NIV).

Judgment was made against the original paradise, the earth is no longer perfect.

2. THE PRESENT HEAVEN AND EARTH WILL SOMEDAY PERISH

The Bible says this cursed earth, along with the present heaven, will one day perish. Isaiah the prophet wrote.

They will perish, but You will endure; all of them will wear out like clothing. You will change them like a garment and they will pass away (Psalm 102:26 HCSB).

The present heaven and the present earth will one day pass away.

Peter also wrote about this. He put it this way.

By the same word the present heavens and earth are reserved for fire, being kept for the day of judgment and destruction of the ungodly.

> But do not forget this one thing, dear friends: With the Lord a day is like a thousand years, and a thousand years are like a day. The Lord is not slow in keeping his promise, as some understand slowness. Instead he is patient with you, not wanting anyone to perish, but everyone to come to repentance. But the day of the Lord will come like a thief. The heavens will disappear with a roar; the elements will be destroyed by fire, and the earth and everything done in it will be laid bare. Since everything will be destroyed in this way, what kind of people ought you to be? You ought to live holy and godly lives as you look forward to the day of God and speed its coming. That day will bring about the destruction of the heavens by fire, and the elements will melt in the heat. But in keeping with his promise we are looking forward to a new heaven and a new earth, where righteousness dwells (2 Peter 3:7-13 NIV).

God, therefore will dissolve the old universe and make it new by means of fire.

3. THERE WILL BE A NEW HEAVEN AND A NEW EARTH

The good news is that there will be a new heaven and a new earth after the present heaven and earth are destroyed. The prophet Isaiah recorded God promising a new heaven and a new earth. He wrote the following.

I will create a new heaven and a new earth. Past things will not be remembered. They will not come to mind (Isaiah 65:17 God's Word).

The glorious promise of God is that this earth will be made new. This will be a reversal of the curse of Eden.

A. JESUS SPOKE OF THE RENEWAL OF ALL THINGS

This seems to be to what Jesus was referring when He returns to the earth. Jesus spoke of the future renewal of all things, or a Messianic Age. It will be the time when all things are made new. Matthew records our Lord saying the following.

Jesus said to them, "Truly I tell you, at the renewal of all things, when the Son of Man sits on his glorious throne, you who have followed me will also sit on twelve thrones, judging the twelve tribes of Israel (Matthew 19:28 NIV).

This can also be referred to as the "Messianic Age." We read.

Jesus said to them, "I assure you: In the Messianic Age, when the Son of Man sits on His glorious throne, you who have followed Me will also sit on 12 thrones, judging the 12 tribes of Israel" (Matthew 19:28 HCSB).

There is a coming "age of the Messiah."

THIS RENEWAL IS TAUGHT IN OTHER PLACES IN SCRIPTURE

We have the same thing taught other places in Scripture. For example, in the Book of Acts we read the following.

Heaven must receive Jesus until the time when everything will be restored as God promised through his holy prophets long ago (Acts 3:21 God's Word).

All things will be renewed or restored. It will be a time of universal restoration.

The Book of Revelation says that God will make all things new.

> Then the one sitting on the throne said: I am making everything new. Write down what I have said. My words are true and can be trusted (Revelation 21:5 CEV).

The present order of creation will be replaced. In this new order, the only people who exist will be God's people. They will live in the closest of relationships.

B. UNBELIEVERS HAVE NO PART IN THIS NEW WORLD

Those who have not trusted God's promises will not take part in the Holy City, the New Jerusalem. We read about this in the Book of Revelation. It says.

> But I will tell you what will happen to cowards and to everyone who is unfaithful or dirty-minded or who murders or is sexually immoral or uses witchcraft or worships idols or tells lies. They will be thrown into that lake of fire and burning sulfur. This is the second death (Revelation 21:8 CEV).

The Holy City is only for believers. Unbelievers are unwelcome.

In the same chapter of the Book of Revelation we read.

> But nothing unworthy will be allowed to enter. No one who is dirty-minded or who tells lies will be there. Only those whose names are written in the Lamb's book of life will be in the city (Revelation 21:27 CEV).

The new world is only for believers.

C. OUR HOPE IS IN AN ETERNAL INHERITANCE

The hope of the believer is in an inheritance that will not fade away. Peter wrote about this promised inheritance for believers. He said.

> Blessed be the God and Father of our Lord Jesus Christ, who according to His abundant mercy has begotten us again to a living hope through the resurrection of Jesus Christ from the dead, to an inheritance incorruptible and undefiled and that does not fade away, reserved in heaven for you, who are kept by the power of God through faith for salvation ready to be revealed in the last time (1 Peter 1:3-5 NKJV).

The hope we have is for an everlasting inheritance.

D. THE REALM OF GOD WILL NOT PASS AWAY

When we say that heaven will pass away this does not mean that the realm of God will cease to exist. As we have earlier noted, the Bible speaks of three heavens. The first is the atmosphere around the earth, the second is the sun moon and stars, while the third heaven is the presence of God.

Consequently, we are not to assume that all three of the heavens will pass away. The physical universe, however, has to be renewed. Therefore, it is the first and second heaven that will be changed but not the third heaven, the realm of God.

SUMMARY TO QUESTION 8
WHAT IS THE NEW HEAVEN AND NEW EARTH?

When Adam and Eve sinned the earth became cursed. We are still living under that curse. However, God has promised to destroy this old earth and heaven making something new. Indeed, the future home of the believer will be in the new heaven and new earth.

We should not, however, assume that this means the realm of God, heaven, will be made new. Indeed, Scripture speaks of three heavens. The realm of God is in the third heaven; a place where the sin of this world did not reach. It is only the first and second heaven, the atmosphere above the earth as well as the stellar heaven which have to be renewed. His throne in heaven is untouched by our sin.

After the final judgment, God will remake the present universe and form a new one; a universe without any remembrance of sin. Though the exact relationship between the old and the new is not entirely clear, it is clear that the new universe will be without sin or any corruption. It will be a wonderful place for believers.

What Are Some Of The Contrasts Between The Old Creation In Genesis And The Future Creation?

The very first verse of the Bible tells us that the Lord originally created the universe.

> In the beginning God created the heavens and the earth (Genesis 1:1 NIV).

The Bible also says that at some time in the future the Lord will create a new heaven and a new earth.

> Then I saw "a new heaven and a new earth," for the first heaven and the first earth had passed away (Revelation 21:1 NIV).

As we examine what the Bible says about the future creation of the Lord, we can make a number of observations and comparisons to the original creation as described in Genesis. They are as follows.

COMPARISON 1: GOD CREATED THE SUN (GENESIS 1:16)

In the original creation, the Lord set the sun in the sky.

> God made the two bright lights: the larger light to rule the day and the smaller light to rule the night (Genesis 1:16 God's Word).

The sun was created to give light to the world.

THERE IS NO NEED OF THE SUN (REVELATION 21:23)

However in the new creation, the sun will not exist. Speaking of the Holy City, the New Jerusalem, John wrote.

> The city does not need the sun or the moon to shine on it, for the glory of God gives it light, and the Lamb is its lamp (Revelation 21:23 NIV).

In God's future creation there will be no need for the sun.

COMPARISON 2: GOD ESTABLISHED THE NIGHT (GENESIS 1:16)

The Lord also made the moon to establish the night.

> God made the two bright lights: the larger light to rule the day and the smaller light to rule the night (Genesis 1:16 God's Word).

The lesser light, the moon was created for the night.

THERE IS NO NIGHT IN ETERNITY (REVELATION 22:5)

There will be no more night. In addition, there will not be any need of light from lamps or the sun because the Lord God will shine on them

> In the eternal realm, there shall never be a night. The Lord will be our light (Revelation 22:5 God's Word).

COMPARISON 3: THE LORD CREATED THE SEAS (GENESIS 1:10)

In the beginning, the Lord created the seas.

> God called the dry ground "land" and the waters "seas." And God saw that it was good (Genesis 1:10 NLT).

THE WILL BE NO MORE SEAS (REVELATION 21:1)

The seas have often caused fear and dread to the people of earth. In the future, there will be no more seas.

> Then I saw a new heaven and a new earth, for the old heaven and the old earth had disappeared. And the sea was also gone (Revelation 21:1 NLT).

Interestingly, the Lord makes this point at the very beginning of His explanation of the new creation; there will be no more seas.

COMPARISON 4: THE LORD ANNOUNCED THE CURSE (GENESIS 3:14-17)

When Adam and Eve sinned, the perfect creation became imperfect. The Lord explained the results of their sin.

> So the LORD God said to the snake: "Because of what you have done, you will be the only animal to suffer this curse— For as long as you live, you will crawl on your stomach and eat dirt. You and this woman will hate each other; your descendants and hers will always be enemies. One of hers will strike you on the head, and you will strike him on the heel." Then the LORD said to the woman, "You will suffer terribly when you give birth. But you will still desire your husband, and he will rule over you." The LORD said to the man, "You listened to your wife and ate fruit from that tree. And so, the ground will be under a curse because of what you did. As long as you live, you will have to struggle to grow enough food. Your food will be plants, but the ground will produce thorns and thistles. You will have to sweat to earn a living (Genesis 3:14-19 CEV).

The original creation had been spoiled by sin. Nothing will be the same as what was originally made.

THE CURSE HAS BEEN REMOVED (REVELATION 22:3)

In the new heaven and new earth there will be no more curse.

> God's curse will no longer be on the people of that city. He and the Lamb will be seated there on their thrones, and its people will worship God and will see him face to face. God's name will be written on the foreheads of the people (Revelation 22:3,4 God's Word).

The curse of Eden will one day be removed! What a wonderful day that will be!

COMPARISON 5: DEATH ENTERS OUR WORLD (GENESIS 3:19)

Death, or separation from God was one of the results of the original curse.

> By the sweat of your brow will you have food to eat until you return to the ground from which you were made. For you were made from dust, and to dust you will return (Genesis 3:19 NLT).

From dust to dust, this is the story of fallen humanity.

THE WILL BE NO MORE DEATH (REVELATION 21:4)

Death will be no more in the new world. No longer will there be any separation of believers from God.

> He will wipe every tear from their eyes, and there will be no more death or sorrow or crying or pain. All these things are gone forever (Revelation 21:4 NLT).

What a wonderful promise of the Lord!

COMPARISON 6: HUMANS ARE DRIVEN FROM PARADISE (GENESIS 3:24)

The sin of Adam and Eve caused the Lord to remove them from the paradise which He created.

After he drove the man out, he placed on the east side of the Garden of Eden cherubim and a flaming sword flashing back and forth to guard the way to the tree of life (Genesis 3:24 NIV).

PARADISE IS RESTORED (REVELATION 22:14)

Though humans were banished from God's presence there will come a day when paradise will be restored and they will return.

Blessed are those who wash their robes so they can have access to the tree of life and can enter into the city by the gates (Revelation 22:14 NET).

The lost paradise will once again be restored.

COMPARISON 7: SORROW AND PAIN BEGIN AS A RESULT OF THE FALL (GENESIS 3:16,17)

Human sorrow began when the first humans rebelled against God.

He said to the woman, "I will increase your pain and your labor when you give birth to children. Yet, you will long for your husband, and he will rule you." Then he said to the man, "You listened to your wife and ate fruit from the tree, although I commanded you, 'You must never eat its fruit.' The ground is cursed because of you. Through hard work you will eat food that comes from it every day of your life" (Genesis 3:16,17 God's Word).

After the sin of Adam and Eve, the Lord told them that sorrow and pain would follow them.

THERE WILL BE NO MORE CRYING OR PAIN (REVELATION 21:4,5)

Yet in the future, there will be no more crying or pain. We read about this in the Book of Revelation.

He will wipe every tear from their eyes. There won't be any more death. There won't be any grief, crying, or pain, because the first things have disappeared." The one sitting on the throne said, "I am making everything new." He said, "Write this: 'These words are faithful and true (Revelation 21:4,5 God's Word).

The wonderful promise of God is that all these things, which were part of the original fallen creation, will now be a thing of the past.

SUMMARY TO QUESTION 9
WHAT ARE SOME OF THE CONTRASTS BETWEEN THE OLD CREATION IN GENESIS AND THE FUTURE CREATION?

The Bible presents quite a contrast between the original creation found in the Book of Genesis and the future creation recorded in the Book of Revelation.

For example, God created the sun and moon in the beginning. However, in the future creation there will be no need for them. There will be no night, for the Lord will shine His light on everything. In addition, the seas which were created in the beginning will be no more.

When Adam and Eve sinned they were judged by the Lord. Among other things, Adam was told that the land would be difficult for him to work, women would experience pain in childbirth, and humanity would have to leave the paradise of God. Paradise was lost.

In the new creation there will be no more sorrow, crying, or pain. In addition, the redeemed human race will be reunited with God. Paradise will be regained.

In sum, there are many contrasts between the old creation and the coming new creation.

QUESTION 10

What Is The
New Jerusalem?

After God remakes the heaven and the earth, the Bible speaks of a city called the "New Jerusalem" coming down out of heaven.

In the Book of Revelation this city is described for us.

> Then I saw New Jerusalem, that holy city, coming down from God in heaven. It was like a bride dressed in her wedding gown and ready to meet her husband (Revelation 21:2 CEV).

The city comes down out of heaven, uniting both heaven and earth. Note that the city is compared to a bride dressed in her wedding gown awaiting to meet her husband. It is where believers will forever live with God.

THE NEW JERUSALEM COMPARED WITH THE OLD

The old city of Jerusalem is where the Lord Jesus will rule from during the Millennium; His one-thousand year reign upon the earth.

The New Jerusalem will be the center of His reign after the Millennium. Indeed, the Lord will rule from this place for all eternity.

It is also called the "Holy City" in contrast to the earthly Jerusalem which was unholy at many times in the past. Indeed, earlier in the Book of Revelation, we read this description of "unholy Jerusalem."

Their bodies will lie in the public square of the great city—which is figuratively called Sodom and Egypt—where also their Lord was crucified (Revelation 11:8 NIV).

What a contrast it will be to the old Jerusalem which is here compared to the evil city of Sodom and the country of Egypt, which is often likened to the unbelieving world system.

As we read the description of the "Holy City" we note that there are some things which are made clear while there is some ambiguity in other descriptions. From Scripture, here is how the city is described.

1. IT IS A LARGE CITY

According to the biblical description, the city is huge. The dimensions are given to us in the Book of Revelation.

> When he measured it, he found it was a square, as wide as it was long. In fact, its length and width and height were each 1,400 miles (Revelation 21:16 NET).

Fourteen hundred miles equals about 2,200 kilometers. The Greek text says the length, width, and height were each 12,000 *stadia*. One *stade* was about 607 feet or 85 meters.

Some English translations use the word "furlongs" to translate the Greek word *stadia*.

> And he measured the city with the reed: twelve thousand furlongs. Its length, breadth, and height are equal (Revelation 21:16 New King James Version).

For most Americans, the term "furlong" would be a bit ambiguous.

A number of English translations merely leave the Greek term stadia in the text without trying translate the word and, therefore, convert the dimensions to miles or kilometers. For example, we read in the

New International Version the following description.

> The city was laid out like a square, as long as it was wide.
> He measured the city with the rod and found it to be
> 12,000 stadia in length, and as wide and high as it is long
> (Revelation 21:16 NIV).

Whatever the case may be, this city is obviously very large.

WHAT IS ITS SHAPE?

The description of the width, height, and length all being the same distance reveal that it as cube-shaped. This is consistent with the dimensions of the Holy of Holies in both the tabernacle and the temple. The Bible say the following about the temple Solomon built.

> He prepared the inner sanctuary at the far end of the Temple,
> where the Ark of the Lord's Covenant would be placed. This
> inner sanctuary was 30 feet long, 30 feet wide, and 30 feet
> high. He overlaid the inside with solid gold. He also overlaid
> the altar made of cedar (1 Kings 6:19,20 NLT).

Although there are those who see it as pyramid-shaped, there seems to be more evidence for it being shaped like a cube.

2. THE CITY HAS HIGH WALLS

John described the walls of the city as follows.

> The city wall was broad and high, with twelve gates guarded
> by twelve angels (Revelation 21:12 NLT).

We are also told of the material in which the wall will be made of as well as the foundation stones in which it will be built upon.

> The wall was made of jasper, and the city was pure gold, as
> clear as glass. The wall of the city was built on foundation

stones inlaid with twelve precious stones: the first was jasper, the second sapphire, the third agate, the fourth emerald, the fifth onyx, the sixth carnelian, the seventh chrysolite, the eighth beryl, the ninth topaz, the tenth chrysoprase, the eleventh jacinth, the twelfth amethyst (Revelation 21:18 NLT).

The description is certainly that of a magnificent-looking wall!

3. THE CITY IS MADE OUT OF GOLD

The heavenly streets of gold will be in this future city. We read the following description of it.

> The city was made of pure gold, as clear as glass (Revelation 21:18 God's Word).

The New Jerusalem is the golden city.

4. IN THE MIDST OF THE CITY IS THE TREE OF LIFE

In the midst of this Holy City is the tree of life, as well as a river which is crystal clear. John describes it this way.

> Then the angel showed me the river of the water of life, as clear as crystal, flowing from the throne of God and of the Lamb down the middle of the great street of the city. On each side of the river stood the tree of life, bearing twelve crops of fruit, yielding its fruit every month. And the leaves of the tree are for the healing of the nations. (Revelation 22:1,2 NIV).

The tree of life in the midst of this Holy City will have different kinds of fruit growing on it.

In addition, we are told that the leaves are for the healing of the nations. As to exactly what that means, we discuss this in appendix four at the end of this book.

5. THE STREETS OF GOLD AND THE PEARLY GATES ARE IN THE NEW JERUSALEM

The Bible says that the New Jerusalem will have streets of gold and gates made of pearls. We read the following in the Book of Revelation.

> The 12 gates are 12 pearls; each individual gate was made of a single pearl. The broad street of the city was pure gold, like transparent glass (Revelation 21:21 HCSB).

Each of the twelve gates is made from one individual pearl. According to this passage, we will actually walk on a golden street in the New Jerusalem!

6. THE NEW JERUSALEM HAS NO TEMPLE

The Bible says that there is no temple in the New Jerusalem. Scripture says that the Lord God, and Jesus the Lamb of God, are themselves the temple. John wrote.

> And I saw no temple in the city, for its temple is the Lord God the Almighty and the Lamb (Revelation 21:22 ESV).

The temple is unnecessary in this city. Indeed, since the presence of God will be among us there is no need of something to represent Him.

7. THIS CITY HAS NO SUN OR MOON

There is no sun or moon the New Jerusalem. The Book of Revelation says.

> The city doesn't need any sun or moon to give it light because the glory of God gave it light. The lamb was its lamp. The nations will walk in its light, and the kings of the earth will bring their glory into it (Revelation 21:23,24 God's Word).

The light will come from God Himself.

This will fulfill a prophecy given by the prophet Isaiah.

The sun will no more be your light by day, nor will the brightness of the moon shine on you, for the LORD will be your everlasting light, and your God will be your glory (Isaiah 60:19 NIV).

The living God will be our glory.

THE GATES OF THE HOLY CITY WILL NEVER CLOSE

We also find that the gates of the city will never close.

Its gates will never be closed at the end of day because there is no night there. And all the nations will bring their glory and honor into the city. Nothing evil will be allowed to enter, nor anyone who practices shameful idolatry and dishonesty—but only those whose names are written in the Lamb's Book of Life (Revelation 21:25 NLT).

In the ancient world, the city gates were always closed at night. This was done to protect the inhabitants from those outside. However, there will be no more night in eternity and no enemies outside. Therefore, there will be no need for the gates to ever close!

The great news about this city is this: those who have placed their faith in the God of the Bible are promised that they will forever be in His presence.

This sums up what the Scripture has to say about this Holy City, the New Jerusalem. From the biblical description is appears to be a place beyond our wildest expectations. Words, most likely, do not even begin to justice in describing this place.

SUMMARY TO QUESTION 10
WHAT IS THE NEW JERUSALEM?

After God makes a new heaven and new earth, the Bible says that the New Jerusalem will come down from heaven. The New Jerusalem, the

Holy City, is where believers will live for all eternity. We are told that outside the city are unbelievers. Only those who have trusted the Lord will be allowed in the Holy City. Nobody else is welcomed.

The glorious description of this city is given to us in Scripture. There are a number of things we are told about this future home for the righteous.

For one thing, it will be an extremely large city with high walls. This emphasizes that heaven will be a safe place for those inside. The Lord Himself protects those who belong to Him.

The New Jerusalem is described as a city of gold with a golden street and twelve huge gates; each made from a single pearl. This speaks of its beauty.

There is no moon or sun in this city because the Lord Himself will provide the light. Jesus Himself said that He was the light of the world. His light will shine in the New Jerusalem. This fulfills a prediction which the Lord made through the prophet Isaiah. God will be our light!

We are also told there is no temple in this heavenly city. The Lord Himself is the temple. Consequently, there is no need for some place to represent Him, for He is there!

Finally, we are told that the gates of the city will never close! There is no need to close the gates at night, as was the practice in the ancient world, because there will be no night and no dangers lurking outside! Believers will safely enter and leave the Holy City.

Indeed, although it will be a city of incomparable beauty, the greatest thing about it is that the Lord will dwell there with His people. This is the fantastic future promised by the God of the Bible.

If Heaven Truly Does Exist,
Then How Does A Person Get There?

We have seen from the Bible that heaven is a genuine place, it really does exist. In fact, it is described for us in quite a bit of detail in Scripture.

The fact that heaven exists brings up some obvious questions, "How does a person go to heaven?" What must we do to go there? Is heaven earned? Do only good people go there? Do followers of all religions go to heaven? What does the Bible have to say about who gets into heaven?

THE BIBLE HAS A UNIQUE VIEW ABOUT HEAVEN

To begin with, we must realize that not all religions agree on the meaning of heaven. The description of heaven, as well as how a person goes there, is a matter of dispute. In fact, the Bible differs from all of them. It has a unique view of God, of heaven, as well as how a person goes to heaven.

THERE IS ONE WAY TO REACH THE ONE GOD

The Bible is very clear on this matter of who enters heaven; it is limited to those who have believed in the God of the Bible. In particular, only those who have trusted Jesus Christ as their Savior are assured of getting into heaven. Jesus said.

I am the way, the truth, and the life. No one goes to the
Father except through me (John 14:6 God's Word).

According to Jesus, there is only one way to reach the one God; it is
through Him and Him alone. These are His unique claims. If they
are true, then all other claims about heaven from other religions and
religious leader are false. In fact, Jesus said.

Truly, truly, I say to you, I am the door of the sheep. All
who came before me are thieves and robbers, but the sheep
did not listen to them. I am the door. If anyone enters by
me, he will be saved and will go in and out and find pasture
(John 10:7-9 ESV).

These are His exclusive claims. Notice that the Lord said that all others are "thieves and robbers." Why? It is because they present another
way by which a person can have a relationship with the True and
Living God. According to Jesus, every other way is false. Indeed, He
is "the" way, the only way!

NOBODY GETS TO HEAVEN BY THEIR GOOD WORKS

Contrary to what many people think, an individual does not go to
heaven because they are "good." Also, a person is not kept out of
heaven because they are "bad." Whoever gets to heaven goes there
because of God's grace, not their own good deeds. The Bible says.

God saved you by his grace when you believed. And you
can't take credit for this; it is a gift from God. Salvation is
not a reward for the good things we have done, so none of
us can boast about it (Ephesians 2:8,9 NLT).

Our salvation from sin, our eventual entrance into heaven, is a "gift"
from God.

Scripture also says.

He saved us, not because of the righteous things we had done, but because of his mercy. He washed away our sins, giving us a new birth and new life through the Holy Spirit (Titus 3:5 NLT).

Jesus Christ has done it all for us. Indeed we cannot add anything to His sacrifice. Our responsibility is to believe in Him as Savior. If so, we are guaranteed eternal life.

THE ROMANS ROAD TO SALVATION

The Apostle Paul, in the Book of Romans, laid it out clearly in what is popularly known as the "Romans Road."

First, we find that all of us have sinned and have come short of God's perfect standard.

For all have sinned and fall short of the glory of God (Romans 3:23 ESV).

Every one of us has fallen short of God's perfect standard. In other words, none of us has the ability to go to heaven based upon our good works. Indeed, we all fall short.

The results of our falling short is death, separation from God.

For the wages of sin is death (Romans 6:23 ESV).

Sin brings death, or separation from God.

However there is good news! In the second half of this verse Paul says the following.

But the free gift of God is eternal life in Christ Jesus our Lord (Romans 6:23 ESV).

God has offered the free gift of salvation to all who believe. Eternal life with the living God will be given to all who believe.

In sum, to get to heaven each of us must place our personal faith in the God of the Bible through Jesus Christ. There is no other way to get to heaven except through belief in Jesus. These are the claims of Scripture.

SUMMARY TO QUESTION 11
IF HEAVEN TRULY DOES EXIST, THEN HOW DOES A PERSON GET THERE?
DO ALL RELIGIONS LEAD TO HEAVEN?

The Bible, the Word of the Living God, makes is clear that heaven truly does exist. It is a special place where God dwells and it will be home for all who have believed in Him.

Yet not everyone is going to go to heaven. Consequently it is absolutely crucial that we understand what is necessary for a person to do in order to go to heaven when they die.

We find that the Bible is clear on this subject. A person gets to heaven by placing their faith in Jesus Christ, God the Son. Jesus paid the penalty for our sins on the cross of Calvary. He died as our substitute. In other words, He suffered on our behalf. In doing so He made heaven available to all.

Our responsibility is to believe in Him; to accept the fact that Christ died in our place and then rose from the dead. If we do this, the Bible guarantees that we will go to heaven.

Therefore, the issue is clear: those who trust Jesus Christ as their Savior go to heaven, those who do not trust Him as Savior will not go to heaven.

In sum, the choice is ours as to where we will spend eternity.

QUESTION 12

Can Anyone Really Know That They Are Going To Heaven? What Assurance Do We Have?

While Christians speak of those who have believed in Jesus Christ as going to heaven, does this really mean that it is true? In other words, what assurance do we have that we will actually go to heaven when we die? Can a person truly know that when they die they will be in the presence of the Lord?

THE BIBLE SAYS THAT WE CAN KNOW WE ARE GOING TO HEAVEN

God's Word is clear on the matter. We can indeed know that we will go to heaven when we die. John wrote.

> This is the testimony: God has given us eternal life, and this life is found in his Son. The person who has the Son has this life. The person who doesn't have the Son of God doesn't have this life. I've written this to those who believe in the Son of God so that they will know that they have eternal life (1 John 5:11-13 God's Word).

John's statement is clear. Believers can "know" that they have eternal life "if" they have believed in Jesus Christ, the Son of God.

Therefore, when Christians speak of knowing that they will go to heaven when they die it is not because of their boasting, their arrogance, or their wishful thinking.

Indeed, it is not our claim, it is the claim of the God of the Bible! He is the One who has given us the assurance that we have eternal life.

JESUS HAS DEMONSTRATED HIS AUTHORITY TO MAKE THESE CLAIMS

There is something else which must be emphasized. Jesus Christ has already demonstrated that He has the authority to make such a claim. Indeed, He provided three lines of evidence that back up His claims as being the one way in which a person can know the one true God.

First, He performed miracles in the sight of the people. These miracles, which were never denied by His enemies, were a sign that Jesus had the authority to make His claims.

Second, Jesus fulfilled a number of Old Testament predictions about the coming Messiah, or Savior. In addition, He Himself also predicted a number of things which have come true. Only God knows the future, only God can accurately predict what will happen. The evidence of fulfilled prophecy shows that Jesus has the authority to make the claims that He made.

Finally, Jesus predicted His death and resurrection from the dead. The fact that He was raised from the dead, conquering death, demonstrates He is exactly whom He claimed to be.

Therefore, the fact that Jesus performed miracles, fulfilled Old Testament prophecy as well as making predictions which have come true, and then came back from the dead after His death, demonstrates that He is the final word on every matter. If He says, or His written Word the Bible says, that we can know that we have eternal life, then we can know. End of story.

So when we speak about Christians going to heaven when we die, we do so on the basis of the clear teaching of the Word of God. As the final authority on all matters of faith and practice, whatever the Bible says on any issue is true. And the Bible says that all those who believe in Jesus are going to heaven someday. Therefore, the issue is settled.

SUMMARY TO QUESTION 12
CAN ANYONE REALLY KNOW THAT THEY ARE GOING TO HEAVEN? WHAT ASSURANCE DO WE HAVE?

It is important to realize that Christians are not the ones making the claim about who gets to heaven and who does not. Indeed, this is not our claim; it is the claim of Jesus Himself. Therefore, if anyone wishes to argue about the existence of heaven, who goes there and who does not, they must confront Jesus about it.

We find that Jesus not only made claims about heaven, He also backed up His claims by three different lines of evidence.

First, He performed miracles in the sight of the people. These miracles, which were never denied by the people of His day, testified to His authority.

In addition, Jesus supernaturally fulfilled a number of Old Testament predictions with respect to the coming Messiah. He also made predictions that have been literally fulfilled.

Above all, Jesus came back from the dead three days after His death. The fact that He conquered death demonstrates that He has the unique authority to make the claims that He did.

Therefore, when His Word, the Bible, says that we can know that we have eternal life if we believe in Him, that settles the matter. Indeed, we can have this assurance based upon what Jesus Christ has done on our behalf.

When Believers In Jesus Christ Die, Will They Go Immediately To Heaven

People who has placed their faith in Jesus Christ are promised heaven in the future. The Bible is clear about this. Indeed, Jesus said that all who believe in Him will have everlasting life.

> The one who believes in the Son has eternal life. The one who rejects the Son will not see life, but God's wrath remains on him (John 3:36 NET).

Furthermore, the Bible says that believers can know they have eternal life if they have trusted Christ as their Savior. This confidence is based upon the fact that Jesus provided convincing evidence that He has the authority to make the claims that He did. Therefore, each of us who have believed in Christ can be confident that heaven awaits us.

But when will we go to heaven? Will this happen immediately upon the death of the believer? The Bible gives a resounding, "Yes!" Scripture has some comforting words for those who have believed in Jesus.

BEING ABSENT FROM OUR BODY MEANS BEING PRESENT WITH THE LORD

Paul made the comparison about being away from the Lord while we are in these bodies with how we shall be at home with the Lord when we leave these bodies through death. He wrote.

So always be cheerful! As long as we are in these bodies, we are away from the Lord. But we live by faith, not by what we see. We should be cheerful, because we would rather leave these bodies and be at home with the Lord (2 Corinthians 5:6-8 CEV).

As we presently live in these earthly bodies we are away from the presence of the Lord. However, the good news is this. One day we will be away from these earthly bodies and then find ourselves in the presence of the Lord! Death will bring us immediately into His presence.

THERE ARE ONLY TWO ALTERNATIVES FOR BELIEVERS

There is something else we learn from this passage. The believer has only two alternatives: either being absent from the Lord while living in this mortal body or being present with the Lord when we leave this mortal body upon death.

Consequently, there will be no such thing as soul sleep or purgatory. We will be immediately in His presence in heaven in a conscious state. In fact, we have these promises elsewhere in Scripture. Paul also wrote.

If I live, it will be for Christ, and if I die, I will gain even more. I don't know what to choose. I could keep on living and doing something useful. It is a hard choice to make. I want to die and be with Christ, because that would be much better (Philippians 1:21-23 CEV).

Notice that Paul believed that if he died he would be with Jesus Christ. In fact, he said he would be "much better" if this happened to him. Therefore, he was confident that death would bring him instantly into the very presence of Christ.

THE CRIMINAL NEXT TO JESUS ON THE CROSS

The man who was crucified next to Jesus on the cross was promised that upon his death he would be in the presence of the Lord. He said the following.

"Jesus, remember me when you enter your kingdom." Jesus said to him, "I can guarantee this truth: Today you will be with me in paradise (Luke 23:42-43 God's Word).

The moment he closed his eyes in death this forgiven criminal was in the presence of the Lord.

THE MARTYR STEPHEN WAS BROUGHT IMMEDIATELY INTO THE PRESENCE OF THE LORD

The Bible records the death of the martyr Stephen. We find that He was immediately welcomed into the presence of the Lord.

> Then Stephen said, "I see heaven open and the Son of Man standing at the right side of God!" . . . As Stephen was being stoned to death, he called out, "Lord Jesus, please welcome me" (Acts 7:56,59 CEV).

Stephen was also received into the presence of the Lord Jesus immediately upon his death.

Therefore, as we study the Scripture, we find that when we believers leave our mortal bodies we are guaranteed that we will go immediately into the presence of the Living God. There will be no delay, no waiting.

SUMMARY TO QUESTION 13
WHEN BELIEVERS IN JESUS CHRIST DIE, WILL THEY GO IMMEDIATELY TO HEAVEN?

There is great news for the believers in Jesus Christ. Not only are they promised heaven in the future, they can also have the assurance that they will have eternal life.

In addition, we find that immediately upon death they are ushered into the presence of the Lord in heaven. In fact, the Bible provides a number of illustrations of people who were about to die who were promised, that upon their death, they would instantaneously be in His presence.

For example, the criminal who died next to Jesus on the cross asked the Lord to remember him when Christ entered His kingdom. Jesus told this repentant man that he would be with Him that very day in paradise, heaven.

The martyr Stephen, as he was being murdered by an angry mob, looked up to heaven and saw Jesus standing at the right hand of God the Father welcoming him into His presence.

The Apostle Paul told the church at Philippi that to die would be profitable for him because he would be "with Christ." He did not envision any waiting period between his death and being in the presence of the Lord.

Therefore, the Scripture is clear on this matter. Immediately upon death the believer is ushered into the presence of the Lord.

QUESTION 14

When We Get To Heaven Will We Immediately Get A New Body?

The Bible says that believers in Jesus Christ will go immediately to heaven when they die. Scripture also promises those who have trusted Jesus will also receive a new body, an immortal incorruptible body.

This brings up a question: do believers receive their new body immediately upon death with their entrance into heaven or is there a waiting period? What does the Bible say?

To answer this question, we will first look at the promises of the Lord with respect to our new body and then discover when we will receive it.

THE PROMISE OF A NEW BODY

To begin with, believers do have the promise that one day we will receive a glorified body.

> For we know that if the earthly tent we live in is destroyed,
> we have a building from God, an eternal house in heaven,
> not built by human hands (2 Corinthians 5:1 NIV).

When these mortal bodies die, we have promised to us an everlasting body. It is called an "eternal house in heaven."

WE CAN BE ASSURED THAT HE WILL DO IT

Since the Lord has given this promise of an eventual transformation of our bodies we can live confidently at all times. Paul wrote.

> God is the one who makes all of this possible. He has given us his Spirit to make us certain that he will do it (2 Corinthians 5:5 CEV).

God always keeps His promises.

THERE IS NO REASON TO FEEL HOPELESS

Once we understand these biblical truths we should never feel hopeless. Indeed, we have an eternal destination waiting for us as well as a new body. In the meantime, we walk by faith looking forward to that day when we are present with the Lord.

> But we live by faith, not by what we see (2 Corinthians 5:7 CEV).

Therefore, when we walk by faith, we are confident of a greater future awaiting us.

THE TIMING OF THE GLORIFIED BODY FOR THE BELIEVER

As we have seen, it is clear from Scripture that we are promised a new body from the Lord. Consequently, we want to know when we will receive it.

NEW TESTAMENT BELIEVERS RECEIVE THEIR NEW BODY AT THE RAPTURE OF THE CHURCH

The timing of the reception of our resurrected or glorified body is explained by Paul.

> Brothers and sisters, we do not want you to be uninformed about those who sleep in death, so that you do not grieve

like the rest of mankind, who have no hope. For we believe that Jesus died and rose again, and so we believe that God will bring with Jesus those who have fallen asleep in him. According to the Lord's word, we tell you that we who are still alive, who are left until the coming of the Lord, will certainly not precede those who have fallen asleep. For the Lord himself will come down from heaven, with a loud command, with the voice of the archangel and with the trumpet call of God, and the dead in Christ will rise first. After that, we who are still alive and are left will be caught up together with them in the clouds to meet the Lord in the air. And so we will be with the Lord forever. Therefore encourage one another with these words (1 Thessalonians 4:13-18 NIV).

Notice the order of events. The dead "in Christ" rise first and then those who remain will be caught up to meet the Lord in the air. At that time the living believers will be given a glorified body. It is at this future time that everyone who has believed in Jesus, whether living or dead, will receive a glorified body. For those who have died "in Christ" it will be a resurrected body.

In sum, when we die our spirit or soul immediately goes to be with the Lord but our body goes to the grave. When Christ comes back for His own, whether alive or dead, we will then receive a glorified body.

Consequently, the promise of that eternal body still awaits us. While we are ushered into the presence of the Lord immediately upon death it is without our glorified body. That takes place at the time of resurrection of the dead with the rapture of the church occurring at the same time.

SUMMARY TO QUESTION 14
WHEN WE GET TO HEAVEN WILL WE IMMEDIATELY GET A NEW BODY?

Among other things, the Bible promises that believers will immediately be ushered into the presence of the Lord upon our death. We are also promised a new body for all eternity. Therefore, the question is this: do we receive that new body immediately upon death or is there some waiting period?

Though believers who die go immediately to be with the Lord, Scripture teaches that the resurrection of bodies of the dead "in Christ" is still a future event. Indeed, at some unknown time in the future, two events will occur simultaneously.

First, those who have died "in Christ" will be raised from the dead. Their dead bodies will join with their spirits which are presently with the Lord.

At the same time, those who are alive will be caught up to meet the Lord in the air. As they are being caught up their bodies will be changed from mortal to immortal, from corruptible to incorruptible.

Therefore, everyone who has believed in Jesus will receive a glorified body at this time. For those who have died, it will be a resurrected body. For those who are alive, they will receive the same type of body, a glorified body. The only difference is that it is not a resurrected body because these people never died.

Therefore, although heaven immediately accepts all those who have died in Christ, the promised resurrected body is still something that awaits believers in the future.

What Are The Heavenly Rewards That Await Believers?

Believers in Jesus Christ are given their resurrected or glorified bodies at the resurrection of the dead and the rapture of the church. The dead are resurrected while the living believers are instantly given a new glorified body. Scripture then explains what happens next.

WE WILL ALL GIVE AN ACCOUNT FOR OUR LIVES

The Bible says that we will give an account of our lives when we are brought into His presence in our glorified bodies. We are told that the Lord will reward believers based upon the deeds they have done after they have trusted Christ as Savior.

This judgment of Christians is one of rewards. It is to determine the extent of rewards each one of us will receive. Paul wrote about this. He said.

> So don't make judgments about anyone ahead of time—before the Lord returns. For he will bring our darkest secrets to light and will reveal our private motives. Then God will give to each one whatever praise is due (1 Corinthians 4:5 NLT).

This process will be an evaluation of what we have done after our conversion to Jesus Christ. It *will* not be a condemnation of our sins.

THE PROCESS IS REVEALED

The illustration used by the Apostle Paul would have been familiar to those whom he wrote. He explained it in this manner.

> For we must all appear before the judgment seat of Christ, so that each of us may receive what is due us for the things done while in the body, whether good or bad (2 Corinthians 5:10 NIV).

It is similar to the process a Roman governor would use to judge those who are accused. He would sit on his tribunal, his judgment seat, to hear both the accusation as well as the defense of an accused person standing before him.

Some years earlier, Paul himself had stood accused before the Roman governor Gallio in the Corinth. Scripture explains it this way.

> While Gallio was proconsul of Achaia, the Jews of Corinth made a united attack on Paul and brought him to the place of judgment. "This man," they charged, "is persuading the people to worship God in ways contrary to the law" (Acts 18:12-13 NIV)

The Greek word *bema*, translated "judgment seat" or "place of judgment," is used for raised platform from which governors would issue decrees or judgments.

Therefore, Paul gave the Corinthians a familiar illustration of what is to come for the believer. Indeed, we all must appear before the tribunal or judgment seat of Christ.

THE REWARD SEAT

The good news for Christians is that this tribunal will not be one of judgment in the negative sense. In other words, believers in Jesus Christ will not face any condemnation at His tribunal. The Judge, in this case, will only be handing out rewards. The Apostle Paul gave this analogy.

> The one who plants and the one who waters work as one, but each will receive his reward according to his work (1 Corinthians 3:8 NET).

Therefore, instead of condemnation, each of us will be evaluated. The goal is to hear Him commend us for our service. Scripture tells us that this commendation may either be given or withheld

Yet we discover from Scripture not all verdicts will be comforting to the believer. Indeed, we are told that we may "suffer loss" of our reward as our words and works will be tested by fire. Paul gave this analogy.

> If what has been built survives, the builder will receive a reward. If it is burned up, the builder will suffer loss but yet will be saved—even though only as one escaping through the flames (1 Corinthians 3:14,15 NIV).

Therefore, our works will be rewarded or they will be discarded.

WORTHLESS WORKS WILL NOT BE REWARDED

Two types of works are listed in Second Corinthians 5:10; those that are bad as well as those who are good. The Greek word translated "bad" has the idea of something that is worthless. These worthless works will not receive any reward. However, neither will it receive any punishment. Indeed, the only penalty believers will receive for these "worthless deeds" is limited to the loss of our heavenly reward.

On the other hand, we find that the Lord will reward us for the worthwhile things we have done after putting our faith in Christ.

In sum, there will be rewards for the faithful works but no reward for the worthless things we did.

WHAT ARE THE GOOD WORKS AND THE BAD WORKS?

The good works for which believers will be rewarded are those things which we have said and done that cause the advancement the message of Jesus Christ to the world. Again, we emphasize that these are works and words that believers do and say *after* they have believed in Christ. There will be no reward for anything done prior to our conversion.

On the other hand, the worthless deeds are those that make no contribution whatsoever to the work of the Christian ministry and the advancement of the kingdom of God.

WE DO NOT WANT TO LOSE OUR REWARD

Believers should desire to receive a full reward for their deeds of faith. In his second letter, John wrote about the possibility of losing that full reward. He put it this way.

> So be sure not to lose what we have worked for. If you do, you won't be given your full reward (2 John 8 CEV).

We can lose our full reward. This is why John encourages believers to work for that reward. In fact, John wrote elsewhere about believers being "in shame" when the Lord judges us.

> Now, dear children, live in Christ. Then, when he appears we will have confidence, and when he comes we won't turn from him in shame (1 John 2:28 God's Word).

What we have done, as well as our motives, will be brought to light. Paul wrote.

> Therefore judge nothing before the appointed time; wait until the Lord comes. He will bring to light what is hidden in darkness and will expose the motives of the heart. At that time each will receive their praise from God (1 Corinthians 4:5 NIV).

Therefore, we should always have these things in mind if we want to receive a full reward from God.

OUR GOAL SHOULD BE TO LIFE A LIFE PLEASING TO GOD

Paul told the Christians in Corinth that their life's ambition should be to live a life pleasing to the Lord.

> So then whether we are alive or away, we make it our ambition to please him (2 Corinthians 5:9 NET).

Above anything else, we should make it our life's ambition to please the Lord in all that we say and do. Paul wrote to the Galatians.

> Am I now trying to win the approval of human beings, or of God? Or am I trying to please people? If I were still trying to please people, I would not be a servant of Christ (Galatians 1:10 NIV).

In his letter to the Philippians, Paul emphasized that his desire was to please God.

> I eagerly expect and hope that I will in no way be ashamed, but will have sufficient courage so that now as always Christ will be exalted in my body, whether by life or by death (Philippians 1:20 NIV).

Certainly, this should be our desire also.

SERVING GOD TO GAIN ETERNAL REWARDS IS A LEGITIMATE MOTIVATION

While some may feel that serving the Lord for the purpose of gaining rewards is not biblical, we find that neither Jesus nor Paul discouraged such a practice.

In fact, Jesus spoke of a great reward for those who endured persecution.

> You are blessed when they insult and persecute you and falsely say every kind of evil against you because of Me.

97

Be glad and rejoice, because your reward is great in heaven (Matthew 5:11,12 HCSB).

Paul wrote about the crown that we may receive that will last "forever."

Do you not know that in a race all the runners run, but only one gets the prize? Run in such a way as to get the prize. Everyone who competes in the games goes into strict training. They do it to get a crown that will not last, but we do it to get a crown that will last forever (1 Corinthians 9:24-25 NIV).

We also read Jesus saying the following in the Book of Revelation.

Look, I am coming soon! My reward is with me, and I will give to each person according to what they have done (Revelation 22:12 NIV).

Therefore, it is certainly biblical for believers to be concerned about earning rewards in this life for the life which is to come.

SUMMARY TO QUESTION 15
WHAT ARE THE HEAVENLY REWARDS THAT AWAIT BELIEVERS?

The Bible teaches that when believers die their souls or spirits immediately go to heaven. However, the body remains in the grave until the time of the resurrection of the dead.

After the dead bodies of the believers are raised and joined with their spirits there comes a time of judgment for believers. This judgment, however, is not one of condemnation but rather for the purpose of reward. Therefore, believers will be evaluated, not condemned.

What will be evaluated? It will be the works which the believers have done after the time they have trusted Jesus Christ as their Savior. Those who are rewarded will receive everything owed to them. We again must emphasize that what they have earned are rewards, not their salvation from sin. Salvation is not earned. It is a free gift for all those who believe.

Scripture says that the "good" works will receive a full reward while the "bad" or worthless works will be "burned up." In other words, they will not rewarded. These worthless works are those things which we have said and done which do not advance the kingdom of God upon the earth.

We also discover that it is possible for believers to lose their full reward. In fact, we are warned about this. Therefore, we should desire to live a life pleasing to God so that we will not be ashamed when the day of evaluation comes.

To sum up, it is possible that some believers will receive few rewards or words of commendation from Christ the Judge.

Since we know that we will appear before the Lord on that day, our goal should be to hear these words from the Him, "Well done, good and faithful servant."

Since Believers Will Receive Different Crowns As Rewards Will There Be Envy In Heaven?

The rewards that believers will receive in heaven are called "crowns." They are known as the crown of righteousness, the crown of glory, and the crown of life.

The idea of believers receiving crowns in heaven brings up a number of questions. What is the difference between the various crowns? Are these literal crowns we will be wearing? If so, would not that cause envy among those who have lesser crowns?

THEY ARE PROBABLY NOT LITERAL CROWNS

The simple answer is that the crowns, which are given to believers as rewards, are probably not actual material crowns. Instead, the crowns promised are most-likely symbolic of the various rewards we will receive.

Why do we conclude this? It is the because the biblical writers described these crowns in figurative language. For example, there is the crown of glory, the crown of life, and the crown of righteousness. In other words, they are not described as being something material such as being a crown of gold or a crown of silver.

Furthermore, a person only wears one crown at a time. Wearing multiple crowns does not seem to be what is being taught here.

We can briefly describe these "crowns" as follows.

THE CROWN OF RIGHTEOUSNESS

Paul wrote of the crown of righteousness when addressing Timothy. He said.

> I have fought a good fight, I have finished *my* course, I have kept the faith: Henceforth there is laid up for me a crown of righteousness, which the Lord, the righteous judge, shall give me at that day: and not to me only, but unto all them also that love his appearing (2 Timothy 4:7,8 KJV).

Paul had been faithful to Jesus Christ in this life. Consequently he was looking forward for the Lord to reward him for his service. This "crown of righteousness" is most likely some type of unspecified reward for his godly conduct on earth.

Since righteousness is something that is non-material, this seems to be a metaphorical crown representing some type of reward Paul will receive rather than a literal material crown that he would wear on his head.

This reward is also known as victor's crown. It is given to those who have lived a victorious Christian life. This verse informs us that it is characterized by a heartfelt desire for the return of the Lord. Therefore, this specific reward will only be given to those who live their lives in anticipation of the Lord's return to the earth.

THE CROWN OF GLORY

Peter wrote of something called the "crown of glory." He put it this way.

> Then, when the chief shepherd appears, you will receive the crown of glory that will never fade away (1 Peter 5:4 God's Word).

The crown of glory is one that does not fade away. We are told that it is received when the Lord returns. It seems to represent those who have been faithful in their work for the Lord in this life.

QUESTION 16

THE CROWN OF LIFE

James mentioned a reward which is known as the "crown of life." He said.

> Blessed is a man who endures trials, because when he passes
> the test he will receive the crown of life that He has prom-
> ised to those who love Him (James 1:12 HCSB).

Jesus also spoke of this crown of life. Indeed, He promised the crown of life for those who were faithful until death. We read of this in the Book of Revelation where it says the following.

> Do not fear any of those things which you are about to
> suffer. Indeed, the devil is about to throw *some* of you into
> prison, that you may be tested, and you will have tribula-
> tion ten days. Be faithful until death, and I will give you the
> crown of life (Revelation 2:10 NKJV).

This crown, or reward, is given for enduring the difficult trials and tests of life. In this verse, these testings can bring one to the point of death.

THERE WILL BE NO ENVY OF OTHER BELIEVERS IN HEAVEN

The fact that there will be different degrees of rewards in heaven always leads to the question about envy. Won't those who receive lesser rewards envy those who receive the greater rewards?

While there may be different degrees of rewards, the Bible says that when one is honored all are honored. Paul wrote.

> If one part suffers, all the parts suffer with it, and if one part
> is honored, all the parts are glad. Now all of you together
> are Christ's body, and each one of you is a separate and nec-
> essary part of it (1 Corinthians 12:26,27 NLT).

There will not be levels or righteousness in heaven. Neither will there be such thing as pride or envy. We read the following in the Book of Revelation.

The 24 leaders bow in front of the one who sits on the throne and worship the one who lives forever and ever. They place their crowns in front of the throne and say, "Our Lord and God, you deserve to receive glory, honor, and power because you created everything. Everything came into existence and was created because of your will (Revelation 4:10,11 God's Word).

Therefore the crowns received as rewards will be thrown at the feet of Jesus. All honor and glory belongs to Him.

This is a further indication that there will be no envy in heaven because the only One who is honored is the Lord Himself.

SUMMARY TO QUESTION 16
SINCE BELIEVERS WILL RECEIVE DIFFERENT CROWNS AS REWARDS WILL THERE BE ENVY IN HEAVEN?

Since believers will be rewarded differently in heaven the question about envy always comes up. We are told that rewards will be given to believers known as "crowns." But everyone will not receive the same reward. Will those with lesser rewards be jealous of those who receive the greater rewards?

There are a number of things we should note in answering this question. First, the crowns are not literal but rather symbolic of the different rewards which we can receive for our faithful service to Christ. Though each person will be rewarded differently, there will be no envy of those who receive greater rewards. In fact, Scripture says when one is honored all are honored.

At the end of the day, all honor will go to the Lord who has done everything on our behalf. Therefore, we do not have to worry about envy or jealously in heaven. It will not exist.

QUESTION 17

Who Is Going
To Live In Heaven?

What will the population of heaven be made up of? Will it be merely humans? Will there be angels in heaven? Will other spirit-beings also be there? What does the Bible have to say on the subject?

Scripture does tell us who will eventually inhabit heaven, the place where the Lord resides in a unique way. They include the following.

1. GOD RESIDES IN HEAVEN

Heaven has been, and always will be, the abode of the Triune God. The Bible teaches that God is a Trinity consisting of Father, Son, and Holy Spirit.

While God is not limited to one specific place in the universe, heaven is His home in a special sense. The psalmist wrote.

> The LORD looked down from his sanctuary on high, from heaven he viewed the earth (Psalm 102:19 NIV).

He resides in this sanctuary on high.

We also read in the Psalms that the throne of the Lord is in heaven. He declared.

> The LORD has established his throne in heaven, and his kingdom rules over all (Psalm 103:19 NIV).

It is from this particular place from where the Lord rules over everyone.

As he was explaining the history of the nation to an unruly crowd, the martyr Stephen quoted the Old Testament. He cited the Lord saying the following.

> Heaven is my throne, and the earth is my footstool. Could you ever build me a temple as good as that?' asks the Lord. 'Could you build a dwelling place for me? (Acts 7:49 NIV).

Heaven is the home of the living God. He will be in heaven.

2. SAVED ISRAEL WILL LIVE IN HEAVEN

Those who have trusted the Lord from the nation Israel make up another part of the heavenly host. After discussing the faithful believers whose exploits are listed in the Old Testament, the writer to the Hebrews concluded the following about them.

> All these people were still living by faith when they died. They did not receive the things promised; they only saw them and welcomed them from a distance, admitting that they were foreigners and strangers on earth. People who say such things show that they are looking for a country of their own. If they had been thinking of the country they had left, they would have had opportunity to return. Instead, they were longing for a better country—a heavenly one. Therefore God is not ashamed to be called their God, for he has prepared a city for them (Hebrews 11:13-16 NIV).

Those from the chosen people, who have trusted in Him, will be with the Lord in heaven.

3. THE NEW TESTAMENT CHURCH WILL BE IN HEAVEN

The New Testament church will also occupy heaven. They consist of all who have believed in Jesus Christ from the day of Pentecost, when the church began, until the time the Lord brings the living believers to Himself, the rapture of the church. They constitute a separate group from believers in other ages.

Paul wrote to the Thessalonians about the time when those who make up this particular group, the living as well as the dead, will all be in the presence of the Lord.

> Brothers and sisters, we do not want you to be uninformed about those who sleep in death, so that you do not grieve like the rest of mankind, who have no hope. For we believe that Jesus died and rose again, and so we believe that God will bring with Jesus those who have fallen asleep in him. According to the Lord's word, we tell you that we who are still alive, who are left until the coming of the Lord, will certainly not precede those who have fallen asleep. For the Lord himself will come down from heaven, with a loud command, with the voice of the archangel and with the trumpet call of God, and the dead in Christ will rise first. After that, we who are still alive and are left will be caught up together with them in the clouds to meet the Lord in the air. And so we will be with the Lord forever. Therefore encourage one another with these words (1 Thessalonians 4:13-18 NIV).

Therefore, the church, the believers who make up the body of Christ, will also be with the Lord forever.

4. GENTILE BELIEVERS WILL BE IN HEAVEN

Apart from saved Israel and the New Testament church, heaven will also consist of Gentile believers who have trusted the promises of God before Christ came into the world. They too will have a place in the heavenly realm.

5. HEAVEN IS THE HOME OF THE TRIBULATION SAINTS

Many people will come to belief in Jesus Christ during the Great Tribulation period. This takes place after the rapture of the church. We read of this in the Book of Revelation. Scripture says.

> I saw thrones, and those who sat on them were allowed to judge. Then I saw the souls of those whose heads had been cut off because of their testimony about Jesus and because of the word of God. They had not worshiped the beast or its statue and were not branded on their foreheads or hands. They lived and ruled with Christ for 1,000 years (Revelation 20:4 God's Word).

These tribulation saints are a distinct group from the New Testament believers, the church. They will also be part of the inhabitants of heaven.

6. THE MILLENNIAL SAINTS WILL INHABIT HEAVEN

There will also be people who put their faith in Christ during the Millennium, the thousand-year reign of Jesus Christ upon the earth. They will be children born to parents who enter the Millennium in non-glorified bodies. These believers will also be in heaven.

7. THERE WILL BE CERTAIN ELDERS IN HEAVEN

There are certain elders, twenty-four, in number, who are in heaven. We read about this in the Book of Revelation. It says.

> Around that throne were 24 other thrones, and on these thrones sat 24 leaders wearing white clothes. They had gold crowns on their heads (Revelation 4:4 God's Word).

Their exact identity is unknown. They could be angels or they could be some special group of humans.

8. ANGELS AND OTHER SPIRIT-BEINGS OCCUPY HEAVEN

There are a number of spirit-beings which the Lord has created which reside in His presence. This includes angels, the cherubim, seraphim, and the "living beings."

Angels, who are ministering spirit-beings, presently occupy heaven. Scripture describes them in heaven as follows.

> Micaiah added, "Then hear the word of the Lord. I saw the Lord sitting on his throne, and the entire army of heaven was standing on his right and his left (2 Chronicles 18:18 God's Word).

They will also occupy heaven in the future. We read about this in the Book of Revelation. It says.

> Then I looked, and I heard the voice of many angels around the throne, the living creatures, and the elders; and the number of them was ten thousand times ten thousand, and thousands of thousands (Revelation 5:11 NKJV).

The holy angels will be with the Lord in heaven.

The cherubim, seraphim, and "living creatures" are created beings; distinct from the angels. While not much is specifically said about them in Scripture, they seem to be a higher class of spirit-being than the angels.

We explain the differences between them and the angels in our three part series on the "Unseen World" (*Angels: God's Invisible Messengers; Evil Angels, Demons, And The Occult; Satan; Our Adversary The Devil*).

This gives us an idea of who will be dwelling in heaven for all eternity. The key, of course, is that the living God will be there. With Him are multitudes of redeemed people, angels and other spirit-beings. For all eternity we will celebrate together. Obviously words cannot begin to describe how wonderful it will be.

SUMMARY TO QUESTION 17
WHO IS GOING TO LIVE IN HEAVEN?

From Scripture we are told who is going to be the occupants of heaven, the eternal realm. We discover that heaven is made up of a number of different personages.

This, of course, includes God Himself (God the Father, God the Son, and God the Holy Spirit). Heaven is His home. First and foremost, heaven is the home of God.

Those who have been saved or redeemed from the chosen people, the nation of Israel, will also inhabit heaven.

There will also be Gentiles, or non-Jews, in heaven. They are those people who believed God's promises before Jesus Christ came into the world.

Heaven will be the home of another group of believers; the New Testament church. These are people who have believed in Christ during the church age. It includes both Jews and Gentiles.

There will be certain people who believe in Christ during the Great Tribulation period, the "tribulation saints." They too will be in heaven.

During the thousand years of peace upon the earth, the Millennium, many will turn to the Lord in belief. Heaven is their home also.

Heaven will be the home of certain elders whose identity is not specified. Finally, the righteous angels, as well as other spirit beings, will also be part of the inhabitants of heaven.

What Will It Be Like Living In Heaven?
(What Will We Do?)

One of the questions about heaven that often arises concerns what we will do once we get there. What will it be like living in our new heavenly home? What will be doing for all eternity?

Fortunately, God has not kept us in the dark about living in heaven. Indeed, the Bible tells us many things about the character, or nature, of heaven, the presence of the Living God. From Scripture we learn the following things.

1. IS WILL BE THE HOME OF RIGHTEOUSNESS

To begin with, the Scripture calls heaven the "home of righteousness" or the place "where righteousness dwells." Peter wrote.

> But in keeping with his promise we are looking forward to a new heaven and a new earth, where righteousness dwells (2 Peter 3:13 NIV).

The New Living Translation puts it this way.

> But we are looking forward to the new heavens and new earth he has promised, a world where everyone is right with God (2 Peter 3:13 NLT).

Everyone in heaven will be in a right relationship with the Lord.

2. THERE WILL BE A REUNION WITH SAVED LOVED ONES

It will be a place where saved loved ones will be re-united. Paul stated this wonderful truth when he wrote to the Thessalonians. He wrote.

> Then we who are alive *and* remain shall be caught up together with them in the clouds to meet the Lord in the air. And thus we shall always be with the Lord. Therefore comfort one another with these words (1 Thessalonians 4:17,18 NKJV).

We will again see those believers in Jesus Christ who have gone before us in death. Consequently heaven will be a place of reunion.

3. THERE WILL BE PERFECT REST

Heaven will be a place of perfect rest for the believer. The Lord spoke to John and told him to write about this truth.

> I heard a voice from heaven saying, "Write this: From now on those who die believing in the Lord are blessed." "Yes," says the Spirit. "Let them rest from their hard work. What they have done goes with them (Revelation 14:13 God's Word).

This rest is not the cessation of activities but rather the completion of a goal. Our earthly labors are finished. We are now in His presence. All of our spiritual battles are over.

4. BELIEVERS WILL BE PERFECTED

Heaven will also be the place where perfected believers will live. The Bible says that every believer who enters heaven will be changed, transformed. We read about this in Paul's first letter to the Corinthians. He explained it this way.

> But let me tell you a wonderful secret God has revealed to us. Not all of us will die, but we will all be transformed (1 Corinthians 15:51 NLT).

Three transformations will take place in heaven. We will have: a change of the body, a change of the mind, and a change of the character.

A. OUR BODIES WILL BE CHANGED IN HEAVEN

The bodies of believers will be changed. They will be like that of the resurrected Christ. The Bible says the following about them.

> Dear friends, we are God's children now, and what we will be has not yet been revealed. We know that when He appears, we will be like Him, because we will see Him as He is (1 John 3:2 HCSB).

We will have bodies like that of the resurrected Christ. This means we will have abilities that our present bodies do not possess. Our new body will be a glorified body.

B. WE WILL HAVE A NEW MIND

Our mind will be free from sin. Paul wrote the following to the church at Corinth about our knowledge when we are in His presence.

> Now we see things imperfectly as in a poor mirror, but then we will see everything with perfect clarity. All that I know now is partial and incomplete, but then I will know everything completely, just as God knows me now (1 Corinthians 13:12 NLT).

We will have a more complete knowledge of God in heaven. However, this does not mean that we will know everything. Indeed, we will never become God-like in knowledge but our knowledge will continue to grow.

C. WE WILL HAVE A NEW CHARACTER

Heaven will also be a place where believers will have a completely new character. Everyone there will be pure. John wrote.

Blessed are those who wash their robes, that they may have the right to the tree of life and may go through the gates into the city (Revelation 22:14 NIV).

Our entire character will be renewed. We will be completely rid of things which cause us to sin against the Lord.

5. ALL OF OUR NEEDS WILL BE MET

Heaven will be a place where all of our needs will be met. We read the following in the Book of Revelation.

They shall neither hunger anymore nor thirst anymore; the sun shall not strike them, nor any heat; "for the Lamb who is in the midst of the throne will shepherd them and lead them to living fountains of waters. And God will wipe away every tear from their eyes (Revelation 7:16-17 NKJV).

We will lack nothing when we are in His holy presence. He will provide everything for us. This is certainly in keeping with His nature as the "providing God."

6. WE SHALL SEE GOD!

In heaven, we shall actually see God. Jesus said.

Blessed *are* the pure in heart: for they shall see God (Matthew 5:8 KJV).

We are promised that we will be in His presence.

WE WILL SEE JESUS ALSO

Not only will we see God the Father, Jesus also said believers will be with Him in heaven. Thus, we are promised to see the First and Second Persons of the Holy Trinity.

On the night of His betrayal, Jesus said the following words to His disciples.

And if I go and prepare a place for you, I will come back and take you to be with me that you also may be where I am (John 14:3 NIV).

He is presently preparing a place for those of us who know Him. When we arrive we will be with Him and He with us.

On that same night, He prayed to His Father about believers being with Him wherever He may be. Jesus said.

I desire those You have given Me to be with Me where I am. Then they will see My glory, which You have given Me because You loved Me before the world's foundation (John 17:24 HCSB).

We will be with Jesus and we will see His glory!

WE WILL BE FACE TO FACE WITH HIM

The Apostle Paul spoke of a day when we will be face to face with God. He wrote the following to the Corinthians.

For now we see only a reflection as in a mirror; then we shall see face to face. Now I know in part; then I shall know fully, even as I am fully known (1 Corinthians 13:12 NIV).

The Book of Revelation also records this happening. John wrote.

I heard a loud shout from the throne, saying, "Look, the home of God is now among his people! He will live with them, and they will be his people. God himself will be with them" (Revelation 21:3 NLT).

The Bible also says that His name will be written on our foreheads. We also read about this in the Book of Revelation.

There will no longer be any curse. The throne of God and the lamb will be in the city. His servants will worship him and see his face. His name will be on their foreheads (Revelation 22:4,5 God's Word).

This is the wonderful promise the Lord has given to those who believe in Him!

7. IT WILL BE A PLACE OF SERVICE

Although heaven will be a place of rest, there is still service to God that will be performed. John wrote about our service in heaven. He said.

> No longer will there be anything accursed, but the throne of God and of the Lamb will be in it, and his servants will worship him (Revelation 22:3 ESV).

We will willingly serve and worship Him.

8. THERE WILL BE WORSHIP OF THE LORD

Heaven is an opportunity where we will have perfect worship of God. There will be nothing distracting us from our worship of Him. Jesus said.

> Indeed, the time is coming, and it is now here, when the true worshipers will worship the Father in spirit and truth. The Father is looking for people like that to worship him (John 4:23 God's Word).

The worship in heaven will be faultless. It will indeed be worship of Him "in truth."

9. THERE WILL BE SINGING

Singing will be a part of our heavenly experience. Scripture records those in heaven singing songs to the Lord. One of them will be the song of Moses and the Song of the Lamb. John wrote about this in the Book of Revelation when he recorded this marvelous sight.

I saw before me what seemed to be a glass sea mixed with fire. And on it stood all the people who had been victorious over the beast and his statue and the number representing his name. They were all holding harps that God had given them. And they were singing the song of Moses, the servant of God, and the song of the Lamb: "Great and marvelous are your works, O Lord God, the Almighty. Just and true are your ways, O King of the nations. Who will not fear you, Lord, and glorify your name? For you alone are holy. All nations will come and worship before you, for your righteous deeds have been revealed (Revelation 15:2,3 NLT).

We will praise God with our singing. Our voices will testify in song to His great and marvelous works.

10. WE WILL EXPERIENCE THE RICHNESS OF HIS GRACE FOREVER

The Bible says that believers will continually experience the riches of God's grace in heaven. Paul wrote the following to the Ephesians about this wonderful promise.

So that in the coming ages He might display the immeasurable riches of His grace in [His] kindness to us in Christ Jesus (Ephesians 2:7 HCSB).

In the ages to come, when everything sinful has forever been removed from the believers, the goodness of God will continually display itself in still higher ways. We cannot even imagine all of the amazing things that the Lord has in store for us!

11. BELIEVERS WILL BE RULING

In some unexplained way, we will rule with the Lord in the next life. Paul wrote the following to Timothy.

If we endure hardship, we will reign with him (2 Timothy 2:12 NLT).

Rulership is part of the future of the believer. We will rule and reign with the Lord in the eternal realm. Again we emphasize that just how we will rule and whom we will rule over is not stated in Scripture.

12. THERE WILL BE EATING AND DRINKING

It is possible, though not necessary, to eat and drink in heaven. We read about this in the Book of Revelation.

> The Spirit and the Bride say, "Come." And let the one who hears say, "Come." And let the one who is thirsty come; let the one who desires take the water of life without price (Revelation 22:17 ESV).

We will have the ability to freely drink the water of life. This seems to refer to actual water which is flowing through the Holy City.

We also read in the Book of Revelation about fruit growing on the tree of life. In the last chapter of this last book of Scripture, it is described for us in this manner.

> Down the middle of the broad street of the city. On both sides of the river was the tree of life bearing 12 kinds of fruit, producing its fruit every month. The leaves of the tree are for healing the nations (Revelation 22:2 HCSB).

This further indicates that we will have the ability to eat and drink.

This is in keeping with what Jesus told His disciples at the Last Supper. He spoke of drinking from the fruit of the vine in the kingdom.

> For I tell you that from now on I will not drink of the fruit of the vine until the kingdom of God comes (Luke 22:18 ESV).

While many interpret this symbolically, there is no apparent reason as to why we shouldn't understand it in a literal manner.

In addition, the Bible speaks of the marriage supper of the Lamb where the believers are banqueting.

> Then the angel said to me, "Write this: 'Blessed are those who are invited to the lamb's wedding banquet. '" He also told me, "These are the true words of God (Revelation 19:9 God's Word).

These passages seem to make it clear that part of the activity in heaven will be eating and drinking.

13. HEAVEN WILL HAVE NO BOREDOM

Contrary to the idea which many people have, eternity will not be boring. Believers will be busy as servants of the Most High God. We read the following in the Book of Revelation.

> Therefore they are before the throne of God, and serve him day and night in his temple; and he who sits on the throne will shelter them with his presence (Revelation 7:15 ESV).

There will be no boredom in heaven. None whatsoever!

These are some of the wonderful truths that the Lord tells us about heaven, our future home. Indeed, what a great place it will be!

SUMMARY TO QUESTION 18
WHAT WILL BE IT LIKE LIVING IN HEAVEN?

We all wonder what it will be like living in heaven. The Bible gives us quite a bit of information about what believers should expect in the next life. We can sum it up as follows.

Heaven will be the home of the righteous. Indeed, those who have trusted in the promises of God will call heaven their eternal home. Heaven will be a place where we feel at home. We know we belong there because of Jesus and our relationship with Him.

Scripture says there will be a reunion with saved loved ones in heaven. Those believers who have gone before us in death will be reunited with us in heaven. This is indeed a comforting thought!

Heaven is also described as a place of perfect rest. Rest means cessation from conflict but not cessation from service. Indeed, we will be serving the Lord in heaven but this service will not involve the conflicts we face down here.

Believers will be perfected in heaven; we will have new bodies, a new mind, and a new heart. Our glorified bodies will be like that of the Lord Jesus. They will be perfect in every respect.

All of our needs will be met in heaven. Since we will be with the Lord, we will lack nothing. He will supply everything necessary.

In heaven, we shall experience God in a personal way. Indeed we will see God the Father and God the Son, Jesus Christ. Consequently, no temple will be necessary since God's presence does not have to be represented to us any longer.

Heaven will be a place where we can serve God. There will be plenty for us to do in this heavenly realm. It will not be boring.

It will also be a place of worship and singing. With our lips we will testify to the goodness of the Lord for all eternity. We will let Him know how much we love Him.

Heaven is a place from where believers will actually rule. What all of this means is not fully explained to us. We are merely told that we will rule and reign with Him.

Such things as eating and drinking will also be a part of heaven. Though not necessary for survival, it seems that we will be able to both eat and drink for all eternity.

Finally, heaven will never be boring. How can it be? The living God is there in its midst!

Will Believers Spend Eternity Playing Harps On Floating Clouds? Will We Have A Halo Above Our Head?

One of the common images of heaven consists of people wearing a white robe with a halo above their head. They are floating on a white cloud out in space and playing a harp. Indeed, to many people this would be the first thing which would come to mind if asked what people will do in heaven.

Is this what heaven consists of? Will we spend all eternity playing a harp while floating on a cloud? Will we be wearing white outfits with a halo above our head while we do this? What does the Bible say?

HEAVEN IS A PLACE OF SERVICE

The biblical description of heaven is one of action, not inaction. We will be serving the Lord in various capacities.

WE WILL JUDGE THE WORLD

For one thing, the Apostle Paul stated that believers will judge the world. He wrote the following to the Corinthians.

> Or do you not know that the saints will judge the world? And if the world is judged by you, are you unworthy to judge the smallest cases? (1 Corinthians 6:2 HCSB).

While we may not exactly know how we will judge the world, it certainly involves doing something.

WE WILL JUDGE ANGELS

Not only are we going to judge the world, the Apostle Paul also said we are to judge angels. To these same Corinthians, he wrote.

> Do you not know that we will judge angels (1 Corinthians 6:3 HCSB).

Again, while we do not understand exactly what this means, it certainly does not give a picture of people inactively playing harps all the time.

JESUS SAID WE WILL BE INVOLVED IN RULERSHIP

Jesus Himself spoke of the rulership of believers in His future kingdom. In a parable, He compared faithfulness in this life to future rule over cities in the next life. Jesus has the Master saying the following to His servants.

> 'Well done, good slave!' he told him. 'Because you have been faithful in a very small matter, have authority over 10 towns (Luke 19:17 HCSB).

Elsewhere Jesus laid down the principle that faithfulness in a few things would allow the believer to be ruler over many things.

> His master replied, 'Well done, good and faithful servant! You have been faithful with a few things; I will put you in charge of many things. Come and share your master's happiness!' (Matthew 25:23 NIV).

Again, this gives us a picture of action, or responsibility; not of passing the time by playing a harp while floating on a cloud. Heaven will not be a boring inactive place.

THERE WILL BE WHITE OUTFITS BUT NO HALOS

Scripture does describe believers as being clothed in white garments. We read of this in the Book of Revelation. It says.

> After this I looked, and there was a great multitude that no one could count, from every nation, from all tribes and peoples and languages, standing before the throne and before the Lamb, robed in white, with palm branches in their hands (Revelation 7:9 NIV).

This represents the fact that we have been cleansed from our sin. However, nowhere in the Bible do we find the idea that there is some type of halo above our head. This idea did not come from God's Word.

MUSICAL INSTRUMENTS ARE PLAYED IN HEAVEN

In heaven, the inhabitants will do many things. One of them is playing musical instruments. We read of harp-playing by the twenty-four elders. The Book of Revelation informs us of this.

> And when he had taken it, the four living creatures and the twenty-four elders fell down before the Lamb. Each one had a harp and they were holding golden bowls full of incense, which are the prayers of God's people (Revelation 5:8 NIV).

The identity of the twenty-four elders is debated. Some believe they are humans while others think they refer to special spirit-beings which the Lord has created. Whatever the case may be, they are playing harps.

In another passage, the martyred saints are pictured as having harps in their hand. This is also found in the Book of Revelation. It says.

> And I saw what appeared to be a sea of glass mingled with fire—and also those who had conquered the beast and its image and the number of its name, standing beside the sea of glass with harps of God in their hands (Revelation 15:2 ESV).

While this passage does not say that these believers actually played the harps the inference is that they certainly did.

Consequently while playing a harp is certainly not everything which we will do in heaven, it seems that it makes up part of the worship which believers will direct to the Lord.

In sum, heaven will be a busy place for believers. It will certainly not consist of floating around on a cloud.

SUMMARY TO QUESTION 19
WILL BELIEVERS SPEND ETERNITY PLAYING HARPS ON FLOATING CLOUDS? WILL WE HAVE A HALO ABOVE OUR HEAD?

A common picture of heaven is one of believers sitting on a floating white cloud with a harp in their hand. Usually the person is dressed in a white robe with a halo above his or her head. This is the idea many people have of heaven. Christians will spend all eternity playing a harp and doing little else. It sounds so boring!

But this is not what the Bible teaches. Heaven will consist of believers serving the Lord in various capacities; we will not be merely sitting around strumming on a harp. This is not what the Scripture says we will be doing.

Indeed, the Apostle Paul said that believers are to judge the world. While we do not know exactly what it means, we do know that it means something.

Paul also said we are to judge angels. Again, it is not explained exactly what that means. However, in some sense, it seems that we will ruler over them.

We know that these illustrations do speak of some sort of rulership in the coming kingdom. This echoes what Jesus taught. He gave a parable about future rulership in His kingdom. Those who were faithful in much would rule over much while those who were faithful in little would have little rule. This is a picture of action and responsibility, not boredom and inaction.

While we are said to be wearing "white clothes" in heaven there is nothing in Scripture that says we will have a halo above our heads.

It does seem possible that we will be playing musical instruments at times. This may include harps. The Book of Revelation tells us that the twenty-four elders were playing harps in worship to the Lord. Their identity is uncertain. They may represent believers or some special spirit-beings which the Lord has created. Therefore, from their particular example we cannot be certain whether or not we will be playing harps. We can only say that it is possible.

Another picture of heaven has those who are martyred for Jesus Christ holding harps in their hands. The inference from this example is that these believers were playing harps in their worship of the Lord.

Consequently it seems that harp playing may indeed be part of our heavenly experience. Yet, as we have emphasized, this is certainly not everything that heaven consists of. We will all be busy and we will all have responsibilities. This is the true picture of heaven.

Will We See God
In Heaven?

While the Bible tells us that heaven consists of a number of truly wonderful things, it also informs of what will *not* be in heaven. There will indeed be things that are missing. They include the following.

1. THERE WILL BE NO UNBELIEVERS IN HEAVEN

First, heaven will consist of only those who have trusted in the God of Scripture. All unbelievers are kept out. We read in the Book of Revelation.

> Outside the city are the dogs—the sorcerers, the sexually immoral, the murderers, the idol worshipers, and all who love to live a lie (Revelation 21:15 NLT).

Unbelievers will be missing from heaven. They have no place with the righteous.

2. SATAN AND HIS ANGELS WILL BE MISSING FROM HEAVEN

Not only will unbelieving humans be kept out of heaven, the same holds true for Satan and the evil spirit-beings which follow him, the evil angels. They too will be denied access to heaven and its glory.

The Bible says the following about the fate of the devil.

Then the Devil, who betrayed them, was thrown into the lake of fire that burns with sulfur, joining the beast and the false prophet. There they will be tormented day and night forever and ever (Revelation 20:10 NLT).

Earlier, Jesus had said that hell, the lake of fire, had been prepared for the devil and his angels.

Then the king will say to those on his left, 'Get away from me! God has cursed you! Go into everlasting fire that was prepared for the devil and his angels' (Matthew 25:41 God's Word).

These beings will be thrown into the lake of fire; eternally separated from God. They will have no place with the righteous.

Therefore, the Bible teaches that all unbelieving creatures, whether human or non-human, will be thrown into the fiery lake.

3. THERE WILL BE NO DEATH IN HEAVEN

In heaven there will be no death. In the Book of Revelation, John described death being thrown into the Lake of Fire. He wrote.

Then Death and Hades were thrown into the lake of fire. This is the second death, the lake of fire (Revelation 20:14 ESV).

Later, it says in the Book of Revelation that death will be no more. We read.

He will wipe away every tear from their eyes. Death will exist no longer; grief, crying, and pain will exist no longer, because the previous things have passed away (Revelation 21:4 HCSB).

Death will be a thing of the past.

Neither will there be an intermediate state between this life and eternity. Hades, which represents this in-between state of the dead, will be no more.

4. THERE WILL BE NO CRYING OR TEARS IN HEAVEN

Sadness and pain will be a thing of the past, for there will be no tears in this new heaven. We read the following in the Book of Revelation.

> He will wipe away every tear from their eyes, and death shall be no more, neither shall there be mourning, nor crying, nor pain anymore, for the former things have passed away (Revelation 21:4 ESV).

This fulfills what the prophet Isaiah said about the future. He wrote.

> He will swallow up death forever. The Sovereign LORD will wipe away the tears from all faces; he will remove the disgrace of his people from all the earth. The LORD has spoken (Isaiah 25:8 NIV).

Death will be swallowed up and tears will be a thing of the past.

5. WE WILL BE FREE FROM ALL IMPURITY

Heaven will be pure; free from all impurity. The Book of Revelation tells us that nothing unclean will be in the Lord's presence. We read.

> But there shall by no means enter it anything that defiles, or causes an abomination or a lie, but only those who are written in the Lamb's Book of Life (Revelation 21:27 NKJV).

Only the things that are pure and holy will be found in heaven. Nothing which is corrupt can exist in the presence of the Lord.

> No longer will anything be cursed. For the throne of God and of the Lamb will be there, and his servants will worship him (Revelation 22:3 NLT).

Nothing that had to do with the cursed earth will exist in heaven. It will be completely free from the curse of sin.

6. THERE WILL BE NO MORE SUN OR MOON

Interestingly, the sun and the moon will not exist in heaven. We read in the Book of Revelation that there is no need for them any longer.

> And the city has no need of sun or moon, for the glory of God illuminates the city, and the Lamb is its light (Revelation 21:23 NLT).

The heavenly bodies will no longer be necessary.

7. IT WILL BE FREE FROM ALL DARKNESS

While there is no sun or moon in heaven, it will be a place that is free from darkness. We read in the Book of Revelation about God being the source of light in heaven.

> There will be no more night, and they will not need any light from lamps or the sun because the Lord God will shine on them (Revelation 22:5 God's Word).

God is light and His presence will lighten everything. Nothing else will be necessary. Indeed all the light which is needed will come from Him.

8. THERE WILL BE NO HEAVENLY TEMPLE

The temple, which represented the presence of God, will no longer be necessary in heaven. John wrote.

> No temple could be seen in the city, for the Lord God Almighty and the Lamb are its temple (Revelation 21:22 NLT).

The Lord will be there in person. Thus, no representation of Him is needed.

Therefore, heaven will be missing a number of things; things which have no place in the presence of God.

SUMMARY TO QUESTION 20
WHAT WON'T WE SEE IN HEAVEN? WHAT WILL BE MISSING?

The Bible informs us what will be in heaven. Indeed, there are many wonderful truths which are given to in Scripture about what heaven will consist of. However, heaven will also be missing a number of things. As we must appreciate what is in heaven, we must also appreciate what is not there. They include the following.

Heaven will be a place where only believers reside. There will be no unbelieving human beings or unbelieving spirit beings such as Satan and his followers. They will be excluded from heaven.

Therefore, certain humans and angels will be missing from God's presence. The only beings in heaven along with the Lord will be the redeemed or saved humans as well as the godly angels and the other spirit-beings the Lord created which did not rebel. Nobody else is allowed.

Death will not exist in heaven. Everyone who resides in heaven will live there eternally. Consequently, death will be a thing of the past. This enemy will be once and for all destroyed.

In addition, Hades, which represents the intermediate state, will also be done away with. Once eternity begins, all things temporary will be gone. There will be no more waiting for anything.

Furthermore, not only will death be a thing of the past, there will not even be any crying or tears in heaven. No sadness of any kind. All of these things will be long gone. Happiness will reign for all eternity.

There is something else which Scripture stresses. Everything impure will be banned from heaven. Things associated with the former cursed earth will be gone from God's presence. Jesus said He will "make all things new."

Neither the sun nor the moon will exist in heaven. They are not necessary because the light of the Lord will illuminate heaven. His light will be sufficient. The heavenly bodies are holdovers from the previous cursed earth. They will no longer be needed.

Finally, there will be no temple in heaven. The various temples which were on earth, as well as the heavenly temple, are representations of the presence of the Lord. Since the Lord Himself will personally be dwelling with believers no temple will be necessary.

This represents some of the things missing in the heavenly realm.

QUESTION 21

Will We See God
In Heaven?

One of the questions which is often-asked about heaven concerns us and God. Will we actually get to see Him when we reach heaven? If so, what will we see? If not, then why won't we see Him? What does the Bible have to say?

OUR DESIRE IS TO SEE GOD

As we read the Scripture, we find that the desire of believers is to see God, to be in His actual presence. The psalmist wrote about this heartfelt longing.

> As a deer longs for streams of water, so I long for you, O God! I thirst for God, for the living God. I say, "When will I be able to go and appear in God's presence?" (Psalm 42:1-2 NET).

Here we have a heartfelt expression of the psalmist. He wanted to actually see God.

The Contemporary English Version puts it this way.

> As a deer gets thirsty for streams of water, I truly am thirsty for you, my God. In my heart, I am thirsty for you, the living God. When will I see your face (Psalm 42:1-2 CEV).

The desire of the psalmist is to be in God's personal presence. Those of us who believe in the God of Scripture through His Son, Jesus Christ, have that same longing as the psalmist. We want to see God; we want to be in His Holy presence.

THE QUESTION OF PHILIP TO JESUS

In the New Testament, we have something similar recorded. Philip, one of Jesus' apostles, asked to see the Father. John records it in this manner.

> Philip said to him, "Lord, show us the Father, and it is enough for us" (John 14:8 ESV).

This question indicates that the people believed they could actually see God the Father. Otherwise, the question would not have been asked.

What does the Scripture say? Will we be able to actually see God, to be in His presence, in the afterlife?

THERE ARE TWO POSSIBLE VIEWS ABOUT BELIEVERS BEING ABLE TO SEE GOD

On the question of actually seeing God when we get to heaven, there are two views on this subject that are held by Bible-believers. Some people believe and teach that we will not see God in heaven while others believe that we will indeed see Him.

We will look at the arguments given by each side to support their case.

OPTION 1: WE WILL NOT SEE GOD IN HEAVEN

There are Christians who believe that we will *not* see God in heaven. A number of arguments are given to support this idea. They are as follows.

1. GOD HAS NO PHYSICAL FORM

The main reason usually given as to why we will not see God in heaven is that God is invisible. Indeed, Jesus said that God is spirit. In the Gospel of John we read the following words of our Lord as He describes God.

> God is spirit, and those who worship him must worship in spirit and truth (John 4:24 ESV).

A spirit, by definition, has no physical form. Since God is spirit, and a spirit does not have any physical or corporeal form, God will not be visible to us. Therefore, we will not see Him in heaven because there is no form to see.

2. HUMANS ARE NOT ALLOWED TO DIRECTLY APPROACH GOD

There is something else which also must be appreciated in attempting to answer this question. Paul the apostle said that the Lord dwells in unapproachable light. He wrote the following description of God in his first letter to Timothy.

> He is the only one who cannot die. He lives in light that no one can come near. No one has seen him, nor can they see him. Honor and power belong to him forever! Amen (1 Timothy 6:16 God's Word).

This, it is argued is another indication that humans will never see God. His character is of such where we humans cannot approach. If we cannot approach Him, then certainly we won't be able to see Him.

In fact, the Lord specifically said this to Moses; humans cannot see the face of God. We read the following in the Book of Exodus.

> But He [God] said, "You cannot see My face; for no man shall see Me, and live" (Exodus 33:20 NKJV).

God Himself has specifically said that we humans cannot see Him and live. This seems to settle the issue.

In the New Testament, the Scripture again makes it clear that no human has ever seen God, or can see God. John wrote.

> No one has ever seen God, but God the One and Only, who is at the Father's side, has made him known (John 1:18 NIV).

Consequently, we will not be able to see Him or be in His actual presence. A study of the Bible precludes this idea.

OPTION 2: WE WILL SEE GOD IN HEAVEN

There is also the perspective that we will indeed see God in heaven. Those who hold this position present the following reasons.

1. WE CANNOT SEE GOD IN THESE SINFUL BODIES

The idea that humans cannot approach God has to do with the situation in which we presently find ourselves. Indeed, we now reside in sinful bodies. As long as we remain in these sinful bodies we cannot come into His holy presence.

Yet the Scripture says that one day our bodies will be changed. Paul wrote the following to the Corinthians.

> I'm telling you a mystery. Not all of us will die, but we will all be changed. It will happen in an instant, in a split second at the sound of the last trumpet. Indeed, that trumpet will sound, and then the dead will come back to life. They will be changed so that they can live forever. This body that decays must be changed into a body that cannot decay. This mortal body must be changed into a body that will live forever. When this body that decays is changed into a body that cannot decay, and this mortal body is changed into a body that will live forever, then the teaching of

Scripture will come true: "Death is turned into victory!
Death, where is your victory? Death, where is your sting
(1 Corinthians 15:51-55 God's Word).

Someday these sinful bodies will undergo a change. When that change
occurs we will then be able to see God. The passages which speak
about not being able to see God, or not being allowed in His presence,
refer to these present bodies.

Today we cannot see God because of our sinful nature. However,
someday we will be changed. When this takes place we will be able to
see Him in our new glorified bodies.

2. THE BIBLE SAYS WE WILL SEE GOD

The other argument used is that there are specific statements in
Scripture which say that we will see God. In the Sermon on the
Mount, Jesus said.

> Blessed *are* the pure in heart: for they shall see God
> (Matthew 5:8 KJV).

Jesus claimed that those who are pure in heart, which every believer
will one day be, will be able to see God. This seems to indicate that we
will be able to see Him in our glorified bodies.

The Apostle Paul, in his first letter to the Corinthians, wrote about
eventually seeing the Lord face to face. He put it this way.

> When I was a child, I talked like a child, I thought like a
> child, I reasoned like a child. When I became a man, I put
> childish ways behind me. Now we see but a poor reflection
> as in a mirror; then we shall see face to face. Now I know
> in part; then I shall know fully, even as I am fully known
> (1 Corinthians 13:11-13 NIV).

Notice that the hope of Paul, to see the Lord face to face, was something to which he looked forward. Yet he believed it would occur after

this life was over. This is in keeping with the idea that we will see the Lord but only when we have our glorified bodies.

In the Book of Revelation, we have a statement of John, the writer of the book, about how he was brought into the presence of God the Father. The Bible says.

> After this I looked, and there in heaven was an open door. The first voice that I had heard speaking to me like a trumpet said, "Come up here, and I will show you what must take place after this." Immediately I was in the Spirit, and there in heaven a throne was set. One was seated on the throne, and the One seated looked like jasper and carnelian stone. A rainbow that looked like an emerald surrounded the throne (Revelation 4:1-3 HCSB).

This is not a reference to seeing the glorified Jesus, but rather it refers to John seeing God the Father. He was allowed to be in the holy presence of the Lord.

Later, in the Book of Revelation, we are told that all believers will eventually see God. The Bible describes what will happen when the Lord creates a new heaven and a new earth. Among other things, we are told the following.

> They will see his face, and his name will be on their foreheads (Revelation 22:4 NIV).

Therefore, these passages have convinced many people that we will indeed see the living God when we get to heaven.

IF WE WILL SEE GOD WHAT EXACTLY WILL WE SEE?

Even if one grants that we will see God the Father in the afterlife, the problem remains as to what we will actually see. God the Father is spirit; He has no physical form.

While the glorified Christ will seemingly remain in the same form for all eternity, God the Father has no definite corporeal form. Therefore, if we do see God the Father we will probably see some representation of His essence. To sum up, we just do not know what exactly we will see when we are in His presence.

WHAT ABOUT THE HOLY SPIRIT?

Interestingly, left out of these discussions is the Third Person of the Trinity, God the Holy Spirit. Nobody ever seems to ask if we will see Him in the afterlife. In fact, Scripture does not seem to single Him out when speaking of the eternal state.

This again points to the fact that there are so many things which we do not know about the afterlife. The answers to these and other questions will have to wait until we the time when we arrive in His presence.

SUMMARY TO QUESTION 21
WILL WE SEE GOD IN HEAVEN?

When we get to heaven it will be an entirely different experience than anything we have ever experienced here upon the earth. There are many questions which remain unanswered.

For one thing, there is the matter as to whether we actually see God the Father when we get to heaven. While we know we are going to see Jesus, God the Son, there is some question as to whether we will see God the Father. Are we going to ever see Him or will He always be invisible to us? Christians are divided on this question.

Those who do not believe that we will ever see Him argue that God the Father, by nature, is invisible. Therefore, we will never see Him because there is no physical or corporeal form to see.

Furthermore, the Bible clearly says that humanity is not allowed to be in His glorious presence. There are direct statements in Scripture, one of them made by God Himself, to the effect that we cannot be in His presence and live. To many, this settles the issue.

Those who do believe that we will one day see God note that it is sinful humanity which is not allowed into God's presence. However, the Bible says that someday we are all going to be changed. Our sinful nature will be transformed into a sinless nature.

Therefore, our present sinful nature will not stop us from seeing the Lord in the future because we will not have it any longer. We will be free from sin.

Furthermore, there are a number of passages which specifically state that we will see God the Father in the afterlife. In the Sermon on the Mount, Jesus said that those who are pure in heart will see God. This describes the transformation through which all of us will undergo. We will become pure in heart in the next world.

If this is the case, and we will be able to see God, then there is still the issue as to what exactly we will see. Since God is spirit, and therefore has no actual form, anything which we do see will likely be some type of representation of His Person. We will not see His actual essence.

Forgotten in this discussion is the Third Person of the Trinity, the Holy Spirit. He seems to be ignored when we ask the question about whether we will see God in heaven.

Nothing in Scripture is said, one way or the other, as to whether or not we will see any representation of Him or actually see Him. We just do not know.

As is true with many questions about the afterlife, there are things which we are not told in this life. Thus, we await the answer to these and other questions. All things will be answered when we get to "the other side."

QUESTION 22

Will We Remember Our Loved Ones In Heaven?

Often we wonder about heaven and the new relationships that will be there. Will we recognize one another in heaven? Will we know our loved ones? Will they know us? The Bible says the following about this subject.

1. DAVID WOULD RECOGNIZE HIS SON

The story of David and his son illustrates the point that we will indeed know our loved ones in the next world. After the child died, we find David giving the following testimony.

> David answered, "As long as the child was alive, I fasted and cried. I thought, 'Who knows? The LORD may be gracious to me and let the child live.' But why should I fast now that he's dead? Can I bring him back? Someday I'll go to him, but he won't come back to me" (2 Samuel 12:22,23 God's Word).

In this statement, David is acknowledging the fact that he will someday be united with his son. If David did not think that he would recognize his son in the next life, then there is no reason he would have made this statement.

There is something else we must consider. Scripture calls David "a prophet." On the Day of Pentecost, Peter gave this testimony to the crowd which gathered.

Brothers, I can tell you confidently that the patriarch David died and was buried, and his tomb is here to this day. But he was a prophet and knew that God had promised him on oath that he would place one of his descendants on his throne (Acts 2:29-30 NIV).

This statement of Peter, calling David a prophet, gives us reason to trust what David said about recognizing his son in heaven.

2. MOSES AND ELIJAH WERE RECOGNIZED AT THE TRANSFIGURATION

At the Mount of Transfiguration, Moses and Elijah appeared with Jesus. Mark records the account as follows.

Then Elijah and Moses appeared and began talking with Jesus. "Teacher, this is wonderful!" Peter exclaimed. "We will make three shrines—one for you, one for Moses, and one for Elijah" (Mark 9:4,5 NLT).

Moses had died centuries before and Elijah was taken to heaven in a whirlwind. Yet they did not lose their individual identity, or their ability to be recognized. Without a formal introduction Moses and Elijah were recognized by Jesus' three disciples.

3. BELIEVERS WILL SIT DOWN WITH THE PATRIARCHS

In another place in Scripture, it is recorded that Jesus mentioned sitting down with the patriarchs in heaven Abraham, Isaac, and Jacob, in the kingdom of God. Matthew reports Jesus saying the following.

I tell you, many will come from east and west and recline at table with Abraham, Isaac, and Jacob in the kingdom of heaven (Matthew 8:11 ESV).

This further demonstrates that each person will keep his or her individual identity. Abraham, Isaac and Jacob would be recognizable.

4. THE RICH MAN RECOGNIZED LAZARUS AND ABRAHAM

In the story that Jesus told of the rich man and the beggar Lazarus, we find the rich man recognizing both Abraham and Lazarus in the next world (Luke 16:19-31). Likewise, Abraham recognized the rich man. In the afterlife, there is obvious recognition of one another. Our identities are kept.

5. WE SHALL BE LIKE JESUS IN OUR RESURRECTED BODIES

The Bible says that we shall be like Jesus in our resurrected body. John wrote that our bodies will be similar to His.

> Dear friends, now we are children of God, and what we will be has not yet been made known. But we know that when Christ appears, we shall be like him, for we shall see him as he is (1 John 3:2 NIV).

We will be like Him. We know from the New Testament that Jesus was recognized after His resurrection. Since His resurrection form was recognizable, so will ours be. Thus, we have another reason to assume that we will be recognizable in the next world.

6. OUR KNOWLEDGE WILL BE GREATER

There is something else which we must consider. The Bible says that our knowledge in heaven will be greater than it is now, not less. Paul emphasized this when he wrote the following to the church in Corinth.

> For now we see only a reflection as in a mirror; then we shall see face to face. Now I know in part; then I shall know fully, even as I am fully known (1 Corinthians 13:12 NIV).

Consequently, if our knowledge is to be greater in the next world, then we should be able to recognize one another in the afterlife since we certainly are able to do this now!

7. PEOPLE WILL SPEAK WITH THE LORD

There is also an indirect reference of people speaking to the Lord in heaven. We read the following in the Book of Revelation.

> And when the Lamb broke the fifth seal, I saw under the altar the souls of all who had been martyred for the word of God and for being faithful in their witness. They called loudly to the Lord and said, "O Sovereign Lord, holy and true, how long will it be before you judge the people who belong to this world for what they have done to us? When will you avenge our blood against these people?" Then a white robe was given to each of them. And they were told to rest a little longer until the full number of their brothers and sisters—their fellow servants of Jesus—had been martyred (Revelation 6:9-11 NLT).

Since these people are able to speak to each other, this seems to give further testimony of recognition of one another in heaven.

Consequently, from the totality of the teachings of Scripture, we find there will be recognition of one another in heaven. We will know our loved ones and they will know us.

SUMMARY TO QUESTION 22
WILL WE REMEMBER OUR LOVED ONES IN HEAVEN?

It seems clear that, in heaven, we will recognize those whom we love as well as those people we are acquainted with here upon the earth. We will all keep our unique identities.

The Bible provides examples of those who had previously died, yet were recognizable in the next world. We know that David believed that his son in the next world would recognize him. Moses and Elijah were recognized at the Mount of Transfiguration. Scripture says that believers will sit down with the patriarchs – this implies recognition of them. Furthermore, the rich man, in Jesus' story, recognized Lazarus and Abraham in the next life.

Those who knew Him recognized Jesus after His resurrection from the dead. Since we are told that we will be like Him in the next life, this means that we too will be recognizable.

That we will recognize our loved ones in heaven is consistent with the fact that we will have greater knowledge in the next life. Since we certainly know our loved ones here on the earth it is reasonable to assume that we will know them in heaven as well.

In Heaven, Will We Have A Memory Of What Happened On Earth? If So, How Can Heaven Be A Place Of Happiness If Our Loved Ones Are Missing?

When we get to heaven will we remember our life upon the earth? In other words, will we have a memory of who we were, whom we were related to, etc.

If so, this brings up a second question. How can heaven really be "heaven" if some of our loved ones, as well as our closest friends, are missing? How will it be possible to enjoy eternity when we know they have been judged and sent away from God's presence? How can heaven be heaven if we know their fate?

THOSE IN HEAVEN DO REMEMBER SOME THINGS

First, we know from Scripture that those in the next world do have some memory of the previous world.

In the famous episode of the dead prophet Samuel appearing to Saul, we find that Samuel, though deceased, had a memory of his time on the earth. Indeed, he knew Saul's identity and of the recent events which had taken place in his life. This includes the Lord refusing to speak to Saul any longer.

Also, in Jesus' story of the rich man and Lazarus we are told that the rich man went to a place of torment after his death. Among other things, he remembered who he was, that he had five brothers who were still living, and the identity of Lazarus.

Therefore, those in the next world do have some memory of this world.

WILL WE FORGET THOSE WHO DID NOT MAKE IT TO HEAVEN?

Even if we remember some things from this life, does it mean that we will know who did not make it to heaven? Is it possible that God will cause us to forget a loved one or friend who is not in heaven?

There are two likely answers to this question. First, it is possible that we will not remember our friends and loved ones who did not make it to heaven. Second, we will remember them but we will understand things from God's perspective.

We will look at the arguments each side offers.

OPTION 1: WE WILL FORGET THOSE IN HELL

A popular answer is that we will forget those friends and loved ones who do not make it to heaven. Those who hold this position argue as follows.

1. ONLY THE RIGHTEOUS ARE REMEMBERED

The Bible says that only the righteous are remembered. Therefore those who are in heaven will forget their sinful loved ones. The Bible says.

> Surely he will never be shaken; a righteous man will be remembered forever (Psalm 112:6 NIV).

If the righteous will be remembered forever, it could be argued that the unrighteous will not be. Somehow and in some way, their memory will be forgotten.

Scripture also says that the memory of Amalek is to be blotted out. We read of this prediction in the Book of Deuteronomy.

> Therefore when the LORD your God has given you rest from all your enemies around you, in the land that the LORD your God is giving you for an inheritance to possess, you shall blot out the memory of Amalek from under heaven; you shall not forget (Deuteronomy 25:19 ESV).

They were to be remembered no more. This seems to mean that they can be forgotten once and for all.

We read the following in the Book of Job about how the evil people are forgotten once they are gone. Scripture says.

> As heat and drought snatch away the melted snow, so the grave snatches away those who have sinned. The womb forgets them, the worm feasts on them; evil men are no longer remembered but are broken like a tree (Job 24:19-20 NIV).

While this speaks of the earthly memories of evil people, the same truths may apply to the next life. There will be no memory of them in the afterlife.

2. THE FORMER THINGS ARE NOT REMEMBERED

Isaiah the prophet spoke of the new heavens and the new earth. He said the former things would not be remembered.

> I will create a new heaven and a new earth. Past things will not be remembered. They will not come to mind. Be glad, and rejoice forever in what I'm going to create, because I'm going to create Jerusalem to be a delight and its people to be a joy. I will rejoice about Jerusalem and be glad about my people. Screaming and crying will no longer be heard in the city (Isaiah 65:17-19 God's Word).

All the things of the former heavens and earth will have been forgotten. This would include all of the evil people.

3. THERE IS NO PAIN IN HEAVEN

Scripture says there will be no pain in heaven, neither will there be tears. In the Book of Revelation, we read the following.

> He will wipe every tear from their eyes. There won't be any more death. There won't be any grief, crying, or pain, because the first things have disappeared (Revelation 21:4 God's Word).

We would assume that there would be pain and tears in heaven if people knew their loved ones were not there. Consequently, it seems that God will somehow remove their memory from our minds. As to how He will do this is not revealed in God's Word. However, we know with God nothing is impossible.

OPTION 2: WE WILL REMEMBER OUR LOST LOVED ONES BUT SEE THEM FROM GOD'S PERSPECTIVE

There is also the option that we will indeed remember those on earth who did not make it to heaven because of their lack of belief in Jesus.

Those who argue for this alternative viewpoint believe that we will not know less in heaven than we do here upon the earth. If we say we will forget our friends and loved ones who do not know Christ then we will have less knowledge in heaven. However, the Bible seems to teach just the opposite. Indeed, our knowledge in heaven will be greater than it is here upon the earth and it will always increase.

How then can we experience all the joys of heaven with the knowledge that certain friends and loved ones did not make it? The answer usually given is that we will see things from God's holy perspective. Once we have the complete divine point of view on sin, we will realize that those in hell are receiving a well-deserved punishment.

In addition, we will more fully appreciate that we are in heaven by God's amazing grace, and by it alone. Thus, there is the possibility that we will remember our lost loved ones when we are in heaven.

To sum up, Scripture does not clearly answer this question. Therefore, we cannot say that either option is the way in which it must be. This is one of these issues which we must wait until we get to heaven before we know the answer.

SUMMARY TO QUESTION 23
IN HEAVEN, WILL WE HAVE A MEMORY OF WHAT HAPPENED ON EARTH? HOW CAN HEAVEN BE A PLACE OF HAPPINESS IF OUR LOVED ONES ARE MISSING?

To many people, heaven would not be heaven if we had memories of our lost loved ones who did not believe in Jesus. We would know that they are spending eternity apart from His presence.

Therefore, many Christians believe that God's answer to the question of the remembrance of the unsaved loved ones is that they will be erased from our memory. Those who have not trusted Jesus Christ as their Savior will be forgotten by believers in the afterlife. Only the righteous will be remembered.

To support this viewpoint, we find that the Bible says that the former things on earth will not be remembered. This is consistent with the idea that there is no pain in heaven and that the unrighteous will go unremembered.

There is another point of view which says we will remember our lost friends and loved ones but we will remember them from the Lord's perspective. In heaven, we will more fully understand the depth of sin against a holy God and what it meant for Jesus to die in our place.

Thus, we will recognize that those who have rejected His free gift of salvation from sin are receiving the punishment they so richly deserve.

On other hand, we will also realize that we too deserve to be punished for our sins. It is only because of God's grace that we ourselves escape the justice of hell.

The Bible does not clearly answer this question for us. Consequently, we will only know the answer to this question when we ourselves arrive in heaven.

Will We Have All Knowledge In Heaven Or Will We Still Be Learning New Things?

There is the idea that when we reach heaven we will know everything. We will be like God. Is this what the Bible teaches? Will we have all knowledge of all things?

ONLY GOD KNOWS EVERYTHING

To begin with, the God of the Bible, and He alone, knows everything. Only He has all knowledge. In other words, no one can teach Him anything. The prophet Isaiah wrote.

> Who has understood the mind of the LORD, or instructed him as his counselor? (Isaiah 40:13 NIV).

There is nobody who can instruct the Lord or give Him advice. He does not need to be taught and cannot learn anything new.

On the other hand, angels, all other created spirit-beings, as well as human beings are creatures, not the Creator. By nature we are limited in what we can know and what we can do. The evidence for this is as follows.

ANGELS, AND OTHER SPIRIT-BEINGS DO NOT KNOW EVERYTHING

We find from Scripture that the angels of God, as well as the other beings the Lord has created, the cherubim, seraphim and living creatures, though perfect beings, do not know everything. Peter wrote the following about the limitations of the knowledge of angels.

> It was revealed to them that they were not serving themselves but you, when they spoke of the things that have now been told you by those who have preached the gospel to you by the Holy Spirit sent from heaven. Even angels long to look into these things (1 Peter 1:12 NIV).

Though the good angels are absolutely perfect creatures, they did not realize certain truths. Even they lack knowledge of some things. In other words, they do not know everything.

We find something similar taught in the Book of Daniel. We read of the following exchange.

> I, Daniel, watched as two others stood there, one on each side of the river. One said to the man clothed in linen who was above the waters of the river, "When will the end of these wondrous events occur?" (Daniel 12:5 NET).

The two others in this context were some type of created spirit-beings. They asked a third personage, the man clothed in linen, as to when certain future events would take place. The fact that they asked the question shows that they did not have this knowledge. This is another indication of the limitations that all created beings have.

HUMANS WILL CONTINUALLY LEARN

The Bible says that our knowledge will certainly be greater in heaven. The Apostle Paul spoke of a day when we will fully know things.

> For now we see only a reflection as in a mirror; then we shall see face to face. Now I know in part; then I shall know fully, even as I am fully known (1 Corinthians 13:12 God's Word).

Full knowledge does not mean "all knowledge." While our knowledge will continue to increase, it will never be exhaustive. In fact, there will always be new things for us to learn.

The Apostle Paul wrote to the Ephesians about how the Lord will reveal the riches of Jesus Christ to us in the coming ages. He stated it this way.

> He also raised us up with Him and seated us with Him in the heavens, in Christ Jesus, so that in the coming ages He might display the immeasurable riches of His grace in [His] kindness to us in Christ Jesus (Ephesians 2:6-8 HCSB).

This is another indication that there is so much for us to learn.

Therefore, while heaven will reveal many things to us which are unknown at this point, we will always be learning. Indeed, for all eternity we will continue to learn the truths of God. What a wonderful thing to look forward to!

SUMMARY TO QUESTION 24
WILL WE HAVE ALL KNOWLEDGE IN HEAVEN OR WILL WE STILL BE LEARNING NEW THINGS?

While some people mistakenly believe that once we reach heaven we will know all things this is not what the Bible teaches. There are several things we need to understand about our future knowledge as well as God's knowledge.

For one thing, only God has all knowledge. As the Creator of the universe, He alone is all-knowing, or omniscient. Everything else is created. As created beings, there are certain things we do not know and never will know.

Even the angels and the other spirit-beings the Lord has created, the cherubim, seraphim, and living creatures, though perfect beings, do not know everything. Scripture says there were things which the angels desired to learn. In the Book of Daniel two spirit-beings ask a question about the future; indicating their lack of knowledge. It is only God who cannot learn new things. All created beings have the capacity to continue to learn. God does not.

Thus, for all eternity, all redeemed humans will continue to learn. The Apostle Paul said that we will know "more fully" when we reach heaven. However, this does not mean we will have exhaustive knowledge. We will always be learning.

Consequently, one of the things we can look forward to in heaven is the knowledge which we will continually gain. We will learn things which we never imagined that we could know. This is what awaits those who believe in Jesus Christ in the afterlife. Heaven, among other things, will be a great learning experience.

QUESTION 25

Who Will Be Married
To Whom In Heaven?

There are a number of common questions which come up about heaven and marriage. What will be the relationship in heaven between people who have been married here upon the earth? What will happen to those who have been married several times? To whom will they be married in heaven if all of the previous spouses are there? What does the Bible have to say about all of this?

NEW MARRIAGES ARE UNNECESSARY IN HEAVEN

From Scripture, we find out a number of things about the relationships in heaven. For one thing, we discover people will not be marrying one another in the next world. There are a couple of reasons for this.

THERE IS NO ADDING OR SUBTRACTING TO THE POPULATION OF HEAVEN

First, we are going to be like angels in heaven. In answering a question from the religious leaders of His day Jesus said the following.

> But those who are counted worthy to take part in that age and in the resurrection from the dead neither marry nor are given in marriage. For they cannot die anymore, because they are like angels and are sons of God, since they are sons of the resurrection (Luke 20:35-36 HCSB).

This does not mean that we are actually going to become angels but rather we are going to be angel-like. In what sense are we going to be like angels?

We should understand this in at least two senses. Angels do not die neither to they have offspring. This being the case, it means that the population of heaven will never increase nor will it decrease.

Therefore, marriage between citizens of heaven will be unnecessary since we will not have to worry about replacing those who have died. We do not have new marriages in heaven, neither do we die.

Furthermore, we find that those who live in heaven will not be able to have children. Scripture teaches that our new glorified bodies will not be able to procreate. Jesus said.

> Jesus answered them, "You are deceived, because you don't know the Scriptures or the power of God. For in the resurrection they neither marry nor are given in marriage but are like angels in heaven" (Matthew 22:29,30 HCSB).

This being the case, there will be no new marriages in heaven. Furthermore, since there are neither births nor deaths in heaven those who are presently married will not be able to have any more children.

This brings up the question about people which have been married here upon the earth? Will they still be married to each other in heaven? Do the relationships here upon the earth carry over into heaven? What does the Bible have to say?

THE QUESTION OF THE RELIGIOUS RULERS: WHO WILL BE MARRIED TO WHOM IN THE NEXT LIFE?

The answer of Jesus, which we just read, was in response to a question He was asked by the religious rulers of His day. Their question dealt with marriage relationships in the next life. They posed a question about a woman who had been married to seven brothers. Assuming they all made it to heaven they wanted to know which of the seven would be married to her in heaven. They asked.

> Now, when the dead come back to life, whose wife will she be? All seven brothers had been married to her (Matthew 22:28 God's Word).

These religious rulers were not really looking for an answer to this question. Indeed they wanted to entrap Jesus. They thought they had the Lord trapped by this question. However, they could not have been more wrong. Jesus answered their disingenuous question and from it we learn a number of things.

The first thing which we must understand about heaven is that it is not merely a continuation of the relationships we have here upon the earth. Relationships will be different.

Thus, Jesus said their problem was a lack of understanding of two basic things; the Scriptures, and the power of God. If they really understood the Scriptures and God's power they would not have asked such a question. The Sadducees, not knowing the Scriptures, mistakenly assumed that the resurrection state was a continuation of our present relationships here upon the earth. It is not.

So what about the husband-wife relationship in the afterlife? What will it be?

THE HUSBAND-WIFE RELATIONSHIP WILL NOT BE DESTROYED

We find that husband-wife relationships will not be destroyed in heaven but they will take upon an entirely new meaning. We will no longer live in the same married state as we do here upon the earth. However we should not assume this means deprivation. We will retain memory of our loved ones and enjoy fellowship with them but we should not assume that husbands and wives or parents and children will have the exact relationship in heaven as they have here upon the earth.

THERE ARE DIFFERENT SETS OF RELATIONSHIPS IN HEAVEN

In heaven there will be a different set of relationships than here upon the earth. For one thing, we are all adopted sons and daughters in God's family. Paul wrote.

> He predestined us for adoption as sons through Jesus Christ, according to the purpose of his will (Ephesians 1:5 ESV).

The relationships are different in heaven because we have one Father, God. We are His children by faith in Christ.

JESUS' COMING CHANGED RELATIONSHIPS

Therefore, we have new family relationships. Jesus said His coming into the world would change relationships. He told His disciples.

> Do not think that I have come to bring peace to the earth. I have not come to bring peace, but a sword. For I have come to set a man against his father, and a daughter against her mother, and a daughter-in-law against her mother-in-law. And a person's enemies will be those of his own household. Whoever loves father or mother more than me is not worthy of me, and whoever loves son or daughter more than me is not worthy of me (Matthew 10:34-37 ESV).

When Jesus came to earth, relationships changed. We are to give our total allegiance to Him. Indeed, everything else is secondary.

WE WILL BE MARRIED TO CHRIST

There is something else that needs to be appreciated. In the next world, believers will be married to Jesus Christ. We are called the "bride of Christ."

We read of this in the Book of Revelation where it speaks of the preparation of the marriage of the Lamb to His bride.

Let us rejoice and be glad and give him glory! For the wedding of the Lamb has come, and his bride has made herself ready. Fine linen, bright and clean, was given her to wear. (Fine linen stands for the righteous acts of God's people.) Then the angel said to me, Write: Blessed are those who are invited to the wedding supper of the Lamb! And he added, "These are the true words of God" (Revelation 19:7-9 NIV).

We are His bride. We will be married to Jesus. This will be our primary relationship in the next world. This is the wonderful truth of Scripture!

Therefore, while heaven will not be a place of deprivation, the relationships we have upon the earth will not be exactly the same in the next world.

SUMMARY TO QUESTION 25
WHO WILL BE MARRIED TO WHOM IN HEAVEN?

There are always questions that arise about marriages and heaven. From Scripture we learn a number of things about marriage and our relationships in the next life.

For one thing, new marriages will not be necessary in heaven because there is no need for continuing the race. Jesus said that we will be like angels in heaven. Among other things, this means that we cannot die but neither can we increase the population. Angels do not marry nor can they have children.

Therefore, since we will be angel-like, the number of people in heaven will neither increase nor decrease; it will remain the same.

Scripture says that believers will be married to Jesus Christ in heaven. Indeed, we are called the "bride of Christ." Therefore, earthly marriages, as we know them, will not exist.

This, however, does not mean that husbands and wives have to live apart in heaven. Quite the contrary. Relationships will be perfect in heaven. However, the relationship between man and wife will not be exactly the same in the afterlife.

There is one more thing. We must remember that everything in heaven will be much greater in every way than what we have here upon the earth. This is something that should always be kept in mind when we think about life in heaven.

Will There Be Physical Pleasures In Heaven?
(Sexual Relations)

One question which comes up from time to time, mostly by men, concerns certain physical pleasures in heaven. Will there be sexual relations between a husband and wife? What does the Bible have to say?

THE MARRIAGE STATE WILL NOT BE THE SAME

We know that there will not be marriage in heaven in the same way as it is here upon the earth. Jesus said the following about the resurrected state.

> But Jesus answered them, "You are wrong, because you know neither the Scriptures nor the power of God. For in the resurrection they neither marry nor are given in marriage, but are like angels in heaven" (Matthew 22:29-30 ESV).

Relationships in heaven will be different than the ones here upon the earth.

MARRIAGE IS OVER WHEN ONE PARTNER DIES

There is no marriage in heaven. According to Scripture, marriage is defined as a physical union between a man and a woman. The Bible says that union ends upon the death of one or both of the people. Paul wrote.

Since I am speaking to those who understand law, brothers, are you unaware that the law has authority over someone as long as he lives? For example, a married woman is legally bound to her husband while he lives. But if her husband dies, she is released from the law regarding the husband (Romans 7:1-3 HCSB).

Paul also wrote to the Corinthians that the marriage bond is over when one of the two dies. He said the following.

A wife is bound as long as her husband is living. But if her husband dies, she is free to be married to anyone she wants—only in the Lord (1 Corinthians 7:39 HCSB).

Marriage on the earth only lasts as long as both partners are alive.

SEXUAL RELATIONS ARE NOT NECESSARY IN HEAVEN

Though not directly stated, passages like these seem to indicate couples will not be having sexual relations in heaven. Furthermore, Scripture emphasizes that sex is restricted to marriage.

Marriage is honorable in every way, so husbands and wives should be faithful to each other. God will judge those who commit sexual sins, especially those who commit adultery (Hebrews 13:4 God's Word).

Since heaven will be a deathless state, there is no need for sexual relations. There is no need for perpetuation of humanity since there will be no adding or subtracting to the number of people in heaven. Since Jesus emphasized there will be no marrying in heaven, then sexual relations seems to be something that is absent. Although there may not be any sexual activity in heaven, there is certainly none in hell!

THINGS WILL BE DIFFERENT IN HEAVEN

While husbands and wives will certainly be together in heaven, they will be together in a different sense. A few other points should be mentioned.

A. IT IS BETTER THAN WE CAN IMAGINE

Whatever God has planned for believers will be something far better than we can imagine. The Bible says.

> That is what the Scriptures mean when they say, "No eye has seen, no ear has heard, and no mind has imagined what God has prepared for those who love him" (1 Corinthians 2:9 NLT).

The Lord always has our best in mind. Indeed, better than we can ever imagine.

PAUL'S VISIT TO HEAVEN

The Apostle Paul wrote about his visit to heaven. While he was not allowed to report on what he saw, he did tell us this.

> I must go on boasting. Although there is nothing to be gained, I will go on to visions and revelations from the Lord. I know a man in Christ who fourteen years ago was caught up to the third heaven. Whether it was in the body or out of the body I do not know—God knows. And I know that this man—whether in the body or apart from the body I do not know, but God knows—was caught up to paradise. He heard inexpressible things, things that man is not permitted to tell (2 Corinthians 12:1-4 NIV).

Notice that he speaks of his experience as inexpressible things that nobody is permitted to speak about. Therefore, whatever does takes place in heaven, it will be better than anything we can ever possibly imagine.

B. EVERYTHING WILL BE CENTERED UPON GOD

It is important that we realize that the resurrected state will be God-centered, not human-centered. The emphasis will be upon God, not humanity.

Therefore many of the questions that we presently have about heaven will not be issues once we come into the presence of God. This includes questions about physical relationships.

SUMMARY TO QUESTION 26
WILL THERE BE PHYSICAL PLEASURES IN HEAVEN? (SEXUAL RELATIONS)

The emphasis in heaven is upon God. Everything will be centered on Him. Scripture also says that God will graciously give believers experiences greater than we can ever imagine. This being said, we should not assume that these will include sexual experiences. They do not seem to be part of the heavenly life that is promised for us in the future.

According to the Bible, sex is limited to marriage and there will not be any marriages in heaven. Jesus made this clear. Marriage is something which is limited to the earth.

There is something else we must remember. Since the total number of people in heaven can never increase or decrease, there will be no need, or possibility or adding to the population. Births and deaths do not occur in heaven. The population of heaven will forever remain the same.

Consequently, while it does not seem like sexual relations between a husband and his wife will be part of life in heaven we should not assume that heaven will somehow be less wonderful by the lack of physical contact. God always has our best in mind. Heaven will certainly not disappoint us in any aspect!

Therefore, we should expect to have experiences in heaven greater than we can ever imagine. The Apostle Paul provides an example of what to look forward to. He spent a short time in the presence of the Lord. While he was not allowed to tell us any specifics about what he experienced, he did say that human words could not express the wonders he saw. This should be enough for us.

Finally, we must remember everything in heaven will be centered on God. Since we will be focusing on the Lord, the idea of certain physical pleasures, which we may or may not experience, will only be secondary.

QUESTION 27

What Will We Look Like In Heaven?

When we get to heaven we will have a different body than the one we have here upon the earth. Indeed, our new body will be one of perfection.

One of the perplexing questions which often arises concerns how we will appear in heaven in that new body. Since there is no aging process in eternity, our looks will seemingly be the same forever.

But what will this body look like? Will we appear the same age as when we died or will we look like we did in the prime of our lives? Or perhaps it will be at some other time in our life.

What about those who have died at a relatively young age? What will they look like? The questions like these go on and on. Does Scripture provide us with any insight on these matters?

THERE ARE NO SPECIFIC STATEMENTS ABOUT OUR LOOKS BUT WE CAN MAKE SOME OBSERVATIONS

To begin with, there are no specific statements in Scripture as to how we are going to look in heaven. Nothing is said as to how old we will look, or how tall or short we will be. Therefore, we must examine a number of general statements in Scripture to discover any information on this subject.

From the Bible, we can make the following observations.

1. OUR BODIES WILL BE RECOGNIZABLE: WE WILL KEEP OUR INDIVIDUAL IDENTITY

There is the indication from Scripture that our glorified bodies will be recognizable. We find that when Jesus was transfigured, Moses and Elijah appeared with Him. The Bible explains what happened as follows.

> After six days Jesus took with him Peter, James and John the brother of James, and led them up a high mountain by themselves. There he was transfigured before them. His face shone like the sun, and his clothes became as white as the light. Just then there appeared before them Moses and Elijah, talking with Jesus. Peter said to Jesus, "Lord, it is good for us to be here. If you wish, I will put up three shelters—one for you, one for Moses and one for Elijah" (Matthew 17:1-4 NIV).

Moses had been dead for over one thousand years while Elijah had ascended into heaven centuries earlier without dying. There is no indication that either of these men had to be introduced to Peter, James and John. Obviously they did not know what these men looked like. Yet it seems that their identity was immediately known.

From this passage, we can probably infer that Moses and Elijah looked somewhat similar to when they had been alive on the earth. They also kept their individual identity as males.

2. THE RICH MAN, LAZARUS, AND ABRAHAM, KEPT THEIR IDENTITIES

In the story Jesus told of two men who died, the rich man and Lazarus, we are told that the rich man recognized Lazarus and Abraham in the afterlife. The rich man is described in this manner.

> And being in torment in Hades, he looked up and saw Abraham a long way off, with Lazarus at his side. 'Father

Abraham!' he called out, 'Have mercy on me and send Lazarus
to dip the tip of his finger in water and cool my tongue,
because I am in agony in this flame!' (Luke 16:23-24 HCSB).

Notice that the rich man saw and recognized both Abraham and
Lazarus. In other words, their individual identities were clear to this
man; he knew who each of them was.

3. THE EXAMPLE OF ADAM AND EVE: FULLY MATURE CREATION

As far as our age in heaven is concerned, we have the example of Adam
and Eve. They were created as fully mature adults. While we have no
description of what they actually looked like, they, along with the rest
of creation was said to be "very good." The Bible says.

> God saw all that He had made, and it was very good.
> Evening came, and then morning: the sixth day (Genesis
> 1:31 HCSB).

All of creation, which includes Adam and Eve, were described as "very
good." The fact that they did not have to go through the various stages
of physical development, like the rest of us have had to endure, may
give us a clue as to how old we will look; fully mature adults at our
prime in life. In fact, immediately upon creation they were told to be
fruitful and multiply. We read of this in Genesis. It says.

> So God created man in His own image; He created him in
> the image of God; He created them male and female. God
> blessed them, and God said to them, "Be fruitful, multiply,
> fill the earth, and subdue it. Rule the fish of the sea, the
> birds of the sky, and every creature that crawls on the earth"
> (Genesis 1:27-28 HCSB).

At the very least, this suggests Adam and Eve did not look like children.

4. JESUS PROVIDES ANOTHER EXAMPLE

There may be a parallel between the creation of Adam and Eve with that of the ministry of Jesus. Scripture says that He did not begin His public ministry until He was about thirty years of age. Luke wrote.

> Now Jesus himself was about thirty years old when he began his ministry (Luke 3:23 NIV).

Upon His death, He was probably somewhere in His mid-thirties. When He came back from the dead His disciples recognized Him.

This indicates that His resurrected body looked similar, in age, to His earthly body at the time in which He died. They recognized Him as Jesus. This seemingly would not have been the case if He looked ten years younger or older than the Jesus they knew. These facts may give us a hint as to what our glorified bodies will look like.

5. WE SHALL BE LIKE HIM

This brings us to our next point. The Bible says that we shall be like Jesus when He returns. John wrote the following.

> My dear friends, we are already God's children, though what we will be hasn't yet been seen. But we do know that when Christ returns, we will be like him, because we will see him as he truly is (1 John 3:2 CEV).

In some sense, we will be like Him.

6. WE WILL HAVE A BODY LIKE JESUS

We know at least one specific way in which we will be like Jesus. The Apostle Paul said that we will have a body like that of the resurrected Christ. He wrote the following to the Philippians.

> But our citizenship is in heaven, and from it we await a Savior, the Lord Jesus Christ, who will transform our lowly body to

be like his glorious body, by the power that enables him even to subject all things to himself (Philippians 3:20-21 ESV).

Therefore, we know that we will be like Him in the sense that we will have a body like His.

To some people, all of these facts indicate that our glorified body will look more or less the same as we looked in our prime. However, this description should certainly be qualified. Our new body will be perfect. None of us, even in our prime, had a perfect body!

There is also the issue of those who never lived to be in their prime. What will God do with them? Some people have assumed they will look the same as they would have looked had they reached their prime. However, again this is just speculation.

7. WE WILL PROBABLY NOT CARE HOW WE LOOK!

There is one last point which needs to be considered. Though we may have the question today about how we are going to look in heaven, this question will most likely not be an issue once we arrive! We will have much better things to think about.

Consequently, some of the things that are issues with us today will probably be non-issues when we meet our Lord face to face.

SUMMARY TO QUESTION 27
WHAT WILL WE LOOK LIKE IN HEAVEN?

When believers get to heaven each of us will have some type of physical form. This form will be ours for all of eternity. Most Christians are somewhat curious as to what they will look like, as well as how old they will appear to be. Consequently, they want to know if the Bible provides any answer to this question.

Scripture does not specifically answer this question. Yet it does say a number of things which indirectly deal with this subject.

For one thing, we will be recognizable in heaven. Moses and Elijah were recognized at Jesus' transfiguration. Abraham, as well as Lazarus, was recognized by the rich man in Jesus' story of the rich man and Lazarus.

Other clues, about what our new bodies will look like can be found in the creation of Adam and Eve. They were created as fully mature adults. Indeed, they were immediately commanded to "be fruitful and multiply." Obviously their bodies had to be to the place where this was possible.

In addition, we find that the Lord testified that their creation was perfect. Among other things, we would assume this also refers to how Adam and Eve looked when creation was finished. These facts may provide further evidence of what we will look like for all of eternity.

We can compare this with Jesus in His earthly body. The Lord did not begin His public ministry until He reached the age of thirty. When Christ came back from the dead in His glorified body He was recognizable by His disciples and others. If He had looked much older or much younger in His glorified body, His identity would probably have been questioned. But it was not. The fact that He looked more or less the same in His glorified body as He did in His earthly body suggests the look of a fully mature adult about the age of thirty.

This may be an indication of how we ourselves will look in eternity; we will look like a fully mature adult in our prime. Scripture does say that we will be like Jesus in the afterlife.

In addition, we are specifically told that this refers to the future body which we will have. Our glorified bodies will be like His glorified body. Therefore, from a reading of the Scripture, it seems that our glorified body will look like a fully mature adult without any of the limitations or imperfections which we now have.

However, it is likely that when we reach heaven we will not really care what we look like. Instead of looking at ourselves we will be looking at Him; the One who died so that we could live!

What Type Of Clothes Will
We Wear In Heaven?

While this may seem like a strange question, it is one which does get asked quite often. Along with what we are going to look like in heaven, people want to know what types of clothes we are going to wear. Is there such thing as a heavenly outfit?

WILL THERE BE NO CLOTHING IN HEAVEN?

There have been those who contend that people will wear no clothing whatsoever in heaven! This comes from the biblical description of Adam and Eve in their pre-fallen state. The Bible says the following about them.

> And they were both naked, the man and his wife, and were not ashamed (Genesis 2:25 KJV).

It is only after sin entered the world that people began to wear clothes. Since humanity is going to return to its original state of perfection it seems to follow that clothes are unnecessary.

BELIEVERS WILL WEAR CLOTHES IN THE NEXT LIFE

While it may seem logical to conclude that believers will be unclothed in heaven, because Adam and Eve were unclothed in the original state, this is not what the Bible teaches. Indeed, we find that everyone mentioned in the afterlife, or in the unseen world, whether it be believers, angels, or Jesus Himself, is depicted as wearing some sort of clothing.

For example, we read the following in the Book of Revelation about those who conquer through Jesus Christ.

> Everyone who wins the victory this way will wear white clothes. I will never erase their names from the Book of Life. I will acknowledge them in the presence of my Father and his angels (Revelation 3:5 God's Word).

Here the believers are said to be given white robes. While they are not described any further, we can at least conclude that they will have some sort of clothing.

Later, in the Book of Revelation, we read the following description of believers.

> After this I saw a vast crowd, too great to count, from every nation and tribe and people and language, standing in front of the throne and before the Lamb. They were clothed in white and held palm branches in their hands (Revelation 7:9 NLT).

Again we find a description of believers being clothed in white.

The Bible later says, in the same Book of Revelation, that the members of the church will be dressed as follows.

> Fine linen, bright and clean, was given her to wear. (Fine linen stands for the righteous acts of the saints.) (Revelation 19:8 NIV).

In this instance, the clothing is fine linen which is bright and clean. Furthermore, we have an explanation of what the fine linen stands for. It is symbolic of the righteous deeds of the believers.

Therefore, in each case where believers are described in the afterlife, we discover that they will be wearing clothes. The clothing they will be wearing is described as white, bright, and clean.

THE CLOTHING OF GOOD ANGELS

We also have the example of the good angels. These particular angels are without sin. Whenever their appearances are described in the Bible these personages are always described as wearing some type of clothing.

For example, on the day of Jesus' resurrection, two angels met certain women at His tomb. They are described in this manner.

> While they were puzzled about this, two men in clothes
> that were as bright as lightning suddenly stood beside them
> (Luke 24:4 God's Word).

Here we have these angels described as wearing dazzling or shining white clothes, bright as lightning. We do not find them unclothed.

Furthermore, in a number of cases when angels appeared to people, they were at first unrecognized as angels. The fact that they looked like ordinary people gives further evidence that they were wearing clothes. Indeed, Scripture never gives the slightest hint that these angelic creatures were unclothed when they appeared.

Thus, whenever we find a description of a righteous angel, they are always clothed. Consequently, lack of clothing is not a sign of righteousness or spirituality.

THE RESURRECTED JESUS WAS CLOTHED

There is no indication whatsoever that the resurrected Jesus was without clothes! Indeed, on the day of His resurrection, when He walked for quite some time with two individuals on the road to Emmaus, there was nothing odd or strange about His appearance. Certainly, this would not have been the case if He was without clothes!

The same is true when He appeared to His disciples in the Upper Room. There is the assumption that He was wearing some type of clothing.

THE GLORIFIED JESUS WILL ALWAYS BE CLOTHED

This is consistent with what the rest of Scripture says of the glorified Christ. In a preview of the coming kingdom, Jesus was transfigured in front of three of His disciples; Peter, James, and John. Matthew records it this way.

> Jesus' appearance changed in front of them. His face became as bright as the sun and his clothes as white as light (Matthew 17:2 God's Word).

In this case, His clothing became white as light.

In the Book of Revelation, the glorified Christ is described in this manner.

> There was someone like the Son of Man among the lamp stands. He was wearing a robe that reached his feet. He wore a gold belt around his waist (Revelation 1:13 God's Word).

The glorified Christ is pictured as wearing a long robe and a golden sash. Again, He is clothed.

Later, in the Book of Revelation, it says of Jesus.

> He was clothed with a robe dipped in blood, and his title was the Word of God. The armies of heaven, dressed in pure white linen, followed him on white horses (Revelation 19:13-14 NLT).

Once again, He is pictured as wearing a robe. Furthermore, His armies are described as wearing white linen.

These passages consistently indicate that the glorified Christ is clothed.

Therefore, from all indications, believers will be wearing some type of clothing for all eternity. This clothing represents the fact that we have been cleansed from our sin. This is why we find it being described as pure and white.

SUMMARY TO QUESTION 28
WHAT TYPE OF CLOTHES WILL WE WEAR IN HEAVEN?

There are many questions which people ask about heaven. This includes such simple things as what we will be wearing in the afterlife.

Some people have assumed that clothing will be unnecessary because the first humans, Adam and Eve, were unclothed in their sinless state. They only wore clothes after they had sinned. Consequently, it is argued that we will return to that unclothed state in our glorified bodies.

However, the Bible does not teach that believers will be unclothed in the afterlife or that being without clothes is somewhat more holy or natural.

Indeed, whenever the righteous angels are described in Scripture it is always with clothing. The same thing holds true for each and every description of believers in the afterlife; they are always clothed.

In addition, we are told that we are going to be like Jesus in the next world. As far as we can tell, every time He appeared in His glorified body it was clothed. Consequently, lack of clothing is not equated with spirituality in Scripture.

Thus, it seems fairly certain that we will wear some type of clothing in the next world. The clothing is usually described as something clean, pure and white. Beyond that, we can only speculate.

Do We Become Angels
When We Go To Heaven?

There is the idea, widely held by many people, that we human beings will actually become angels when we get to heaven. Is this what the Bible teaches? The answer is a clear, "No." Human beings will not become angels when we reach heaven.

JESUS' STATEMENT IS MISUNDERSTOOD

Possibly the reason why some people think humans will become angels at death is because of a misunderstanding of a statement of Jesus. Jesus spoke of the state of the righteous in heaven when it comes to marriage and having children. He said believers will be *like* angels. Matthew records Him saying.

> At the resurrection people will neither marry nor be given in marriage; they will be like the angels in heaven (Matthew 22:30 NIV).

According to Jesus, we will be like angels, we will not become angels. This distinction must be understood.

A number of other points need to be made about the differences between humans and angels. They can be summed up as follows.

1. ANGELS AND HUMANS ARE DIFFERENT ORDERS OF BEINGS

The Bible makes the distinction between humans and angels. We are different orders of beings. Humans, for example, have been made in the image of God. The Bible says.

> Then God said, "Let us make human beings in our image, to be like us. They will reign over the fish in the sea, the birds in the sky, the livestock, all the wild animals on the earth, and the small animals that scurry along the ground." So God created human beings in his own image. In the image of God he created them; male and female he created them (Genesis 1:26-27 NLT).

Angels, on the other hand, are ministering spirits. They have been created to do God's bidding. The writer to the Hebrew said.

> But angels are only servants. They are spirits sent from God to care for those who will receive salvation (Hebrews 1:14 NLT).

We have been made as different orders of beings.

Indeed, the Bible says that humans are a lower form of creation than angels and a separate form of being. The psalmist wrote of humans in the following way.

> For You have made him a little lower than the angels, And You have crowned him with glory and honor (Psalm 8:5 NKJV).

We read the same thing in the letter to the Hebrews. It says.

> You made him a little lower than the angels; you crowned him with glory and honor (Hebrews 2:7 NIV).

Humans, by nature, are an order of beings which are lower than angels. We are not angels and will never become angels.

In addition, human beings come about as the result of a relationship between a man and a woman. Angels, on the other hand, were not born. They were created as ministering spirits. They did not have to grow up.

Furthermore, angels are deathless and sexless creatures. They cannot die and they cannot procreate. Human beings can do both. This is another indication of the different orders of beings which God has made. While humans will not be able to have children or to die in the eternal state, the fact that we are now able to do this points out the difference "in kind" between angels and humans.

2. ANGELS WERE CREATED PERFECT WHILE HUMANS ARE NOW BORN SINFUL

Another difference between humans and angels concerns choice. When the angels were created they were created as intelligent beings which were perfect in their nature. Each of them was given a choice as to whether or not they would serve God. It seems that about one third of them decided to rebel against God. Thus, a great number of them fell from their original perfection because of their own choice.

Humans, on the other hand, are born separated from God. Indeed, all of us come into this world with a sin nature. Because of the sin of Adam and Eve, we are born in a state of rebellion. Paul wrote.

> Wherefore, as by one man sin entered into the world, and death by sin; and so death passed upon all men, for that all have sinned (Romans 5:12 KJV).

Therefore, angels had a clear choice to follow the Lord while they were in a state of perfection while humans make their choice in a state of sin and separation. This is another distinction between us and angels.

3. WE NOW HAVE AND WILL HAVE A DIFFERENT BODY THAN ANGELS

In this life, as well as in the next, believers will have a different body or form than the angels. The Bible says that we will receive a new body. Paul wrote.

> But someone may ask, "How will the dead be raised? What kind of bodies will they have?" What a foolish question! When you put a seed into the ground, it doesn't grow into a plant unless it dies first. And what you put in the ground is not the plant that will grow, but only a dry little seed of wheat or whatever it is you are planting. Then God gives it a new body—just the kind he wants it to have. A different kind of plant grows from each kind of seed. And just as there are different kinds of seeds and plants, so also there are different kinds of flesh—whether of humans, animals, birds, or fish. There are bodies in the heavens, and there are bodies on earth. The glory of the heavenly bodies is different from the beauty of the earthly bodies (1 Corinthians 15:35-40 NLT).

This new body will be similar to our present body but not molecule for molecule the same. Angels do not have bodies like humans. They are ministering spirits who have no physical or corporeal form. This is another difference between human beings and angels.

4. LAZARUS WAS CARRIED BY ANGELS TO GOD'S PRESENCE, HE DID NOT BECOME AN ANGEL

In Jesus' story of the rich man and Lazarus, when Lazarus the beggar died, he was carried by angels to Abraham. Jesus said.

> The time came when the beggar died and the angels carried him to Abraham's side (Luke 16:22 NIV).

The fact that he was carried by angels shows that he did not become an angel! Again, angels are distinguished from humans.

5. BELIEVERS WILL JUDGE ANGELS IN THE AFTERLIFE, NOT BECOME ANGELS

A further distinction between believers and angels is made by the Apostle Paul. He said that believers will one day judge angels. He wrote.

> Don't you realize that we will judge angels? So you should surely be able to resolve ordinary disputes in this life (1 Corinthians 6:3 NLT).

While we are not certain as to what all of this means, one obvious meaning is that humans are considered different from angels in the afterlife if we are to judge them.

6. THERE IS A DISTINCTION MADE BETWEEN HUMANS AND ANGELS IN THE AFTERLIFE

The distinction is specifically made between angels and humans in the afterlife. The writer to the Hebrews put it this way.

> Instead, you have come to Mount Zion, to the city of the living God (the heavenly Jerusalem), to myriads of angels in festive gathering, (to the assembly of the firstborn whose names have been written in heaven, to God who is the judge of all, to the spirits of righteous people made perfect, to Jesus (mediator of a new covenant, and to the sprinkled blood, which says better things than the [blood] of Abel (Hebrews 12:22-24 HCSB).

In this passage, we find angels distinguished from humans in the next world.

Therefore, as the totality of Scripture is examined, it becomes clear that we will not become angels in the afterlife. We will keep our identity as humans but with a new glorified body.

SUMMARY TO QUESTION 29
DO WE BECOME ANGELS WHEN WE GO TO HEAVEN?

It is a common misconception that when we humans die we will actually become angels in the next life. However, the Bible teaches no such thing. While Jesus said we will be "like angels" in the heavenly kingdom it does not mean that we will become angels. There are a number of reasons as to why this is the case.

For one thing, angels and humans are different orders of beings. Angels are created beings while humans are conceived through relations between a man and a woman. Angels themselves are deathless and sexless creatures. Indeed, they cannot die neither can they have children. Humans can do both. While humans will not be able to die or have children in the next world, the fact that we are now able to do this points out the distinction between us and angels.

In addition, the Bible says that humans were created a little lower than the angels. This again shows the distinction between us and them. We are of a different order.

There is something else. Angels were all created perfect while all humans, after Adam and Eve, were born with a sinful nature. Angels cannot be forgiven of their sins but human beings can.

Add to this the fact that we have a different physical form than angels in this life and that we will also have a different form in the next life. We are promised a glorified body. Angels, on the other hand, do not have any physical form.

In Jesus' story of the rich man and Lazarus, He said that angels carried the beggar Lazarus, after his death, to the place of blessing in next world. If Lazarus became an angel upon his death then there would have been no need to be carried by one. This is another indication of the distinction between humans and angels.

While humans are different from angels in this life the Bible also makes the specific distinction between humans and angels in the afterlife. They are never spoken of as equals.

In addition, Scripture says that some day we will actually judge angels. This proves the distinction between angels and humans will remain for all of eternity.

All of these things make it clear that believing humans will not become angels upon death.

Does Time Exist
In Heaven?

We reckon our lives in days, months, years, hours, minutes and seconds. We live in time. What about heaven? Will time as we know it exist in heaven? What does the Bible say?

WHAT IS TIME?

It is important to understand what we mean by time. Events occur in succession. This succession of events is known as time. This is how we humans have always lived. We have always been bound by time. In fact, the Bible starts out with a reference to time. Genesis 1:1 reads.

> In the beginning God created the heavens and the earth (Genesis 1:1 KJV).

The phrase, "In the beginning" starts the time references in Scripture. Throughout the Bible, events are reckoned in succession, by time. Since this is the case in human history, does it mean we will still be bound by time in heaven?

GOD IS TIMELESS

While human beings are bound by time or events which occur in succession, the God of the Bible is not. He is not bound by anything. In fact, Scripture testifies that He sees both the beginning and the end. We read in Isaiah the Lord saying the following.

> Remember the former things of old; for I am God, and
> there is no other; I am God, and there is none like me,
> declaring the end from the beginning and from ancient
> times things not yet done, saying, 'My counsel shall stand,
> and I will accomplish all my purpose,' . . . I have spoken,
> and I will bring it to pass; I have purposed, and I will do it
> (Isaiah 48:9-11 ESV).

It is clear that God is not bound by time. He declares the end from the beginning. He knows what has happened, what is happening and what will happen. Does this mean there will not be any time in heaven?

TIME REFERENCES IN HEAVEN

We actually find a couple of time references in heaven. Scripture says.

> They cried out with a loud voice: "O Lord, holy and true,
> how long until You judge and avenge our blood from those
> who live on the earth?" (Revelation 6:10 HCSB).

The martyrs in heaven are wondering how long it will take to avenge their deaths. This indicates that they are aware of time in some sense.

We also read the following in Revelation.

> When He opened the seventh seal, there was silence in
> heaven for about half an hour (Revelation 8:1 HCSB).

Again we appear to have another reference to time in heaven. In this case, the time reference is to events going on in heaven. However, it could merely be John's perspective here upon the earth that is in view.

Consequently, it seems that time exists in heaven in some sense while these events are occurring upon the earth. Whether or not this will continue for all eternity is not certain.

TIME MAY BE A FACTOR IN ETERNITY

There is an indication that time will actually be a factor in eternity. We are told that there will be a tree of life in the New Jerusalem which yields fruit each month. The Book of Revelation says.

> Then the angel showed me the river of the water of life, bright as crystal, flowing from the throne of God and of the Lamb through the middle of the street of the city; also, on either side of the river, the tree of life with its twelve kinds of fruit, yielding its fruit each month. The leaves of the tree were for the healing of the nations (Revelation 22:1-2 ESV).

It has been contended that people who lived in biblical times thought of eternity as an extension of time as far back and as far forward as anyone could imagine. In other words, they did not think of eternity as timelessness or absence of time as much as time extending forever.

Indeed, the fact that this tree yields fruit each month seems to indicate that some type of time exists in heaven. Beyond this, there is nothing else we can say with certainty.

SUMMARY TO QUESTION 30
DOES TIME EXIST IN HEAVEN?

We human beings are restricted to time. We have no choice. Does this mean it will be the same in heaven? Will we be bound to experiencing events one after another?

While some think there will be no time in heaven, as we now know it, this is not necessarily the case. Indeed, there are certain parts of Scripture that seem to assume those in heaven are in the same time sequence as those upon the earth.

In the Book of Revelation we find a number of references to time from the perspective of those in heaven. This seems to indicate that they are viewing the same events at the same time, in the same sequence, in which they are occurring.

Furthermore, in the eternal realm, we are told that the tree of life yields new fruit each month. This possibly indicates that there is some type of time that exists in eternity. Indeed, it has been argued that people who lived in biblical times saw eternity as time extending as far as one can imagine. Thus, they had no idea of timelessness or absence of time.

This is one of these issues where the information seems insufficient to come up with any final answer. The ultimate answer will only be known when we arrive in heaven. Until then, we can only speculate.

Will Jesus Still Have
His Scars In Heaven?

When Jesus Christ returned from the dead in His resurrected body, He still had the scars from His wounds on the cross. In fact, He used these scars to prove to doubting Thomas that it was actually He Himself which rose from the dead. The Bible describes it this way.

> Then he [Jesus] said to Thomas, "Put your finger here and see my hands. Reach out your hand and put it in my side. Do not doubt but believe" (John 20:27 NIV).

Since He had these scars immediately after His resurrection, does this mean they will remain for all eternity in the form in which we shall see Him? Will the scars remain?

HE WILL HAVE THE SCARS AT HIS SECOND COMING

Scripture says that Jesus will show these same scars to the nation of Israel when He returns again. We read the following words of the Lord in the Book of Zechariah.

> Then I will pour out a spirit of grace and prayer on the house of David and the residents of Jerusalem, and they will look at Me whom they pierced. They will mourn for Him as one mourns for an only child and weep bitterly for Him as one weeps for a firstborn (Zechariah 12:10 HCSB).

The nation which rejected Jesus as their Messiah will recognize Him at His Second Coming. One of the things they will recognize are the wounds which He still carries. This speaks of their rejection of Him when He came the first time.

Not only Israel will see Christ when He returns, the Bible says every eye will see Him. We read the following in the Book of Revelation.

> Look, he is coming with the clouds, and every eye will see him, even those who pierced him; and all the peoples of the earth will mourn because of him. So shall it be! Amen (Revelation 1:7 NIV).

Again, we are reminded that Jesus was pierced in His body. Indeed, He was pierced for all of us.

JESUS PAID THE INFINITE PRICE

These scars will remain as a testimony of the infinite price Jesus paid for our sins. Peter emphasized that Jesus paid the penalty for our sins by shedding His own blood on the cross. He wrote the following to the believers.

> You were rescued from the useless way of life that you learned from your ancestors. But you know that you were not rescued by such things as silver or gold that don't last forever. You were rescued by the precious blood of Christ, that spotless and innocent lamb (1 Peter 1:18-19 HCSB).

Indeed, in the Book of Revelation Jesus is often referred to as "the Lamb." This again stresses the fact that He paid the ultimate price for our sins. He died in our place and we will be reminded of that glorious fact forever and ever. May we give Him all the honor which is due to Him!

SUMMARY TO QUESTION 31
WILL JESUS STILL HAVE HIS SCARS IN HEAVEN?

The Bible says that the glorified body of the resurrected Christ had the scars from His crucifixion. In fact, Jesus showed them to Thomas to prove it was actually Him who came back from the dead. These scars will seemingly remain on His glorified body for all eternity.

When Jesus returns to the earth, we are told that the nation of Israel will see these scars and recognize that they crucified their promised Messiah. The Book of Revelation also emphasizes that the entire world will see the One who was pierced.

The purpose of this is to remind us, for all eternity, of the ultimate price Jesus paid for our sins. He gave the most precious thing He had, His life. As we see Him in eternity we will be forever reminded of the wonderful gift of salvation He has provided for us when He sacrificed His own life. Consequently, none of us will ever forget what He has done. Indeed, we never should forget.

QUESTION 32

Do Animals Go To Heaven?
Will We See Our Pets In The Afterlife?

What is the ultimate fate of animals? Do they go to heaven? If so, then which animals go to heaven? What, if anything, does the Bible have to say about this subject?

This question gets asked quite often. People want to know if heaven will consist of life-forms other than humans. The real question which is asked is not so much about animals in general but rather a certain pet we have had or may now have. Will *that* particular animal join us in the afterlife? Since many of us have had or do have an emotional attachment with an animal this is more than a mere academic question.

THERE IS NO DIRECT STATEMENT ANSWERING THIS QUESTION

To begin with, there is no direct statement, one way or the other about the presence or absence of animals in heaven. Scripture is silent on the matter. Whenever the Bible is silent on a particular matter we should be careful in drawing conclusions. Indeed, whatever conclusions we may draw have to be held with uncertainty.

The best way to go about looking at this issue is to consider arguments which have been offered on both sides of this issue.

THE CASE FOR ANIMALS BEING IN HEAVEN

First, we will look at some of the arguments given for the inclusion of animals in heaven. They can be summed up as follows.

1. BELIEVERS WILL RETURN ON HORSES

Often people bring up the following passage in the Book of Revelation to say there must be animals in heaven. We read of them at the return of Christ.

> The armies of heaven were following him, riding on white horses and dressed in fine linen, white and clean (Revelation 19:14 NIV).

Does not the appearance of horses at the Second Coming of Christ show that animals will be in heaven? Not really. For one thing, these animals are coming down to earth to judge the nations at the return of Christ.

Furthermore, most interpreters of the Book of Revelation see these as figurative creatures, not real horses. Indeed, it is difficult to imagine how horses can ride on clouds!

2. THERE WILL BE ANIMALS IN THE MILLENNIUM

In the Book of Isaiah, it speaks of animals living peacefully with each other in a future period of peace which will engulf the entire earth. The Bible says.

> The wolf will live with the lamb, and the leopard will lie down with the goat. The calf, the young lion, and the fatling will be together, and a child will lead them. The cow and the bear will graze, their young ones will lie down together, and the lion will eat straw like an ox. An infant will play beside the cobra's pit, and a toddler will put his hand into a snake's den. No one will harm or destroy on My entire holy mountain, for

the land will be as full of the knowledge of the LORD as the
sea is filled with water (Isaiah 11:6-9 HCSB).

This passage refers to a future state where humans and animals are
together. However, there are a couple of problems with using this passage to assume animals will be in heaven.

For one thing, many Christians do not believe that these passages
are to be interpreted literally. Indeed, they do not assume that a literal thousand year rule of Christ upon the earth is actually taught in
Scripture.

Even for those who do accept a literal Millennium, all this passage
states is that animals will exist at that time. This is before the final judgment of human beings. Therefore, the situation in the Millennium
does not really say anything final about the eternal state.

3. ANIMALS HAVE SELF-AWARENESS

There is also the argument that animals have self-awareness. While animals are different from humans in that they do not have an eternal
spirit, they are different from non-living things such as trees and plants.

While this is true, it does not mean they are meant to live eternally.
Indeed, the only reason humans are immortal is because God has
made us such. We are not by nature immortal beings. Nothing in
Scripture indicates animals have some sort of immortality.

4. PARADISE WILL BE REGAINED

One could argue that animals will be in heaven since animals existed
in the Garden of Eden before sin entered the world. The Bible says.

> God made every type of wild animal, every type of domestic
> animal, and every type of creature that crawls on the ground.
> God saw that they were good (Genesis 1:25 God's Word).

199

If paradise is going to be restored, then it could be assumed that it will be restored with animals. John wrote.

> I saw a new heaven and a new earth, because the first heaven and earth had disappeared, and the sea was gone (Revelation 21:1 God's Word).

The eternal state seems to be a return to the original state in Eden. Yet there will be a difference between humans living in the eternal state and Adam and Eve.

Adam and Eve were created perfect; we will have new bodies which are perfect. Adam and Eve, while perfect, had the possibility of sinning. Indeed, they did sin. However, the bodies of believers in the eternal state will be incapable of sinning.

In addition, even if animals do make it to the eternal state, it says nothing about animals which presently exist or have once existed.

While these points may indicate there will be animals in heaven, there is certainly nothing conclusive in the biblical evidence.

WHY ANIMALS MAY NOT BE IN HEAVEN

There are a number of reasons often given as to why animals may not be part of God's eternal kingdom. We can list them as follows.

1. ONLY HUMANS HAVE AN ETERNAL SPIRIT

The Bible says that only humans have an eternal spirit. On the other hand, animals are not made for eternity. The Bible makes the distinction between human life and all other forms of life. In describing the creation of the first man, Adam, the Bible says the following.

> Then the Lord God formed the man from the dust of the ground. He breathed the breath of life into the man's nostrils, and the man became a living person (Genesis 2:7 NLT).

God breathed the breath of life into humans. However, He did not do this when He created the animals. Furthermore, in every promise or picture of heaven there is never any description of animals. Of course, this does not mean animals are not there. We do not expect Scripture to describe everything which heaven will consist of.

2. IN HEAVEN OUR ATTENTION WILL BE ON JESUS

It also should be emphasized that the attention in heaven will not be on ourselves or our surroundings. Instead the attention will be on the Lord Jesus. Our hearts and minds will be centered on Him. This being the case, some people regard the question of animals as a rather trivial question.

Yet, this does not really answer the question. The fact that we will rightly center our attention on Him does not indicate, one way or the other, whether there will be animals in heaven.

CONCLUSION: SCRIPTURE DOES NOT ANSWER THE QUESTION

Therefore, we conclude that Scripture is silent on this matter. One certainly cannot rule out the possibility of animals being in heaven but since there is no direct teaching on this issue it is best to not come to any conclusion.

SUMMARY TO QUESTION 32
DO ANIMALS GO TO HEAVEN? WILL WE SEE OUR PETS IN THE AFTERLIFE?

One of the most common questions about heaven concerns animals in general and, in particular, a certain pet which we had in the past or may have right now. People want to know if these pets will join them in the next world.

The Scripture does not say anything specific on the subject. Some have thought the passage in the Book of Revelation about the saints returning on white horses is an illustration that animals will be in heaven. There is also a passage in Isaiah about the future time of animals living peaceably together. However, these passages do not clearly state that animals will be with humans in the eternal state.

It is often pointed out that animals do have a consciousness of their own existence. While this is true it does not mean that they are immortal. Only humans have been granted immortality. Immortality is not something which we naturally have.

It has also been argued that since humans will return to an original paradise, there must be animals in this new paradise since animals were part of the original setting in Eden. Even if one granted that possibility it says nothing about animals which now exist or have existed.

Those who argue against animals in heaven point out that in all the descriptions of heaven, animals are nowhere to be found. While true, this does not mean they are not there.

There is also the fact that the focus in heaven will be Jesus Himself. Again, this is true but it does not answer the question, one way or the other, as to whether or not animals will be part of that experience.

When all is said and done we have to say that our answer to this question must be one of uncertainty. Heaven is going to be such a wonderful place with things waiting for us which we cannot even imagine!

Therefore, the answer to this question will only be known when we arrive in His presence. Yet, when we do finally arrive in the presence of the living God there will be other things on our mind.

Why Is It Assumed By Some That Peter Is Sitting At The Gates Of Heaven?

Heaven is often characterized by the Apostle Peter, or Saint Peter, sitting at the pearly gates. He is the one who either allows people to enter, or to turn them away. Where does this idea come from? Is it biblical? Did the Lord give Peter this honor? What does the Bible have to say?

PETER WAS GIVEN THE KEYS TO THE KINGDOM

The idea that Peter has some sort of authority to determine who enters heaven comes from a statement by Jesus to Simon Peter which is only recorded in Matthew's gospel. The account reads as follows.

> Now when Jesus came into the district of Caesarea Philippi, he asked his disciples, "Who do people say that the Son of Man is?" And they said, "Some say John the Baptist, others say Elijah, and others Jeremiah or one of the prophets." He said to them, "But who do you say that I am?" Simon Peter replied, "You are the Christ, the Son of the living God." And Jesus answered him, "Blessed are you, Simon Bar-Jonah! For flesh and blood has not revealed this to you, but my Father who is in heaven. And I tell you, you are Peter, and on this rock I will build my church, and the gates of hell shall not prevail against it. I will give you the keys of the kingdom of heaven, and whatever you bind on earth shall be bound in

heaven, and whatever you loose on earth shall be loosed in heaven." Then he strictly charged the disciples to tell no one that he was the Christ (Matthew 16:13-19 ESV).

This passage has been used to argue that Peter, one of Jesus' apostles, was given the right to determine who could enter heaven and who could not. Is this what the passage teaches?

PETER WAS NOT GIVEN AUTHORITY OVER ENTRANCE TO HEAVEN

Peter was indeed given the "keys to the kingdom." This has been misinterpreted to mean that he has been given the right to determine who enters heaven and who is excluded.

However, a simple reading of this passage will show that this is not what it says. The authority given to Peter was here upon the earth, not in heaven. He was told whatever he bound on earth would be bound in heaven. Nothing is said about any authority he would possess in the next life.

WE DETERMINE OUR DESTINY WHILE WE ARE HERE UPON THE EARTH

Indeed, the only determinative factor as to who goes to heaven and who does not is made by each of us here upon the earth. It depends on what we do with Jesus. If we believe in Him, we have everlasting life but if we reject Him, God's wrath or punishment will continue to remain on us. John wrote.

> Whoever believes in the Son has eternal life; whoever does not obey the Son shall not see life, but the wrath of God remains on him (John 3:36 ESV).

Therefore, the entrance to heaven is not determined by Saint Peter when one reaches the pearly gates, it is determined by each of us based upon what we do with God the Son.

THE UNBELIEVERS WILL BE JUDGED AT THE LAST JUDGMENT

One more thing needs to be mentioned. The judgment of unbelievers takes place at the Last Judgment. We read of this in the Book of Revelation. It says the following.

> Then I saw a great white throne and him who was seated on it. Earth and sky fled from his presence, and there was no place for them. And I saw the dead, great and small, standing before the throne, and books were opened. Another book was opened, which is the book of life. The dead were judged according to what they had done as recorded in the books. The sea gave up the dead that were in it, and death and Hades gave up the dead that were in them, and each person was judged according to what he had done. Then death and Hades were thrown into the lake of fire. The lake of fire is the second death. If anyone's name was not found written in the book of life, he was thrown into the lake of fire (Revelation 20:11-15 NIV).

This judgment occurs *before* the New Jerusalem comes down from heaven. It is in the New Jerusalem where we find the pearly gates. Therefore, even if Peter was sitting at the pearly gates, the judgment as to whom will enter heaven has already been completed. Peter has no say so in the matter.

Therefore, the idea that Simon Peter, a fallible disciple of Jesus, would have any determination as to who will enter heaven is a complete myth with no biblical basis whatsoever.

SUMMARY TO QUESTION 33
WHY IS IT ASSUMED BY SOME THAT PETER IS SITTING AT THE GATES OF HEAVEN?

In Matthew chapter sixteen, it is recorded that Jesus told one of His disciples, Simon Peter, that he was to be given the keys to the kingdom of heaven. This has been wrongly understood to mean that Peter will eventually determine who enters heaven and who does not. In other words, he had the authority to allow certain people to enter and to shut others out.

A simple reading of the passage in context will reveal that the authority granted to Peter was limited to events here upon the earth. Nowhere does the Scripture remotely teach that Peter has any authority to determine who is saved and who is lost.

The entrance to heaven is determined by the Lord and by Him alone. Human beings have no say so in the matter. He has set the standard as to who will enter heaven and who will not. His standard is Jesus Christ. Entrance to heaven all depends upon how we respond to Jesus. The Bible says that if we believe in Him then we will have everlasting life, namely heaven.

On the other hand, if we reject Him, only judgment awaits us. This determination is made in this life only and it is made by the Lord Himself. There is no second chance and there certainly is no audience before Saint Peter at the pearly gates.

Furthermore, the pearly gates belong to the New Jerusalem. This is the Holy City which comes down from heaven. This city is only revealed after the Last Judgment. The Last Judgment means simply that; there is no judgment after this.

Consequently, there is no judgment occurring by anyone when a person arrives at the "pearly gates." Entrance or non-entrance has already been determined.

Thus, all unbelievers are already outside of the pearly gates when the Holy City with its gates of pearls comes down from above. Simon Peter has nothing to do with any judgment at any pearly gates. None.

Is There A Chance That Believers Can Be Sent Away From Heaven At Some Time In The Future?

While the Bible says that those who believe in Jesus Christ will spend eternity in heaven, there are some people who question if we will truly be there forever. Indeed, they wonder if somehow their experience will end. Will there be another rebellion like that of Adam and Eve? If we have free will, is it possible that we will rebel like what happened in the beginning? Should we be concerned about this?

There are several points which we need to make.

GOD HAS PROMISED ETERNAL LIFE FOR THOSE WHO BELIEVE

To begin with, God has promised eternal life to those who believe in Jesus Christ.

> For God loved the world so much that he gave his one and only Son, so that everyone who believes in him will not perish but have eternal life (John 3:16 NLT).

Eternal life means forever. If God has promised that we will be with Him "for all eternity," then we can be confident that this will indeed happen.

GOD CANNOT LIE

In addition, we find that the Bible says that God is not able to lie. Paul wrote.

This truth gives them confidence that they have eternal life, which God—who does not lie—promised them before the world began (Titus 1:2 NLT).

When God promises something, He keeps His promise.

HE KNOWS ALL THINGS, PAST, PRESENT, AND FUTURE

There is something else. The Bible says that God knows "all things." This includes the past, present, and future. In other words, He knows everything that has happened, that is happening, and that will happen in the future. Everything!

When we put all of these facts together we can conclude the following: nobody should be concerned about the possibility of ever being sent away from heaven. Indeed, once a person has trusted Jesus Christ and enters heaven, they are guaranteed by the Word of God to spend eternity in the presence of the Lord. Consequently, there is nothing that will ever keep this from happening.

SUMMARY TO QUESTION 34
IS THERE A CHANCE THAT BELIEVERS CAN BE SENT AWAY FROM HEAVEN AT SOME TIME IN THE FUTURE?

There are some people who worry that heaven might not be the everlasting home of believers. They wonder if it is possible that people will rebel at some point and then be banished from heaven. Is this possible?

There are several reasons why we know that this is not possible.

First, the Lord promised eternal life to all those who believe in Him. Eternal life means just that, for all eternity.

Add to this that God cannot lie. If He promises something it will come to pass. End of story.

Finally, God's knowledge covers all eternity. He knows everything that will happen in the future. There is no indication in the Bible that another rebellion can or will take place.

Therefore, when we consider the promises of God, the character of God, and the knowledge of God, we conclude that there is no possibility that heaven will end someday for those enter into it.

Are We To Believe The Testimonies Of People Who Claimed To Have Visited Heaven?

There are various ways in which people claim to have personal knowledge of heaven. Some have claimed to have had near death experiences where they have died and come back to life. Then they supposedly relate what it is like in the afterlife.

Others claim to have been contacted by beings from the spirit world. From them, they believe that accurate information about heaven is derived.

Add to this people who have claimed to have actually visited heaven. Their visit did not occur when they had a near death experience, they claim that God Himself transported them to His presence.

Many of these people claim to be Bible-believing Christians. What are we to make of this type of claim? Should they be believed?

1. THREE BIBLICAL CHARACTERS HAVE BEEN GIVEN A GLIMPSE OF HEAVEN

When we search the Scriptures we find that there are only three people in the Bible who were actually given a glimpse into heaven; Isaiah the prophet, the Apostle Paul, and John, the disciple of Jesus. We can learn some interesting facts when we examine their testimony.

A. ISAIAH SAW THE THRONE OF GOD

Isaiah the prophet was given a vision of heaven. This is recorded in the sixth chapter of the Book of Isaiah. It reads as follows.

> In the year King Uzziah died, I saw the Lord. He was sitting on a lofty throne, and the train of his robe filled the Temple. Hovering around him were mighty seraphim, each with six wings. With two wings they covered their faces, with two they covered their feet, and with the remaining two they flew. In a great chorus they sang, "Holy, holy, holy is the LORD Almighty! The whole earth is filled with his glory!" The glorious singing shook the Temple to its foundations, and the entire sanctuary was filled with smoke. Then I said, "My destruction is sealed, for I am a sinful man and a member of a sinful race. Yet I have seen the King, the LORD Almighty!" Then one of the seraphim flew over to the altar, and he picked up a burning coal with a pair of tongs. He touched my lips with it and said, "See, this coal has touched your lips. Now your guilt is removed, and your sins are forgiven." Then I heard the Lord asking, "Whom should I send as a messenger to my people? Who will go for us?" And I said, "Lord, I'll go! Send me" (Isaiah 6:1-8 NLT).

Notice that Isaiah was given a "vision" of heaven. In other words, he was not transported there. His description of his vision is very brief.

Furthermore, his response to this vision was one of utter humility. He realized the depth of his sinfulness in the presence of the Lord. Through all of this, Isaiah was humbled by the experience.

B. THE APOSTLE PAUL DID NOT DESCRIBE HIS EXPERIENCE IN THE WORLD OF THE DEAD

The Apostle Paul was given a glimpse of the afterlife. However, there are several interesting things we discover from his experience.

To begin with, he did not write about it to anyone about his experience until fourteen years *after* it occurred. He said the following to the Corinthians.

> I was caught up into the third heaven fourteen years ago (2 Corinthians 12:2 NLT).

Second, he was "not allowed" to reveal any of the things he saw or heard. He further wrote to the Corinthians.

> But I do know that I was caught up into paradise and heard things so astounding that they cannot be told (2 Corinthians 12: 4 NLT).

This should give us pause. If the Apostle Paul waited fourteen years to even mention this experience, and then said that he was not permitted to provide any of the details. What then should we make of people who immediately relate their so-called visit to heaven and then provide us with graphic details?

If the greatest missionary in the history of the church, the man who was give unique authority to write a large portion of the New Testament, was not allowed to reveal what he saw and heard, what makes anyone suppose that someone else would be given such an honor that the Apostle Paul was not given?

Furthermore, Paul explicitly said the details "cannot be told." Why then should we now believe someone who says that they can be told?

There is something else we should consider. After Paul's experience he was given a "thorn in the flesh." He said it was given for the following reason.

> Especially because of the extraordinary revelations. Therefore, so that I would not exalt myself, a thorn in the flesh was given to me, a of Satan to torment me so I would not exalt myself (2 Corinthians 12:7 HCSB).

We do not know the exact nature of this "thorn in the flesh." Many things have been suggested. Whatever it was, it kept him from boasting of his experience.

We again contrast Paul with those who claim to have had a similar experience as his. There does not seem to be much humility on the part of those who have claimed to be ushered into heaven by God Himself! Neither do we find them being given a similar "thorn in the flesh." Their stories are simply not believable.

C. JOHN HAD VISIONS OF HEAVEN BUT DID NOT GO THERE

The man who gives us the fullest description of the unseen world is the Apostle John. However, he was not allowed to personally visit heaven but rather was merely given a vision of it. This is also fascinating.

If John was allowed to write what heaven was actually like, but was not permitted to go there for a firsthand look, why again should we believe the testimony of anyone else who claims to have gone to heaven and been given a firsthand look; something John was not given? It does not make any sense.

OBSERVATIONS ON THOSE WHO HAVE CLAIMED TO VISITED HEAVEN

There are three observations we can make about people who have claimed to have had the privilege of visiting heaven.

1. WHY SHOULD WE BELIEVE THEIR CLAIM? WHERE'S THE EVIDENCE?

To begin with, we must ask the obvious question, "Why should we believe their claim?" What evidence is there, apart from their own personal testimony, that they have actually visited the presence of God? There is none.

Basically, we have to take the word of this person that they have had an honor which was not afforded the greatest of biblical characters. Since there is no way to prove or disprove their claim, it is basically meaningless.

2. THEIR SO-CALLED EXPERIENCE IS CONTRARY TO SCRIPTURE

Furthermore, any claim to have visited heaven and return with the details is contrary to the teaching of the Word of God. Only three individuals were allowed to get a glimpse of heaven; Isaiah, John and Paul. Isaiah gave only a brief description while John provided a few more details. However, neither of these men was permitted to visit heaven. What we learn about heaven from them was by means of a vision.

On the other hand, Paul actually visited the righteous realm of the dead but was not permitted to give us any details. Therefore, for a person today to claim to have been personally transported to heaven contradicts the teaching of Scripture. Humans were not permitted to tell us about heaven from firsthand experience.

3. THEY FALSELY CLAIM TO ADD TO OUR KNOWLEDGE OF HEAVEN

This is our biggest concern. Those who make these sorts of claims are basically saying that they are adding to our knowledge of heaven. They are telling us things which none of the biblical characters were allowed to tell us. In other words, they are giving us further divine revelation.

Yet the Bible warns us not to go beyond what is written in Scripture. Paul made this clear when he wrote to the Corinthians. He said.

> I have applied all these things to myself and Apollos for your benefit, brothers, that you may learn by us not to go beyond what is written (1 Corinthians 4:6 ESV).

This is an important principle, as well as a stern warning! We are not to go beyond what is written in Holy Scripture. In one of the first books of the Bible we have a similar warning from Moses. He wrote.

> You shall not add to the word that I command you, nor take from it, that you may keep the commandments of the Lord your God that I command you (Deuteronomy 4:2 ESV).

God's words are important to Him. We are not to add to them. However, people who have claimed to have visited heaven do exactly that! Indeed, they add to God's words. In fact, what they are saying is what we have in Scripture is not sufficient! Supposedly, we need their testimony as well. This is a dangerous claim to make!

Moreover, those who make such claims need to heed the warning which John gave at the end of the Book of Revelation. The man who had been given the most details about heaven penned the following words of warning.

> I warn everyone who hears the words of the prophecy of this book: if anyone adds to them, God will add to him the plagues described in this book (Revelation 22:18 ESV).

God's Word is clear. We are not to add to it. If anyone does, God will add the plagues described in the Book of Revelation to that person. God's Word is not to be trifled with.

For these reasons we should not accept the claims of anyone who says that they visited heaven and has now returned to share the details with us. This is wrongfully adding to God's truth.

SUMMARY TO QUESTION 35
ARE WE TO BELIEVE THE TESTIMONIES OF PEOPLE WHO CLAIMED TO HAVE VISITED HEAVEN?

There have been a number of individuals who have claimed to have been given a special visit to heaven. For whatever reason, without having to die, they were allowed to view the next life as well as the presence of the Lord firsthand.

There are a number of reasons why these claims of visitation to heaven should be soundly rejected. For one thing, only three biblical characters were given a glimpse of heaven. One of them, Isaiah, wrote about it briefly. However, he did not actually visit heaven but only received a vision of the throne of God.

Another person, John, gave a number of details of heaven. Yet like Isaiah he too was shown these truths in a vision. The Apostle Paul visited heaven but he did not tell anyone about it for fourteen years after it took place. In addition, he was not allowed to reveal any specifics of his visit. He was commanded to keep silent on the details.

These facts should make it clear that modern claims to have visited heaven should not be taken seriously. For one thing, such claims cannot be proven or disproven. There is no evidence someone can bring back to demonstrate they have the right to make such a claim. Consequently, their claims are meaningless.

Furthermore, these claims contradict what we know to be true. God did not allow any of His great saints to personally visit heaven and then bring back the details of their visit. There is no reason whatsoever to assume that the Lord has done this now in the cases of these people who make such a claim.

There is something else. The individuals who make such claims are adding to God's revealed truth. They say that they have been given details of the unseen world that God did not allow the Apostle Paul, Peter, John or anyone else to give. In other words, they have placed themselves in a position greater than all of the biblical characters!

This is adding to the Word of God. This is the real worry that we have here. Indeed, we have stern warnings in the Bible from God Himself about adding to His Word. The Bible says that those who falsely claim to add to God's revealed Word are subject to His severe judgment. The people who make the claim to have visited heaven should keep this in mind.

Will Everyone Eventually Go To Heaven? (Universalism)

There is a belief that sometime in the future everyone will be released from the penalty of sin and restored to God. This includes all human souls, Satan and his evil angels. The entire universe will be reconciled to God. Any type of hell, that may have existed, will eventually be destroyed. This belief is known as "universalism."

THIS DOCTRINE TAKES DIFFERENT FORMS

Universalism takes on a number of different forms. We can sum up the most popular ones in the following manner.

VIEW 1: THE WICKED WILL BE SAVED AFTER UNDERGOING PUNISHMENT

Some hold that the wicked will automatically be saved after undergoing a period of punishment in the afterlife. The punishment in hell is conscious, but not eternal. Future punishment is measured for each sin. After the person has been sufficiently punished for their sin they will then be saved. Hell then becomes purgatory; a place of purging to get the person ready for heaven. Once purged, they enter heaven.

VIEW 2: EVERYONE IS ALREADY SAVED

Others teach that everyone is already saved without even realizing it. This view denies any type of hell for the wicked. Since everyone is already saved, it is the job of the Christians to go into the world and tell everyone that they are already saved. Jesus Christ has paid the penalty for their sins so they do not any sin to suffer for. Christians are to preach this message of salvation which everyone now has.

VIEW 3: EVERY PERSON IN HELL WILL EVENTUALLY REPENT

There is also the view that after a period of time in hell, every person will see the light, repent of their sins, and then go to heaven. Nobody will desire to stay in hell forever.

VIEW 4: THERE IS NO JUDGMENT AT ALL FOR THE WICKED

Religious pluralism is the belief that all religions are equally valid and there is no judgment for the wicked. Therefore, the idea of a heaven for believers and a hell for unbelievers has no basis in reality. Those who hold this position see nothing special about Jesus or the Christian faith. They may believe in some god but it is not the God of the Bible. Consequently, they reject the idea of hell.

THE BIBLICAL ARGUMENTS FOR UNIVERSALISM: CHRISTIAN UNIVERSALISTS

Some universalists actually appeal to the Bible to support their case. Among other things, they are known as "Christian universalists." They believe that the Bible teaches that everyone will be eventually become saved. They argue in the following manner.

1. EVERYONE WILL BOW TO JESUS

The Bible says that everyone will eventually bow to Jesus. Paul wrote the following to the church at Philippi.

> Therefore God also has highly exalted Him and given Him the name which is above every name, that at the name of Jesus every knee should bow, of those in heaven, and of those on earth, and of those under the earth, and *that* every tongue should confess that Jesus Christ is Lord, to the glory of God the Father (Philippians 2:9-11 NKJV).

Since everyone will bow, they believe that this means everyone will eventually be saved.

2. ALL PEOPLE WITH BE WITH JESUS

In addition, Jesus said that He would bring all people to Himself. We read of this claim in the Gospel of John. Jesus said.

> And I, when I am lifted up from the earth, will draw all people to myself (John 12:32 NIV).

This indicates that all people will eventually come to Him.

3. GOD WANTS EVERYONE TO BE SAVED

Furthermore, the Bible also says that God wants everyone to be saved. Paul wrote the following to Timothy.

> This is good, and it pleases God our Savior, who wants everyone to be saved and to come to the knowledge of the truth (1 Timothy 2:3,4 HCSB).

Since God always gets what He wants, everyone will eventually be saved. It is not possible for God's will to be frustrated.

4. ALL THINGS WILL BE GATHERED TOGETHER TO JESUS CHRIST

The Bible also says that all things will be gathered to Jesus Christ. Paul wrote the following to the Ephesians.

> God's secret plan has now been revealed to us; it is a plan centered on Christ, designed long ago according to his good pleasure. And this is his plan: At the right time he will bring everything together under the authority of Christ—everything in heaven and on earth (Ephesians 1:9,10 NLT).

All things in heaven and earth will Jesus Christ gather together. This includes Satan, the sinning angels, and all wicked humans. Therefore everyone will come to know Him.

5. CHRIST WILL MAKE ALL ALIVE

The Bible also says that Christ will make "all" alive in Himself. Paul wrote to the Corinthians about this.

> For as in Adam all die, even so in Christ all shall be made alive (1 Corinthians 15:22 NKJV).

All are to be made alive. This means "all" will be saved.

6. HE WILL MAKE ALL THE PEOPLE RIGHTEOUS

We again discover that all, or everyone, will be made righteous in Jesus Christ. Paul wrote to the Romans.

> Therefore, everyone was condemned through one failure, and everyone received God's life-giving approval through one verdict. Clearly, through one person's disobedience humanity became sinful, and through one person's obedience humanity will receive God's approval (Romans 5:18,19 God's Word).

Everyone means everyone! Jesus Christ has made it a reality that everyone will eventually get to heaven. His death made the unrighteous righteous.

7. THE WORD TRANSLATED ETERNAL DOES NOT MEAN EVERLASTING

The Greek word *aionios*, which is often translated as "eternal," does not always mean "everlasting" or "forever," For example we read the following instances of its use.

> Who saved us and called us to a holy calling, not because of our works but because of his own purpose and grace, which he gave us in Christ Jesus before the ages began (2 Timothy 1:9 ESV).

The word translated "ages" in this verse is elsewhere translated as "eternal." Therefore, we are not to assume that this word always speaks of something everlasting.

The same holds true when Paul wrote to Titus. He talks about a time before the "world" or "ages" began. He said.

> My message is based on the confidence of eternal life. God, who never lies, promised this eternal life before the world began (Titus 1:2 God's Word).

The writer to the Hebrews spoke of the end of the "age."

> If that had been necessary, he would have had to die again and again, ever since the world began. But no! He came once for all time, at the end of the age, to remove the power of sin forever by his sacrificial death for us (Hebrews 9:26 NLT).

In these instances, the Greek word *aionios* does not mean "everlasting." If the word can mean something apart from everlasting in these contexts, it can also refer to something other than everlasting punishment.

Therefore, it is thought by some people that the Bible teaches the doctrine of universalism.

SUMMARY TO QUESTION 36
WHAT ARGUMENTS ARE GIVEN THAT EVERYONE WILL ULTIMATELY GO TO HEAVEN? (UNIVERSALISM)

Universalism is the belief that there is no eternal suffering in hell. Everyone will eventually end up in heaven. This includes the devil and his evil angels. This belief is usually found in one of four ways.

Some believe that all will eventually be saved. After there is a certain amount of suffering in the next life, the sins of the wicked will have been paid for. At that time, they will be able to enter into heaven.

Others believe that everyone is already saved. There is no such place as hell. Yet the unbelievers in Jesus Christ do not now know this yet. The message is that Jesus has already paid the penalty for their sins. Consequently, people need to understand that they have already been forgiven and heaven awaits them. This is the good news of the gospel according to those who hold this theory.

There are others who think that every person in hell will eventually repent and become saved. After a time of suffering, they will turn to Jesus and ask His forgiveness. Since God is a gracious God He will indeed forgive them.

Finally, there are those who do not believe God will judge unbelievers at all. This is the perspective of those who reject the Bible, as well as the God whom the Bible portrays. To them, God does not exist so there will be no judgment.

Others may believe that there is some God who exists. Yet this God, whoever He might be, will certainly not eternally punish anyone. Therefore, these people, though they believe in some God, do not believe in the God of the Bible.

Whatever the case may be, those holding this view believe that an eternal hell does not exist.

Some appeal to the Bible to support their position on universalism. They argue as follows.

The Bible says that everyone will eventually bow to Jesus. This must mean that everyone will be saved one day if they are to bow to Him.

The Word of God also says that the Lord wants everyone to be saved. Since God always get what he wants, everyone will be saved. This should settle the matter.

Scripture teaches that all things will be gathered to Jesus Christ. He will make everyone righteous. Therefore, everyone must be saved, either now or at sometime in the future.

In addition, it is argued that the word translated "eternal" does not mean everlasting. It does not necessarily mean "without end." Therefore, hell can be temporary.

All of these things, it is contended, show that there is no eternal punishment for the wicked. Instead everyone will one day end up in heaven. This is the doctrine of universalism.

Will God Allow Everyone To Everyone Eventually Enter Heaven? (Universalism)

The doctrine of universalism says that every human being will eventually enter heaven. While universalists all agree that there is no such thing as an eternal hell, they do not agree how everyone will eventually get to heaven. "Christian universalists" appeal to the Bible to support the idea that everyone will eventually go to heaven.

Yet the Bible teaches no such thing. Universalism is not the biblical teaching on the subject of the ultimate destination of the lost. We can make the following observations as to why universalism contradicts the Scripture.

1. ACCORDING TO SCRIPTURE, THERE ARE TWO TYPES OF PEOPLE: SAVED AND LOST

The idea that the Bible somehow teaches that everyone is already saved is nonsensical. The Bible makes it clear that humanity is divided between those who are saved and those who are lost. The lost are already in a state of condemnation. John wrote.

> Anyone who believes in Him is not judged, but anyone who does not believe is already judged, because he has not believed in the name of the One and Only Son of God (John 3:18 HCSB).

A person is either saved or lost; there is no third possibility.

2. THERE ARE NO PASSAGES IN SCRIPTURE THAT TEACH UNIVERSALISM

Not only does the Scripture make a distinction between the saved and the lost, nowhere does it teach that everyone will someday be saved. The passages used by universalists do not teach what they claim it teaches.

3. SALVATION IS POSSIBLE FOR EVERYONE BUT EVERYONE WON'T BE SAVED

For example, John 12:32 says that Christ makes salvation possible. It does not say that everyone will eventually be saved. Later on in the same passage, Jesus made the following declaration about those who reject Him.

> The one who rejects me and does not receive my words has a judge; the word that I have spoken will judge him on the last day (John 12:48 ESV).

Not everyone will become a believer. Those who reject His Word must face Christ as the "Judge."

4. EVERYONE WILL BOW BUT NOT EVERYONE WILL BE SAVED

Although every one will eventually confess Jesus Christ, not even one will be reconciled, or made right, with Him. Everyone will bow to Him. The believer will bow in adoration while the unbeliever bows in defeat. Paul wrote the following to the Colossians.

> And through Him to reconcile everything to Himself by making peace through the blood of His cross whether things on earth or things in heaven (Colossians 1:20 HCSB).

Scripture clearly says that heaven and earth are reconciled to Christ. What is absent from this passage are the things "under the earth." This is the unseen realm of the wicked dead and the fallen angels. They have not been reconciled to Him. The Bible specifically omits these personages when it speaks of whom Christ reconciled to Himself. He did not reconcile them. They are lost and they will remain lost!

5. ONLY THE ONES "IN CHRIST" ARE SAVED

Paul says that all those "in Christ" are to be made alive. He wrote the following to the Corinthians.

> For as in Adam all die, so in Christ all will be made alive (First Corinthians 15:22 NIV).

However, the phrase "in Christ" refers only to believers. The same holds true for the statement of Paul that "all" will be made righteous "in Christ." Only those who have believed in Jesus are "in Christ." They alone are the righteous ones. The wicked dead will never be made righteous.

6. THERE ARE PEOPLE WHO ARE OUTSIDE OF THE HOLY CITY

In speaking of the Holy City, the New Jerusalem, which is the future home of believers, we are told this.

> Blessed are those who wash their robes, so that they may have the right to the tree of life and may enter the city by the gates. Outside are the dogs, the sorcerers, the sexually immoral, the murderers, the idolaters, and everyone who loves and practices lying (Revelation 22:14,15 HCSB).

We should note the distinction. There are those inside the Holy City and there are those "outside." Those outside are never allowed inside. This will be the situation for all eternity. This passage alone refutes the idea of any type of universalism.

7. GOD DOES NOT PROMISE SALVATION FOR EVERYONE

First Timothy 2:4 says that God "desires" all people to be saved. However, this is not a promise of salvation for everyone. Human beings still have a choice to believe or not to believe.

While the Lord desires their salvation He has left the choice up to each individual concerning whether or not to believe. He will not make anyone believe in Him or love Him. Heaven will not be a place where people are forced to attend. All those who are there are there by their own choice.

8. GOD GATHERS THE UNBELIEVERS FOR JUDGMENT

The Bible does say that all things will be gathered to Christ on the earth. However the Bible also says that some things are gathered for judgment. In Matthew, we read the following statement of Jesus.

> When the Son of Man comes in his glory, and all the angels with him, then he will sit on his glorious throne. Before him will be gathered all the nations, and he will separate people one from another as a shepherd separates the sheep from the goats (Matthew 25:31,32 ESV).

This separation is for judgment, for condemnation. It is not for salvation.

Therefore, we have no passages in Scripture which teach universalism.

9. THERE ARE PASSAGES THAT TEACH EVERLASTING PUNISHMENT FOR THE WICKED

Not only doesn't the Scripture teach universalism, there are passages that clearly teach the everlasting punishment of the wicked. In John's gospel we read of two types of people. There are those who have life and those who must endure the wrath of God.

> Whoever believes in the Son has eternal life; whoever does not obey the Son shall not see life, but the wrath of God remains on him (John 3:36 ESV).

Note that the disobedient ones will never see life. Never means never.

The Apostle Paul wrote that unbelievers will face everlasting punishment. He wrote the following to the Thessalonians.

> . . .This will take place at the revelation of the Lord Jesus from heaven with His powerful angels, taking vengeance with flaming fire on those who don't know God and on those who don't obey the gospel of our Lord Jesus. These will pay the penalty of eternal destruction from the Lord's presence and from His glorious strength (2 Thessalonians 1:6-9 God's Word).

The penalty for the lost is everlasting separation from the Lord's presence. This does not allow for any type of universalism.

We are also told that people who are apart from Jesus Christ are in the process of perishing. Paul wrote the following to the Corinthians.

> For the word of the cross is folly to those who are perishing, but to us who are being saved it is the power of God (1 Corinthians 1:18 ESV).

The writer to the Hebrews said that unbelievers will never enter into God's rest. Scripture puts it this way.

> For only we who believe can enter his place of rest. As for those who didn't believe, God said, "In my anger I made a vow: 'They will never enter my place of rest,' even though his place of rest has been ready since he made the world" (Hebrews 4:3 NLT).

There is no rest for the wicked. Not here, not in the next life. Never!

10. WE NEED GOD'S VIEW OF SIN

There is something else which we must stress. Those who advocate universalism do not have an appreciation of God's view of sin. To find out what God thinks of sin, one only needs to look at the cross of

Jesus Christ. The Bible says that God has a just or righteous reason for everything that He does. Indeed, we read in the Book of Ezekiel about the disasters that God has brought upon Jerusalem.

> Yet there will be some survivors—sons and daughters who will be brought out of it. They will come to you, and when you see their conduct and their actions, you will be consoled regarding the disaster I have brought upon Jerusalem— every disaster I have brought upon it. You will be consoled when you see their conduct and their actions, for you will know that I have done nothing in it without cause, declares the Sovereign LORD (Ezekiel 14:22,23 NIV).

Nothing God does is without a cause. There is always a wise reason for His acts.

We also discover something else very important with respect to sin. Ultimately we sin against God. In his prayer of confession, David acknowledged this. He wrote.

> Against you, you only, have I sinned and done what is evil in your sight, so that you are proved right when you speak and justified when you judge (Psalm 51:4 NIV).

Since human beings have sinned against an infinite, personal God they should receive infinite punishment. Furthermore, it is God alone who decides what a fitting punishment consists of. It is not our business because people are not sinning or rebelling against us.

11. THE GREEK WORD AION SPEAKS OF THE LONGEST POSSIBLE DURATION

With respect to the Greek word *aionios*, we should note the following. While it is true that the word *aionios* does not always mean "everlasting," it does refer to the longest possible duration that the Greek language can express.

Furthermore, in the great majority of the passages where it is used, the meaning is "everlasting or without end." It is the common meaning for the term.

In addition, this same word is used in explaining the duration of time in heaven. It is everlasting. Jesus said.

> These people will go away into eternal punishment, but those with God's approval will go into eternal life (Matthew 25:46 God's Word).

Note well the parallel. There is everlasting punishment for unbelievers and everlasting life for believers.

Moreover, Scripture gives no hope for those who have not believed in Jesus Christ. Jesus Himself said.

> Truly I tell you, people can be forgiven all their sins and every slander they utter, but whoever blasphemes against the Holy Spirit will never be forgiven; they are guilty of an eternal sin (Mark 3:28 NIV).

Note that these people are guilty of an "eternal" sin. Therefore, the Greek term used when describing the length of punishment, *aionios*, lends further support for the idea of everlasting punishment, not one of limited duration.

12. THE PURPOSE OF JUDGMENT IS PUNISHMENT

Those who advocate universalism miss the point of punishment. It is not reformatory but punitive. God is punishing the unbeliever for their forsaking of Him. Sin has to be punished. Indeed, there is always a penalty to pay.

13. THERE IS NO WORK OF THE HOLY SPIRIT ON THE DEAD

There is more evidence against universalism. There is no biblical evidence that the Holy Spirit works His influence upon anyone after death in order to convince them to be saved. On the contrary, the Bible says to let these evil people remain evil. We read the following in the Book of Revelation.

> Let the evildoer still do evil, and the filthy still be filthy, and the righteous still do right, and the holy still be holy (Revelation 22:11 ESV).

Those who are lost will never repent.

14. WHY DID CHRIST DESCRIBE JUDAS IN THE WAY HE DID?

We also have the description of the traitor Judas by Jesus. Why did Jesus say what He did about Judas if there was some final restoration? Jesus said the following concerning the traitor.

> The Son of Man goes as it is written of him, but woe to that man by whom the Son of Man is betrayed! It would have been better for that man if he had not been born (Matthew 26:24 ESV).

If Judas eventually joins everyone else in heaven, then why do we have this solemn statement of Jesus? Why would it have been better if he had never been born?

15. WHY DID PAUL SUFFER?

If everyone was eventually to end up in heaven, then why did the Apostle Paul suffer so? According to his own testimony, the following things happened to him as he was going about his evangelism of the lost.

> Five times I received at the hands of the Jews the forty lashes less one. Three times I was beaten with rods. Once I was stoned. Three times I was shipwrecked; a night and a day I was adrift at sea; on frequent journeys, in danger from rivers, danger from robbers, danger from my own people, danger from Gentiles, danger in the city, danger

in the wilderness, danger at sea, danger from false brothers; in toil and hardship, through many a sleepless night, in
hunger and thirst, often without food, in cold and exposure
(2 Corinthians 11:23-27 ESV).

Why go through all of this if everyone is going to end up in heaven?
What would be the purpose of all this suffering?

16. THERE IS NO MOTIVATION FOR EVANGELISM

Why try to reach the lost if they are not really lost? There is no motive
for evangelism if everyone will ultimately be saved. Why waste the
effort? We should spend our time doing other things.

Yet we see the constant preaching of the gospel by the apostles of
Christ. In addition, we find that the Bible commands us to preach the
gospel. Jesus said.

Go therefore and make disciples of all the nations, baptiz-
ing them in the name of the Father and of the Son and of
the Holy Spirit (Matthew 28:19 NKJV).

The urgency of the gospel message is because people are lost. Unless
they repent they will remain lost forever.

17. IT DENIES PEOPLE THEIR RIGHT TO CHOOSE

Scripture gives certain conditions for salvation. People have to turn
to God for forgiveness. For universalism to be true God, would have
to force His will on everyone. No one has any choice. Not Satan, not
the most evil person who has ever lived. They will all be forced to be
in God's presence forever. This would mean eternity would consist of
a number of beings in God's presence who have no desire to be there!

18. WE ARE SAVED FROM SOMETHING

Our last two points should drive home this truth. The Bible says
that those who trust Jesus Christ are "saved." It also says that Jesus

is our only Savior. Well, if we are saved, then we must be saved from something!

However, if universalism is true, and everyone ends up in heaven, then there is really nothing to ultimately be saved from. In other words, Christ really didn't save us from anything eternal.

19. WHAT IS THE POINT OF EVERYTHING?

Finally, if universalism is true, then what is the point of everything that happens here upon the earth? No matter what people do, whether good or evil, it will eventually mean nothing because everyone ends up in the same place.

Why not then sin as much as possible? If there is not going to be a final, or eternal, judgment of the wicked, then why should we ask people to behave? There is no reason that they should.

The answer to this question is that the doctrine of universalism is simply not biblical. It should not be preached or taught by those who call themselves Christians. It is not a Christian doctrine!

SUMMARY TO QUESTION 37
WILL GOD ALLOW EVERYONE TO EVERYONE EVENTUALLY ENTER HEAVEN? (UNIVERSALISM)

There are many people who hold to the doctrine of universalism. This is the belief that everyone will someday end up in heaven. While there are a number of arguments put forward for this theory all of these arguments are unconvincing. We can respond to them as follows.

For one thing there is not one passage in Scripture that teaches the doctrine of universalism. None.

Not only is there no passage of Scripture that teaches universalism, there are many passages that speak of an everlasting punishment of the wicked. There is no way of getting around the plain meaning of these passages.

The Bible does say that everyone will bow to Jesus as the universalists point out, but it does not say that everyone will be saved. The wicked will bow down in recognition of Jesus' Lordship but they will not become part of the company of the saved.

It also seems clear that universalists do not appreciate the horrible reality of sin. Ultimately all sin is directed at God our Maker. As such, it deserves punishment in proportion to the crime. Furthermore, since sin is ultimately against Him, then He is to be the Judge of what is the proper punishment for the wicked.

In addition, Scripture says that the eternal home of believers will be in the New Jerusalem, the Holy City. In describing the Holy City, we find that there are people who live outside of it. They are never allowed in! In fact, Scripture describes them in the strongest of terms to indicate their sinful condition. This fact alone should make it clear that not everyone will eventually be allowed into God's holy presence.

There is more. The Greek word used to describe the eternal suffering of the wicked means the punishment is of the longest possible duration. It is endless suffering. It has no idea of ceasing.

There is also the purpose of divine judgment. The Bible says that it is to punish the unbelievers, not to reform them. Scripture is clear that sin must be punished. Jesus suffered the punishment for our sins by His death on the cross. However, it does not do any of us any good unless we personally choose to apply it to ourselves. This comes about by believing in Him.

Furthermore there is no indication that the Holy Spirit works with those who are dead. It is only the living with whom He deals. Once a person dies in unbelief of Jesus there is no hope for them. None whatsoever!

There is also the matter of Judas Iscariot. Jesus' description of Judas does not make sense if there was to be some final restoration of the wicked dead. Indeed, Jesus said it would have been better if Judas had never been born. This does not sound like somebody who will eventually be restored to a proper relationship with the Lord.

If universalism is true then why did the Apostle Paul suffer in the manner in which the Bible records? Why did he go through the beatings, the shipwrecks, the periods of hunger and thirst, and the times in prison? If everyone would eventually end up in heaven why go through such suffering? Why not relax and enjoy life?

Indeed, why should we evangelize the lost? The gospel would seemingly be pointless. What's the use?

If everyone eventually went to heaven then it would be denying them the right to choose. Indeed, it would force people to be in God's presence against their will. What kind of heaven would that be?

There is one other thing. Christ came to earth to save us. If there is no everlasting punishment of the wicked then what is He saving us from? The word "saved" has the idea that a person is saved from something. Yet if universalism is true there is nothing to be eventually saved from.

Finally, what is the point of anything? This entire existence on earth would seemingly be without any real meaning.

Consequently we conclude that the idea of universalism is not something that fits with the Bible. Thus, it should not be believed, preached, or taught.

QUESTION 38

Can The Spirits Of The Dead Tell Us What It Is Like In Heaven? (Spiritism)

To gain information about what it is like in heaven, some people attempt to contact the spirits of the dead. They believe this to be an authoritative source of information.

Indeed, who would know better as to what goes on in the world of the dead than those who are dead? They are in the best position to tell us about heaven and what goes on there. Therefore, the spirits of the dead are often contacted to gain accurate information about the unseen world.

Should we then attempt to contact these deceased spirits to gain information on heaven? Does the Bible have anything to say about it?

THE BIBLE WARNS AGAINST THIS PRACTICE

The Bible does indeed have much to say about this practice. For example, it warns us about mediums; a person who claims to be able to contact the dead. In the strongest of terms, Scripture tells believers to avoid consulting such people. We read the following in Deuteronomy.

> For example, never sacrifice your son or daughter as a burnt offering. And do not let your people practice fortune-telling, or use sorcery, or interpret omens, or engage in witchcraft, or cast spells, or function as mediums or psychics, or call

forth the spirits of the dead. Anyone who does these things is detestable to the Lord. It is because the other nations have done these detestable things that the Lord your God will drive them out ahead of you. But you must be blameless before the Lord your God (Deuteronomy 18:10-13 NLT).

This sort of practice is strictly forbidden by the God of the Bible. Indeed, the Lord says that such practices are detestable to Him.

Elsewhere the Lord says in Leviticus that He will become the enemy of those who claim to speak with the dead. The Bible says.

I will be your enemy if you go to someone who claims to speak with the dead, and I will destroy you from among my people (Leviticus 20:6 CEV).

The Lord promised to destroy those who attempt to contact the spirits of the dead! Obviously, this type of practice is something which God hates.

There is indeed the strongest of punishments coming for those who try receive messages from those who are dead. We also read in Leviticus.

If you claim to receive messages from the dead, you will be put to death by stoning, just as you deserve (Leviticus 20:27 CEV)

Through his spokesmen, the prophets, God has already told us what we need to know about heaven. We do not consult the dead.

WHY WE SHOULD NOT GET OUR INFORMATION ABOUT HEAVEN FROM SPIRITS

There are a number of reasons as to why we should not seek information about heaven by consulting the spirits of the dead. They are as follows.

1. WE DO NOT KNOW WHO WE ARE CONTACTING

For one thing, we have no way of knowing who we are contacting. It is possible that the medium is actually a fraud. He or she is not contacting the spirits of the dead but rather is faking the entire episode. No spirits are involved. This is a distinct possibility.

If this is the case, then any message received is actually from a deceiver who is pretending to be a go-between for the spirits and those here upon the earth. Obviously, any message from this sort of person is worthless.

2. ANY SPIRIT CONTACTED WILL BE LYING

If there is any genuine contact with the spirit world we can be assured that they are lying. Indeed, the Bible warns us against these "deceiving spirits." In addition, there is no human being who has any way of knowing whether or not they getting correct information. There is really nothing anyone can do to check out what is said. Their word is all that we have and their word is not good!

3. THE MESSAGE THEY GIVE CONTRADICTS SCRIPTURE

There is also the message that comes from the supposed contact with evil spirits. These "spirits" never warn of judgment for disbelief in Jesus Christ. They do not speak of hell or any type of endless separation from God because of sin. These spirits never speak of a need for a Savior to escape the wrath of God.

Instead, they always seem to have positive messages about the afterlife. In other words, they tell people what they want to hear about the next life. According to these spirits, everything is fine in the next world so no one need worry about death and dying. This type of message is a blatant lie!

WHAT WE LEARN ABOUT THE SPIRIT WORLD BIBLICAL EXAMPLES

There are a number of things learned about the spirit realm from biblical examples. They include the following.

LAZARUS WAS SEEMINGLY UNABLE TO GO BACK AND SPEAK TO THE BROTHERS OF THE RICH MAN

In Jesus' story of the rich man and Lazarus, there is no indication that Lazarus could communicate with the brothers of the rich man. It seems that he was unable to do such a thing. Abraham did say it was impossible for Lazarus to cross over to the world of the unbelieving dead. This seems to indicate the impossibility of the believing dead contacting the living.

THE EXAMPLE OF SAUL AND SAMUEL: WE SHOULD NOT ATTEMPT TO COMMUNICATE TO THE DEAD

The only time God allowed a spirit to communicate from the dead is the case of Samuel. His message was one of judgment for King Saul. When Samuel did appear, he told Saul that he would join him in the realm of the dead the next day!

Therefore, the only biblical example of the believing dead communicating to the living resulted in the judgment of the one who was disobedient to God and contacted the dead. Saul received the death sentence.

In contrast to being guided by spirits, we should let the Word of the living God guide us. The Bible says the following about the Word of God.

> Your word is a lamp for my feet and a light for my path (Psalm 119:105 NLT).

God's Word must be our guide. It will never lead us astray. Spirits of the dead cannot give us any guidance. Thus, we should never try to contact them about heaven or any other subject. Never!

SUMMARY TO QUESTION 38
CAN THE SPIRITS OF THE DEAD TELL US WHAT IT IS LIKE IN HEAVEN? (SPIRITISM)

There are those who turn to speaking to the spirits of the dead in order to obtain information about heaven. They believe humans can get a firsthand account of heaven from those who are presently there. If there is a heaven, a place where people go after this life is over, then it seemingly makes sense to ask those who are already there. Certainly, they will tell us about life in the next world.

This is usually attempted by using the services of a person known as a medium. The medium claims to be able to reach those in the next world. Through the help of the medium the dead are contacted and information about the next life is gathered and provided to the one seeking the truth.

Yet the Bible warns against this in the strongest of terms. Indeed, in the Old Testament the death penalty was given for those who attempted to contact evil spirits. The Lord said such practices were abhorrent to Him. They were an abomination!

Apart from God's specific words on the subject, there are also a number of practical reasons as to why we should not try to contact the spirits of the dead to give us information about heaven. They are as follows.

For one thing, we don't know if we are truly contacting these spirits. It is possible, even likely, that the medium is faking the entire episode. Nobody can really be sure. If the medium is a fraud then any message received comes from a liar who has no contact whatsoever with the next world.

Even if the medium does actually contact some spirit there are further problems. How does anyone know if these spirits are telling the truth about the situation in the next world? On what basis can we test their claims? There is none. We have to take their word for it. This is especially worrisome because Scripture speaks of them as "lying spirits."

A further problem concerns the message these spirits give. They are always positive, never negative. We never hear of these spirits preaching the gospel of Jesus Christ or warning people of the coming punishment of an everlasting hell. Instead their message always contradicts what the Bible has to say about the afterlife. These "spirits" provide false comfort to the living in their description of the next world. They are not to be believed.

We also learn things about contacting the dead from a couple of biblical examples. In the story of the rich man and Lazarus which Jesus told, Lazarus was not allowed to cross over to the realm of the dead where unbelievers resided. While this does not necessarily mean that he could not contact the living on the earth, in the story which Jesus gave it was emphasized that such contact would not help the living. They must make their decisions based upon God's Word. They are not to get their information about the unseen world by having contact with the dead.

In the only biblical example of a dead believer being contacted by the living, we find the dead prophet Samuel pronouncing judgment upon King Saul. When Samuel spoke to Saul from the realm of the dead it was to announce his death in battle the next day.

Thus, the only biblical example of genuine contact with the dead resulted in judgment for the one who made the request. This should serve as a further warning as to why we should not try to contact the dead.

These reasons make it clear that information about heaven should be gathered from a study of Scripture and not from attempts to contact those who have died. They cannot provide us any new information. Everything we need to know about heaven is found in the Bible. This alone is the place where we should get our information

Why Should We Focus Our Thoughts On Heaven?

Is it practical to spend our time on earth thinking about the next life? Does the Bible tell us to think about heavenly things? Indeed, it does. Paul the Apostle wrote to the Colossians and commanded them to set their mind on heavenly things.

> Since, then, you have been raised with Christ, set your hearts on things above, where Christ is seated at the right hand of God. Set your minds on things above, not on earthly things (Colossians 3:1,2 NIV).

We are told to make heaven the focus of our attention while we are living here upon the earth. We should truly concentrate on the things which are above.

LIFE IS SHORT

The Bible emphasizes that life is short. In Job, our life is compared to a flower which rises up and withers away, or as a shadow which does not last. It says.

> He springs up like a flower and withers away; like a fleeting shadow, he does not endure (Job 14:2 NIV).

Life is like a fleeting shadow.

The psalmist also compared life to dreams that disappear and grass that springs up in the morning but is withered by the evening. He put it this way.

> You sweep people away like dreams that disappear or like grass that springs up in the morning. In the morning it blooms and flourishes, but by evening it is dry and withered (Psalm 90:5-6 NLT).

As the flower has only one short day of life, we human beings are on this earth for precious little time.

The Book of James compares life to a fog or a mist that comes up for a little while and then disappears. He wrote.

> You should know better than to say, "Today or tomorrow we will go to the city. We will do business there for a year and make a lot of money!" What do you know about tomorrow? How can you be so sure about your life? It is nothing more than mist that appears for only a little while before it disappears. You should say, "If the Lord lets us live, we will do these things" (James 4:13-15 CEV).

Since life is short, we are to make the most of it. We should think on those things which are above. Nothing else really matters.

WHAT HAPPENS WHEN WE FOCUS OUR ATTENTION UPON HEAVEN?

There are a number of practical things which happen when we focus our attention on the afterlife and not upon this life. We can sum them up as follows.

1. WE REMIND OURSELVES THAT THIS WORLD IS NOT OUR HOME

The Bible emphasizes that the believer's home is not here upon the earth but rather in heaven. Paul wrote to the Philippians.

But we are citizens of heaven, where the Lord Jesus Christ lives. And we are eagerly waiting for him to return as our Savior (Philippians 3:20 NLT).

When we think about heaven we are reminded that this earth is not our real home. This helps us put things in perspective. Whatever happens to us here is only temporary; whether good or bad. Heaven is where we belong.

2. WE REMIND OURSELVES THAT HEAVEN IS WHERE WE WILL LIVE FOREVER

If we are going to live forever in heaven, then certainly we should desire to know as much about it as we are able. The more we realize that heaven is our eternal home the more we will think about it. In turn, we will become much more productive in our lives here upon the earth as we think of our heavenly home. This is how it works.

3. WE REMIND OURSELVES WHERE OUR GENUINE TREASURE RESIDES

The genuine treasures of those who believe in Jesus are not here upon this earth but rather with God the Father in heaven. Jesus said.

> Don't store up treasures here on earth, where they can be eaten by moths and get rusty, and where thieves break in and steal. Store your treasures in heaven, where they will never become moth-eaten or rusty and where they will be safe from thieves. Wherever your treasure is, there your heart and thoughts will also be (Matthew 6:19-21 NLT).

We should constantly remind ourselves of this. We need to make certain our efforts are to earn treasures in the heavenly realm, not the earthly realm.

4. WE REMIND OURSELVES TO BE THANKFUL THAT WE HAVE BEEN SPARED FROM JUDGMENT

When we think of heaven we become thankful that we have been spared the judgment of hell, a punishment which we all richly deserve. Whenever we think about heaven we are reminded that we are going there because of God's mercy. This should cause us to continually give thanks to the Lord. Indeed, Paul wrote.

> In every thing give thanks: for this is the will of God in Christ Jesus concerning you (1 Thessalonians 5:18 KJV).

Among the things for which we should be thankful is that we have been spared the judgment of God. This is truly something we should never forget.

5. WE REMIND OURSELVES THAT THE GOD OF THE BIBLE IS STILL IN CONTROL OF ALL THINGS

The God of the Bible not only exists; He is in control of all things. When we think about heaven we recognize the fact God is still on the throne, He is still running the universe and it's running exactly the way He desires. This is another practical benefit of thinking about heaven. Paul wrote these important words to the Romans.

> We know that all things work together for the good of those who love God: those who are called according to His purpose (Romans 8:28 HCSB).

We must continually remind ourselves that God is causing all things to work together for good. He has a purpose in all things which go one.

6. WE REMIND OURSELVES THAT WE HAVE A GENUINE HOPE

Finally, we should spend our time focusing on heaven as a reminder that we do have a realistic hope for the future. Paul noted that we do suffer in this life but these sufferings do not compare to what is coming. He wrote.

> For I consider that the sufferings of this present time are not worth comparing with the glory that is going to be revealed to us (Romans 8:18 HCSB).

The difficult times will indeed come. Thinking of our heavenly future can make these times easier to endure. The present suffering does not compare to the future glory.

These are some of the reasons as to why believers should focus on their heavenly home. We should indeed make it a regular part of our life to think on the things which are above. Before we know it, we will actually be there!

SUMMARY TO QUESTION 39
WHY SHOULD WE FOCUS OUR THOUGHTS ON HEAVEN?

Scripture emphasizes the shortness of human life. Indeed, there are a number of analogies which the Bible gives which reminds us that life is short.

We find that life is compared to a mist that fades away with the morning sun or a flower which blooms in the morning and then withers by evening. Since life is short, we need to make the most of it. One of the ways we can accomplish that is to set our minds upon heaven.

There are a number of practical benefits when we do this. For one thing, it helps us realize that this world is not our home. We are only visiting here.

Since heaven is our eternal home, we should spend our time thinking about it and finding out as much about it as we possibly can. There is no need for us to be ignorant about the world to come.

In addition, we should be storing up treasures in our eternal home as opposed to storing them up here upon this earth. Earthly wealth will fade, heavenly wealth will not.

Thinking about heaven also causes us to be thankful that we are going to spend eternity there rather than being separated from the Lord in hell. Indeed, this should cause us to be thankful constantly.

Furthermore, thinking about heaven reminds us that God is still in control of all things. He is the One who runs the universe and ultimately controls every aspect of it. This is a comforting thought for believers; God is still on the throne.

There is also the fact that we have a genuine hope for something better after this life is over. Setting our mind on heaven makes us realize that the problems we face here are only temporary. Better things await us.

Consequently, thinking about heaven has some very practical benefits.

What Observations And Conclusions Should We Make About Heaven?

From Scripture, we can make a number of general observations and conclusions concerning what it says about heaven.

OBSERVATION 1: HEAVEN IS REAL

While God is everywhere present in the universe, there is a place where the He dwells in a special sense. Among other things, it is called heaven. Heaven is not a mythological place. Neither is it somewhere that we humans merely wish would exist. It does exist, it is real. The Bible makes this clear.

OBSERVATION 2: HEAVEN COMPLETES THE PROMISES OF GOD TO THE BELIEVER

Presently believers in Jesus Christ are in states of incompleteness. Those who are alive are waiting to be in His presence. Those who have died are in His presence but still have not received all that God has promised. This will happen at the resurrection of the dead when the Lord raises the believers and then rewards them. When this occurs, the promises that God has made to us will be fully realized.

OBSERVATION 3: ONLY BELIEVERS IN THE GOD OF THE BIBLE GO TO HEAVEN

While heaven is a real place, not everyone will go there. Indeed, only those who have believed in the God of Scripture will be in heaven.

Unbelievers will spend their eternity apart from Him. Consequently, the only way in which a person in this day and age can get to heaven is to trust Jesus Christ as their Savior.

OBSERVATION 4: WE CAN HAVE ASSURANCE THAT WE ARE GOING TO HEAVEN

The Bible says that we can know that we are going to heaven, we can know that we have eternal life. In other words, we can have the assurance that when we die, we believers will be immediately in the presence of the Lord. These are not our claims, our boasts, this is what the Bible says!

OBSERVATION 5: WE CAN KNOW MANY THINGS ABOUT HEAVEN

While God has not revealed everything about heaven, He has told us a number of things that we can know about it. These truths should encourage us as we go through this life. Indeed, heaven, for each of us, is only a breath away!

SUMMARY TO QUESTION 40
WHAT OBSERVATIONS AND CONCLUSIONS SHOULD WE MAKE ABOUT HEAVEN?

There are a number of conclusions that we can make about heaven when we consider what the Bible has to say on the topic.

To begin with, heaven is real. There is a God who exists who has a special place where He dwells in a unique way. The Bible calls it heaven.

Each human being, whether living or dead, is in a state of incompleteness. For believers, heaven will be the place where the promises of God, to those who have believed, will be fulfilled.

Heaven is certainly real but not every human will go to heaven. The Bible tells us that God has made only one way for a person to reach Him; this is through belief in God the Son, Jesus Christ.

In addition, Scripture says that each of us who believe can know that we are going to heaven. His Word gives us that assurance.

Finally, though many things about heaven have not been revealed, there are many things we can know. Indeed, and what we do know of heaven causes us to want to go there. Recognizing these truths about heaven can certainly help us in our daily lives in this difficult world in which we live.

In sum, heaven should always be on our mind.

Don't Statements In The Book Of Ecclesiastes Contradict Other Parts Of Scripture About Heaven?

We have seen that the Bible, from beginning to end, speaks of a place called heaven. Heaven is where God dwells in a unique way and heaven will be the place where all believers in Him will eventually go.

However, the Book of Ecclesiastes contains some statements about the afterlife that seem to be at variance with what other portions of Holy Scripture. What are we to make of them?

For example, the writer says the following.

> I thought to myself, "God is going to test humans in order to show them that they are like animals." Humans and animals have the same destiny. One dies just like the other. All of them have the same breath of life. Humans have no advantage over animals. All of life is pointless. All life goes to the same place. All life comes from the ground, and all of it goes back to the ground. Who knows whether a human spirit goes upward or whether an animal spirit goes downward to the earth? (Ecclesiastes 3:18-21 God's Word).

According to this passage, humans have no advantage over animals at death. Indeed, the writer says that there is no difference between them; they all go to the same place. No one can know whether the spirit of humans goes upward toward God, or downward toward extinction. Elsewhere we read in Ecclesiastes.

> The living know that they will die, but the dead don't know anything. There is no more reward for the dead when the memory of them has faded. Their love, their hate, and their passions have already vanished. They will never again take part in anything that happens under the sun. Go, enjoy eating your food, and drink your wine cheerfully, because God has already accepted what you've done (Ecclesiastes 9:5-7 God's Word).

How can we explain these passages in light of other portions of Scripture? Doesn't this contradict what the Lord says about our hope for heaven?

THERE ARE TWO POSSIBLE EXPLANATIONS

Generally there are two different explanations that have been given to this question. One view says that all these statements can be harmonized with the rest of Scripture when we understand the context in which they are made.

Others see these as contradictory statements because of the perspective of the writer. He is "under the sun." In other words, he is speaking as a person who is giving us a fallible human answer to these questions; he is not speaking for God.

OPTION 1: THEY CAN BE HARMONIZED

There are some who believe these statements can be harmonized with the rest of Scripture. If the passages are taken out of context, then Ecclesiastes seems to be a book of skepticism. Once the context is understood, the statements are compatible with the rest of Scripture. The proper way to interpret these passages is follows.

ECCLESIASTES 3:18-21

In Ecclesiastes 3:18-21, the author is saying that similar things happen to humans and animals. Each is born, each die, and each do not come back in the same form. Yet what he is emphasizing is that the dead presently have no knowledge *in* our world, not *of* our world. The reason they have no knowledge in our world is because they are dead. In addition, the passage refers to the lifelessness of the human body, not the human soul. It is only the body that he is speaking of.

ECCLESIASTES 9:5,6

The statements in Ecclesiastes 9:5,6 need to be understood in light of verse ten of that chapter. The subject is the grave.

> Whatever your hand finds to do, do it with all your might, for in the grave, where you are going, there is neither working nor planning nor knowledge nor wisdom (Ecclesiastes 9:10 NIV).

There is no more working in this world once you are dead. This is the main thought in 9:5-6. Consequently, there is no conflict.

A. THERE WILL BE JUDGMENT IN THE FUTURE

The writer of Ecclesiastes does say there is judgment in the future.

> Be happy, young man, while you are young, and let your heart give you joy in the days of your youth. Follow the ways of your heart and whatever your eyes see, but know that for all these things God will bring you to judgment (Ecclesiastes 11:9 NIV).

He believed in a future judgment.

B. THOSE WHO DIE HAVE SOMEWHERE TO GO

He also says that those who die go to their eternal home.

When men are afraid of heights and of dangers in the streets; when the almond tree blossoms and the grasshopper drags himself along and desire no longer is stirred. Then man goes to his eternal home and mourners go about the streets (Ecclesiastes 12:5 NIV).

The writer concludes.

Having heard everything, I have reached this conclusion: Fear God and keep his commandments, because this is the whole duty of man. For God will evaluate every deed (Ecclesiastes 12:13 NET).

Therefore, when the book is understood correctly, there is no denying of life after death. Consequently, the Book of Ecclesiastes does not contradict the rest of Scripture when it is properly understood.

OPTION 2: THE PERSPECTIVE IS UNDER THE SUN

There is another way in which to view these statements in Ecclesiastes. If we understand that the perspective of the author is from "under the sun," then the problems disappear. The writer is making his judgments without the aid of divine revelation. From a human perspective, or under the sun, there is no difference between an animal and a human.

One does not know if the spirit of the human goes up, and the animal goes down. What is needed is divine revelation to tell us the answer. Otherwise we would have no answer.

No matter which option one chooses to take, there is no need to assume we have a contradiction in Scripture.

SUMMARY TO APPENDIX 1
DON'T STATEMENTS IN THE BOOK OF ECCLESIASTES CONTRADICT OTHER PARTS OF SCRIPTURE ABOUT HEAVEN?

Some of the statements in the Book of Ecclesiastes seem to contradict other parts of Scripture about the subject of the afterlife. Indeed, they appear to teach that the dead know nothing once they are dead.

How can we reconcile these passages, which apparently teach opposite things about heaven and hell, from other passages in Scripture? Does this mean the Bible has contradictions? Does this mean we do not have any solid information about what happens after death?

We must stress that the Bible contains no contradictions. We find that there are two possible ways of reconciling these statements without assuming error in Scripture.

One possible solution concerns the understanding of the perspective of the writer of Ecclesiastes. It is from "under the sun." In other words, without the aid of divine revelation he is trying to understand truths about life and death.

Basically, he cannot know the answers because there is not any way he could possible know them. Indeed, none of us can know. Without divine revelation we are only guessing. This is why he comes up with such statements about life, death and the afterlife.

Thus, when the perspective of the writer is understood along with the overall message of Ecclesiastes, then there is no contradiction. The writer does make contradictory statements to the rest of Scripture. The reason he does so is his perspective; under the sun or without divine revelation. Therefore, the purpose of the book is to teach the futility of life without God.

However, there is another way of understanding the statements in Ecclesiastes without assuming contradictions. If the context is properly understood, and we discover what the author is actually saying, then we do not find contradictions. Basically, what the writer is talking about is that the dead know nothing about what occurs in this life. He is not speaking about what they know in the next life.

Thus, the so-called contradictions disappear when Ecclesiastes is correctly interpreted.

Either solution is possible. Whatever the case may be, we do not have to assume that God, speaking through the writer of Ecclesiastes, is teaching us different things about the afterlife than what we find in the rest of Scripture. He is not.

APPENDIX 2

How Will God Judge Babies And Young Children Who Die As Well As The Mentally Challenged? Will They Go To Heaven?

The Bible teaches that unless a person accepts Jesus Christ as their Savior, they cannot go to heaven, they will go to hell. John wrote.

> Whoever believes in the Son has eternal life; whoever does not obey the Son shall not see life, but the wrath of God remains on him (John 3:36 ESV).

Those who believe in Christ have eternal life but those who do not believe will suffer God's punishment. This is the clear message of Scripture.

But what about children who die too young to make such a decision, or people whose mental capacity is such that they are unable to make any decisions, much less spiritual ones? Will God damn them, or will they go to heaven? This question of their accountability has puzzled many.

We will consider a number of the most popular answers that have been given to this question as well as a response to each of these answers. We will conclude with what we believe is the "best" answer to this question.

SUGGESTED ANSWERS TO THIS QUESTION OF THE FATE OF BABIES WHO DIE

When it comes to discovering a biblical answer to the destiny of babies or young children who die, there have been a number of responses put forward that do not fit the facts. We will look at seven suggested answers by Christians that we believe to be inadequate.

1. Unbaptized Infants Go To Limbo, A Place On The Outskirts Of Hell

2. God's Love Prevents Him From Sending Children To Hell

3. God Judges Them Based Upon The Decision They Would Have Made

4. Only The Children Of Believers Are Saved

5. All Infants Who Died Are Predestined To Salvation

6. The Souls Of Infants Are Treated As If They Did Not Exist

7. Infants Who Die Are Not Part Of The Elect Therefore They Are Lost

We will consider the arguments provided by those who hold each of these views and then provide a brief response.

After we examine each of these suggestions, we will then give what we believe to be the best answer to the question.

OPTION 1: THEY GO TO LIMBO

The Roman Catholic Church says that all infants who die unbaptized enter a place called limbo (*Limbus Infantum*). Limbo is said to be on the outskirts of hell.

These infants do suffer in this place, but their suffering is from a lack of baptism, not because of the particular sins they committed.

PROBLEMS WITH LIMBO

Scripture speaks of no such place as limbo. Neither does the Bible place such importance on water baptism. Since no place as limbo exists, and water baptism is not crucial to salvation, this answer is insufficient as to the fate of infants who die. We have to find a better answer.

OPTION 2: A GOD OF LOVE WOULD NOT ALLOW CHILDREN TO GO TO HELL

This view holds that God's love prevents Him from sending infants who die to hell. The Bible does say that God is love.

> Anyone who does not love does not know God, because God is love (1 John 4:8 ESV).

A God of love, it is contended, would not do this.

RESPONSE

Yet the Bible also says that God is holy. He is a God of justice. Peter cited the Lord saying.

> Since it is written, "You shall be holy, for I am holy" (1 Peter 1:16 ESV).

God could not overcome the sin of infants merely because He is a God of love. His justice demands that the sin must be dealt with. We still need a better answer.

OPTION 3: GOD JUDGES BASED UPON WHAT THEY WOULD HAVE DONE

Another view emphasizes the foreknowledge of God in an attempt to solve this question of babies who die in infancy. This view says that God judges all infants based upon what He foreknew they would have done. The Bible teaches that God knows everything. He knows everything that will happen, as well as everything that might happen. Nothing escapes His knowledge.

HE WOULD KNOW HOW THEY WOULD HAVE LIVED

Consequently, it is argued, that He knows which infant would have been saved had they lived. Therefore, He will judge them, not according to what they have done, but rather according to what they would have done, had they lived. Those who would have believed in Jesus Christ are saved, while those who would have not believed are lost.

RESPONSE

This would have God judging infants for some hypothetical, conscious rejection of Christ. Since this rejection never actually occurred, they would be held responsible for something they never did. This is inconsistent with the biblical portrayal of God.

OPTION 4: ONLY CHILDREN OF BELIEVERS ARE SAVED

There are some who have argued that only the children of believers are saved if they die in infancy. There is no such guarantee for the children of unbelievers.

It is true that Scripture says that the believing spouse can sanctify or "set apart" the unbelieving mate and that also touches their children. Paul wrote the following.

> For the unbelieving husband is sanctified by the wife, and the unbelieving wife is sanctified by the Christian husband. Otherwise your children would be unclean, but now they are holy (1 Corinthians 7:14 HCSB).

The children are called "holy." This is taken to mean that believing infants are treated differently than infants whose parents are unbelievers.

RESPONSE

This passage does not mean that the children of unbelievers are necessarily lost. The issue of their salvation is not in view in this passage.

Consequently, there is nothing in Scripture which separates the children of believers from unbelievers as far as eternal salvation is concerned.

OPTION 5: THEY ARE UNCONDITIONALLY PREDESTINED TO SALVATION

Some Bible students believe that infants who die were unconditionally predestined for salvation before the foundation of the world. Their destiny was determined before they were born, not upon their death. God, knowing that they would die before having any chance to decide for Him or against Him, predetermined their fate long before they were born. All of them will be saved.

RESPONSE

When this view is logically carried out, it incorrectly assumes that people do not have any choice in the matter of salvation. This is not what the Bible has to say on the matter. Human beings do have choice and they will be judged accordingly.

OPTION 6: THEY WILL BE TREATED AS THOUGH THEY DID NOT EXIST

This position argues that God would treat infants who die as though they did not ever exist. Since they never reached an age to make a choice, it would not be fair to either reward them or condemn them. Consequently their souls cease to exist.

THE SPIRIT LASTS FOREVER

The Bible, however, says that the immaterial part of us, the soul or spirit, will last forever. There is no idea in Scripture that somehow our spirit will ever cease to exist. The spirits of these dead infants must go somewhere. This is the question which must be answered.

OPTION 7: INFANTS WHO DIE ARE LOST BECAUSE THEY DID NOT BELIEVE IN JESUS

This view is by far the harshest and the most distasteful. It basically says that infants who die will go to hell because they are not part of the elect. If they had been part of the elect, then they would have reached an age where they could have made a decision for Christ. The fact that they never reached that age shows they are not part of those chosen by God. Thus, they will spend eternity in hell.

RESPONSE

Those who hold this view should read the entire Bible. If anything stands out in Scripture it is that the God of the Bible is righteous and fair. His judgments are always perfect.

Furthermore, Scripture emphasizes His love for humankind. One wonders what kind of love God would have if this were the way in which He dealt with the eternal souls or spirits of young children. This is a monstrous idea and it certainly does not reflect the God of Scripture.

BABIES CANNOT BE DECLARED INNOCENT, THEY HAVE A SIN NATURE

There is one more issue that we will deal with before we provide an answer to this question. The obstacle is this: babies are born with a sin nature so how can they enter heaven if their sins have not been forgiven?

They are obviously not innocent in the sense of not having a sin nature. Therefore, they need a Savior.

ALL HAVE SINNED ARE GUILTY

The Bible says that all of us are born with a sinful nature, and are guilty before God. Paul wrote to the Romans.

> For all have sinned and fall short of the glory of God (Romans 3:23 HCSB).

Children are never in a sinless state. Indeed, we are born into the world as sinners. This is the consistent teaching of both testaments.

ADAM'S CHILDREN ARE IN THEIR LIKENESS

The reason that children are born sinful has to do with our inherited nature. At the very beginning of the Bible, it says that after Adam and Eve sinned, they bore children in their likeness. We read in Genesis.

> Adam was 130 years old when he fathered a child in his likeness, according to his image, and named him Seth (Genesis 5:3 HCSB).

This likeness was a sinful likeness. All of us who have been born since that time have the same sin nature. David said.

> Indeed, I was guilty when I was born; I was sinful when my mother conceived me (Psalm 51:5 HCSB).

Thus, from the Old Testament, there is no such idea that children are born in some type of state of sinlessness.

THE NEW TESTAMENT SAYS SIN HAS BEEN PASSED ON

The New Testament also makes it clear that the sin nature has been passed on to all of us. Paul wrote.

> When Adam sinned, sin entered the world. Adam's sin brought death, so death spread to everyone, for everyone sinned . . . Yes, Adam's one sin brings condemnation for everyone, but Christ's one act of righteousness brings a right relationship with God and new life for everyone. Because one person disobeyed God, many became sinners. But because one other person obeyed God, many will be made righteous (Romans 5:12,18,19 God's Word).

The sin nature is alive and well in all of us.

ALL PEOPLE NEED TO BE SAVED

Because children are born with a sin nature, they are lost in sin and need to be saved. Jesus explained why He came into this world.

For the Son of Man came to seek and save those who are lost (Luke 19:10 NLT).

In another place, the New Testament declares.

The one who believes in the Son has eternal life, but the one who refuses to believe in the Son will not see life; instead, the wrath of God remains on him (John 3:36 HCSB).

Those who refuse to believe in Jesus Christ are already in a state of condemnation.

Paul wrote to the Romans emphasizing that none of us are righteous. He said.

None is righteous, no, not one (Romans 3:10 ESV).

Since all infants are born with a sin nature, and are under the condemnation that Adam brought, they need a Savior. It is contended that we cannot lessen their guilt before God.

Therefore, to call them innocent, is not an option to answer the question as to what will happen to babies that die. We cannot declare them innocent. They are not innocent; none of us are.

RESPONSE TO THIS OBJECTION AND AN ANSWER TO THIS QUESTION

Nobody doubts that children are born with a sin nature. However, this is not the real question. The question is this: "Does the Bible hold them responsible before they reach an age of understanding right from wrong?" In other words, is there a time where babies or young children, although having a sin nature, do not knowingly sin against the commandments of God? If so, what does the Bible say about their responsibility?

What we will find is that, according to the Bible, there is an age where children begin to understand what is right and what is wrong. Before

APPENDIX 2

they reach that age, they do not have this understanding, and therefore, are not held to be accountable before God.

We will support this answer in two different ways. First, we will consider the attributes of God as revealed in Scripture. Second, we will examine specific passages that shine light on this difficult question.

POINT 1: THE ATTRIBUTES OF GOD SHOULD BE CONSIDERED

When considering this question, we must look at the nature or attributes of God. Indeed, the character of God must enter into the discussion. As we will see, it is inconsistent with God's character of condemn those who cannot be held responsible.

GOD IS GOOD

First, we emphasize that God is a good God. The Bible says.

> Taste and see that the Lord is good; blessed is the one who takes refuge in him (Psalm 34:8 NIV).

The psalmist encourages people to taste and see the goodness of the Lord.

GOD IS A GOD OF JUSTICE

The Bible also emphasizes the fairness and justice of God. The psalmist wrote.

> The LORD gives righteousness and justice to all who are treated unfairly (Psalm 103:6 NLT).

God is a righteous God. He looks after those who are unfairly treated.

The Lord is a God of justice. The prophet Zephaniah wrote.

> The LORD within her is righteous; he does no wrong. Morning by morning he dispenses his justice, and every

new day he does not fail, yet the unrighteous know no shame (Zephaniah 3:5 NIV).

The God of the Bible does only that which is right.

Paul, in speaking of a future time of judgment for the world, emphasized that God will be righteous in His judging.

> For he has set a day when he will judge the world with justice by the man he has appointed. He has given proof of this to all men by raising him from the dead (Acts 17:31 NIV).

The Lord will judge the world with justice.

Unbelievers choose to reject Jesus Christ, infants do not. Justice needs to be fairly given to both for their actions.

To sum up, when we consider this question of the fate of babies and infants who die, we must take into account the attributes of the God of the Bible. As we have just seen, the God of the Bible is a good God, a God who always does the right thing, and a God of justice.

With this in mind, let us now look at a number of specific passages in Scripture that touch upon this issue.

POINT 2: BIBLE PASSAGES THAT SHED LIGHT ON THIS ISSUE

Apart from looking at the character of God, there are passages in both testaments that shed light on the issue of the responsibility of children before they reach an age of understanding right from wrong.

EXAMPLE 1: YOUNGER ONES FROM ISRAEL WERE NOT JUDGED FOR THE SINS OF THE MULTITUDE (NUMBERS 14:29)

In the Book of Numbers, we have an account that sheds some light on this topic. The children of Israel were taken to the borders of the Promised Land, but did not enter in because of their unbelief. God, therefore, commanded that these people would wander for forty years in the desert, and then die as a punishment for their sin.

However, He specified that only those from age twenty and over be held accountable, while others would survive.

> Your corpses will fall in this wilderness—all of you who were registered in the census, the entire number of you 20 years old or more—because you have complained about Me (Numbers 14:29 HCSB).

Thus, we see God making a distinction of who was held accountable for their actions and who was not. At that time, those twenty years and above were considered accountable. While the judgment for lack of faith was physical death, and not eternal death, the principle still applies.

These people from the nation of Israel "knew" what was right, yet they did not do it. Consequently, God held them accountable. However, there were others, the younger ones, who were not held accountable.

EXAMPLE 2: DAVID'S CHILD WHO DIED IN INFANCY

The Old Testament relates the story of one of the children of David and Bathsheba. Their child became very ill. David fasted and prayed in order that God might spare the life of his son.

When the son died, the people were afraid to tell David because of how he might take the news. When David found out, he washed himself, changed his clothes, and asked for food. His servants were astonished at his change of attitude. David explained why he did what he did.

> He answered, "While the baby was alive, I fasted and wept because I thought, 'Who knows? The LORD may be gracious to me and let him live.' But now that he is dead, why should I fast? Can I bring him back again? I'll go to him, but he will never return to me" (2 Samuel 12:22,23 HCSB).

The fact that David said that he would join his son someday shows that he believed in life after death and that he would be with his infant son in the afterlife.

Some argue that David was only saying that he would join his son in death someday, nothing more. However, there is no comfort whatsoever in that. David believed that he would see his young son again.

Among other reasons, we know that David is in heaven from what he wrote in the famous 23rd Psalm.

> Certainly, goodness and mercy will stay close to me all the days of my life, and I will remain in the LORD's house for days without end (Psalm 23:6 God's Word).

Furthermore, we know that David was a prophet. On the Day of Pentecost, Peter, when addressing the crowd, spoke of David as a prophet of God.

> Brothers, I can confidently speak to you about the patriarch David: he is both dead and buried, and his tomb is with us to this day. Since he was a prophet, he knew that God had sworn an oath to him to seat one of his descendants on his throne. Seeing this in advance, he spoke concerning the resurrection of the Messiah (Acts 2:29-31 HCSB).

Speaking as God's prophet, David said that someday he would go to be with his son. Therefore, this indicates that his deceased son was with the Lord.

This becomes even more evident when we contrast this attitude with the attitude he showed at the death of another son, Absalom. David expressed hope that he would be reunited with the infant son but showed no such optimism for his wicked son.

This is a further indication that David believed that his young son went to be in the presence of the Lord.

Add to this the fact that David was able to console his wife Bathsheba after the death of his young son.

> So David comforted his wife Bathsheba (2 Samuel 12:24 NET).

What consolation could he give to her? It was the comfort of knowing that she too, along with King David, would see their son again.

EXAMPLE 3: THE BURIAL OF THE LITTLE CHILD IN THE CURSED LINE (1 KINGS 14:13)

The Lord harshly judged the line of the evil King Jeroboam for their wickedness. While all of the males would die and animals would feed on their dead bodies, we are told that one child would receive a proper burial.

> Then Ahijah said to Jeroboam's wife, "Go on home, and when you enter the city, the child will die. All Israel will mourn for him and bury him. He is the only member of your family who will have a proper burial, for this child is the only good thing that the Lord, the God of Israel, sees in the entire family of Jeroboam" (1 Kings 14:13 NLT).

The obvious question here is, "why?" What made this child different from all the other males in the line of Jeroboam?

Was he given a proper burial because he was a baby, or an infant, in contrast to all the rest of the males in the family? If he was a baby then how could he have manifested "something good" in his life? What is the good that the Lord saw in him?

It is possible that "the good" He saw in the child was his lack of understanding of right from wrong. This child had not reached an age where he could appreciate the difference. This is why he was not held personally responsible. Consequently, his body was buried and the people mourned his death.

EXAMPLE 4: THE CHILD IN ISAIAH

There is one particular passage that sheds much light on this issue. We read of a certain child in the Book of Isaiah. The Bible says the following of him.

> By the time he learns to reject what is bad and choose what is good, he will be eating butter and honey. For before the boy knows to reject what is bad and choose what is good, the land of the two kings you dread will be abandoned (Isaiah 7:15,16 HCSB).

Twice, this passage clearly states that until this child reaches a certain age, he is considered distinct from an adult. In particular, the child is considered different from adults in his ability to make moral choices. Indeed, it speak of an age that he will reach when he "knows" to reject the bad and "choose the good." Before he reaches that age, the child does not know the difference.

This is not denying the child has a sin nature. What it is doing is telling us that there is an age when children, as opposed to adults, do no understand the consequences of their actions. The boy, in this verse, had not reached an age where he had the capacity to choose the good but reject the evil.

EXAMPLE 5: GOD'S CONCERN FOR THE CHILDREN IN NINEVEH

In another example, we find that Scripture emphasizes God's concern young children. In the Book of Jonah, God specifically told that prophet that there were innocent children in Nineveh, that would perish with the guilty, if the Lord destroyed the city. In fact, notice how the following two Bible translations render this verse.

> Should I not be even more concerned about Nineveh, this enormous city? There are more than one hundred twenty thousand people in it who do not know right from wrong, as well as many animals (Jonah 4:11 NET).

In that city of Nineveh there are more than a hundred twenty thousand people who cannot tell right from wrong, and many cattle are also there. Don't you think I should be concerned about that big city (Jonah 4:11 CEV).

Each of these translations sees this as young children, infants or babies, who do not know "right from wrong." Again, this seems to indicate that they are at an age where they would not be held accountable to God if they died.

Another translation renders it as follows.

And should I not have concern for the great city of Nineveh, in which there are more than a hundred and twenty thousand people who cannot tell their right hand from their left—and also many animals (Jonah 4:11 NIV).

The ESV and NKJV also translate this verse in the same manner.

Not being able to know the difference between their right and left hand is another way of saying they are babies or infants. The fact that God singled out certain little ones as non-responsible shows that they did not have the same responsibility as the older people. The Bible does not say they were sinless, merely that they were innocent of the sins for which Nineveh was to be judged.

EXAMPLE 6: JOB'S DESIRE THAT HE WOULD HAVE BEEN STILLBORN

Another example, that is consistent with the biblical teaching on the destiny of those who die, before understanding good from evil, is the lament of the patriarch Job. After suffering loss of his family, his wealth, and finally his health, Job mused as follows.

Why did I not perish at birth, and die as I came from the womb . . . For now I would be lying down in peace; I would be asleep and at rest with kings and rulers of the earth, who

> built for themselves places now lying in ruins . . . Or why was
> I not hidden away in the ground like a stillborn child, like an
> infant who never saw the light of day? (Job 3:11,13-14 NIV).

With all of his troubles in life, Job said it would have been better if he had died at birth, that he was stillborn. If that had happened, he assumed that he would have been at peace in the next life.

We find that Job's view of death, and what would have happened in the afterlife, applies only to those who die in the Lord. We read about this in the Book of Revelation.

> Then I heard a voice from heaven say, "Write this: Blessed
> are the dead who die in the Lord from now on." "Yes," says
> the Spirit, "they will rest from their labor, for their deeds
> will follow them" (Revelation 14:13 NIV).

Those who die in the Lord are "at rest." Therefore, it seems that Job assumed that if he had died as a baby, he would be in that place of rest, like the believers referred to here in the Book of Revelation who die "in the Lord." In other words, Job believed that infants who died would be "at peace" with the Lord.

In contrast to what Job said, we compare it to the destiny of the wicked dead. The Bible is clear: there is "no rest" in death for the wicked. None whatsoever.

In Jesus' story of the ungodly rich man and the righteous man Lazarus, when each of them die, Lazarus is at peace in the next world but the rich man is not. In fact, he is consciously suffering. There is no peace, or rest, whatsoever for this man in the afterlife.

This is the consistent teaching of Scripture with respect to those who have died apart from the Lord, they are in a state of judgment and condemnation in the next world. While the righteous are at rest, the unrighteous are never at rest.

There is one final thing to note. In Job's lament, there is nothing whatsoever said about the possibility of him not being at rest in the next world, had he died in infancy. It seems that the thought never crossed his mind that, if he had died at birth, he would have been apart from the Lord. He assumed he would have been in the wonderful presence of the Lord.

Therefore, Job's description, of what would have happened to him had he died at birth, is consistent with the rest of Scripture. He would have been in a state of rest, in the presence of the Lord.

This is further confirmation that those who die, before they reach an age of understanding right from wrong, will be in heaven.

EXAMPLE 7: JESUS AND THE CHILDREN

We now come to the life and ministry of Jesus. There is a passage in Luke that also seems to speak to this issue. We will look how a number of translations render these verses.

> Now people were even bringing their babies to him for him to touch. But when the disciples saw it, they began to scold those who brought them. But Jesus called for the children, saying, "Let the little children come to me and do not try to stop them, for the kingdom of God belongs to such as these. I tell you the truth, whoever does not receive the kingdom of God like a child will never enter it (Luke 18:15-17 NET).

> Then Jesus called for the children and said to the disciples, "Let the children come to me. Don't stop them! For the Kingdom of God belongs to those who are like these children (Luke 18:16-17 NLT).

> But Jesus called the infants to him and said, "Don't stop the children from coming to me! Children like these are part of the kingdom of God. I can guarantee this truth: Whoever

doesn't receive the kingdom of God as a little child receives
it will never enter it (Luke 18:16-17 God's Word).

Notice that the translations see these as "babies" (NET) or "infants" (God's Word) that are brought to Jesus. Jesus obviously sees something distinct in these very young children. In fact, He says "the kingdom of heaven belongs to them," or "they are part of the kingdom of heaven."

If a little child, a baby or an infant, could not enter the kingdom of God because he or she died in infancy, then this statement of Jesus would not make sense.

In fact, in what sense would the kingdom belong to them if they could not enter because their lack of putting their trust in Christ; something that they would not have the capacity to do?

Consequently, there seems to be a presumption here that children are part of the kingdom. Dying in infancy would not preclude this.

EXAMPLE 8: JAMES SPEAKS OF THOSE WHO KNOW TO DO GOOD

James spoke of this same principle, knowing to do good. He wrote.

So, for the person who knows to do good and doesn't do it,
it is a sin (James 4:17 HCSB).

While there are people who do indeed "know" to do that which is good, babies and infants do not. Again, we have the distinction between those who know and those who do not.

EXAMPLE 9: THE FINAL JUDGMENT: THE BASIS OF CONDEMNATION

These eight preceding examples from Scripture fit with what the Bible says about the final judgment. Scripture indicates that people will be judged for what they have done, not for what they did not do, or could not do. We read about this in the Book of Revelation. It says.

Then I saw a great white throne and One seated on it. Earth and heaven fled from His presence, and no place was found for them. I also saw the dead, the great and the small, standing before the throne, and books were opened. Another book was opened, which is the book of life, and the dead were judged according to their works by what was written in the books. Then the sea gave up its dead, and Death and Hades gave up their dead; all were judged according to their works (Revelation 20:11-13 HCSB).

Note their judgment is "according to their works." Indeed, they are not sent to the lake of fire because they have a sin nature. This seems to rule out those who were unable to choose or reject God's offer of salvation if they had not reached the age of knowing right from wrong.

Let us again recall the description of the child in Isaiah, as well as the description of those children in Nineveh, "before the boy knows to reject what is bad and choose what is good," "there are more than one hundred twenty thousand people in it who do not know right from wrong."

There is an age where babies and infants do not understand the difference between right and wrong. Therefore, this final judgment would seem to exclude infants because they were not capable of doing "evil works."

THIS IS CONSISTENT WITH GOD'S CHARACTER

As we have stressed, this is consistent with the character of God. The Bible says that God does not like to judge those whom He created. Yet sin calls for judgment. Scripture, however, teaches that God is compassionate to His creation. The psalmist wrote.

The Lord is good to everyone. He showers compassion on all his creation (Psalm 145:9 NLT).

The God of the Bible is a God of compassion.

THE LORD WANTS ALL TO BE SAVED

Furthermore it is the desire of God that everyone comes to Him in faith. Paul wrote the following to Timothy expressing this characteristic or attribute of God.

> This is good and pleases God our Savior, who wants everyone to be saved and to understand the truth (1 Timothy 2:3-4 NLT).

Peter also emphasized that the Lord desires all to come to Him in repentance. He wrote.

> The Lord is not slow in keeping his promise, as some understand slowness. Instead he is patient with you, not wanting anyone to perish, but everyone to come to repentance (2 Peter 3:9 NIV).

The Lord wants all of humanity to believe in Him, to repent. However, babies and infants do not have that capacity.

Therefore, the Bible strongly indicates that those who have died before they know the difference between right and wrong will enter the kingdom of heaven because of the justice and compassion of God.

CONCLUSION: BABIES AND YOUNG CHILDREN WHO DIE WILL BE IN HEAVEN

From a study of the totality of Scripture, we find that children who die in infancy will not be condemned by God. Though they are born with a sinful nature, they will not be condemned. God will not hold them responsible because they have not yet reached the age to make a decision for or against Him. This includes all children, those who are born to both believers and unbelievers. The mentally challenged will also fall into this category.

WHAT IS THAT SPECIAL AGE?

Is there a special age that a person reaches when they become accountable to God? Although the answer is yes, the age is different for each person. People mature at different rates, so it would be wrong to insist on one particular age that a person reaches when they are held accountable.

Yet before anyone reaches that age, God will not hold them accountable for something which, by definition, they are incapable of doing.

WHAT ABOUT ABORTED AND MISCARRIED BABIES?

This also brings up the issue of aborted babies along with those who have died before birth. What will be their fate?

THEY ARE SOULS AT CREATION

The Bible indicates that upon conception the soul or spirit joins the unborn child. Scripture says that God breathed the breath of life into Adam.

> Then the LORD God formed the man of dust from the ground and breathed into his nostrils the breath of life, and the man became a living creature (Genesis 2:7 ESV).

Adam became human when God breathed life into him.

HIS LIKENESS

Since Adam, all children have been conceived, are born with his likeness.

> Adam was 130 years old when he fathered a child in his likeness, according to his image, and named him Seth (Genesis 5:3 HCSB).

This indicates both the body and spirit are passed on. In other words, at the moment of conception they are fully human with a body and a spirit.

Therefore, aborted and miscarried babies would seem to fall into the same category as babies and infants. In other words, God's grace will cover them also.

SUMMARY TO APPENDIX 2
HOW WILL GOD JUDGE BABIES AND YOUNG CHILDREN WHO DIE AS WELL AS THE MENTALLY CHALLENGED? WILL THEY GO TO HEAVEN?

One of the most common questions about the afterlife concerns the fate of those who die in infancy as well as those who are not mentally capable of making a rational decision to believe in God. What will happen to them?

There have been a number of popular solutions to this question of what happens to these individuals that do not fit with the Bible.

Some argue that unbaptized infants who die go to a place on the outskirts of Hell called Limbo. Yet the Bible knows of no such place. In addition, baptism is not necessary for salvation.

It has been argued that God's love will overlook the sin of infants. But Scripture says God cannot overlook any sin.

One clever solution says that God will determine the fate of each infant based upon what they would have done had they have been given the chance. Yet this idea cannot be sustained biblically.

Some Christians claim that only the children of believers are guaranteed salvation. Children of unbelievers have no such guarantee. This, however, is not taught in Scripture.

There are Bible-believers who argue that infants who die were predestined to salvation before the foundation of the world. Again, this is taught nowhere in Scripture and causes more problems than it solves.

Some treat these children as though they never existed. Yet, the Bible is clear that each of us has a soul or spirit which will never cease to exist. So this option does not answer the question.

The worst option says God will damn these infants because they are obviously not part of the elect. If they were, then they would have lived long enough to make a decision for Christ.

None of these answers fit the Scripture.

What the Bible does say is as follows: children are not accountable until they reach a certain age, and are able to understand right from wrong. When they reach this age to know the difference between the two, then they must make a decision.

However, if they die before this time God will not hold them responsible In fact, we find a number of passages in the Old Testament as well as the New Testament that supports this idea. Indeed, Scripture specifically says in two different places, Isaiah and Jonah, that infants were not able to know good from evil.

We couple this with what the Bible says about the last judgment. At that time, people will be judged according to the evil deeds they have committed. If a child does not reach the age where they know the difference between right and wrong, then it seems they cannot be held accountable for doing evil deeds if they did not understand at all what they were doing.

We can also appeal to the nature of God in answering this question. God is a God of love, justice, and compassion. Judgment is something He does not like to do. Those who are judged in Scripture are judged based upon their evil choices.

Children who die in infancy have not had the capacity to make evil choices. It is not because they are born innocent, or without a sin nature. It is because they did not reach an age where they could appreciate the consequences of their actions. They are not born in a state of being saved, but rather are saved through God's grace at the moment of death.

This would also fit those babies who are aborted or miscarried as well as those who do not have the mental capacity to make a decision for or against Christ.

This, we believe, is the best answer to this difficult question.

What Is The Book Of Life? Is It The Same As The Lamb's Book Of Life? Can Believers Have Their Name Erased From This Book?

The Bible speaks of a special book that exists called the "Book of Life." What exactly is it? Is it an actual book or is it symbolic of something? Whose names are in it? Whose names are not?

Furthermore, there is also the mention in Scripture of a Lamb's Book of Life. Is this the same book, or is it another book? And one final question, "Can the name of a believer be removed from this Book of Life?"

A few preliminary observations need to be made.

GOD DOES NOT NEED TO WRITE THINGS DOWN!

People write down things in books, or ledgers, for later recollection. Since God is all-knowing, He does not need to write things down. So when we read about these various "books of God" we are dealing with a figure of speech.

Indeed, this is an example of the Lord illustrating something humans do, recording in a book. God uses this figure of speech so that we can understand that He separates humanity into two groups, the righteous and the unrighteous. Hence the reference to books.

With this in mind, let us look at the various "books" which the Bible ascribes to God.

THE BOOKS THAT GOD KEEPS: THE DIVINE LEDGER

There appear to be several "books," or records, that God keeps in heaven. In fact, there are a number of references in each testament to these writings.

THE "BOOKS OF GOD" IN THE OLD TESTAMENT

There are references in the Old Testament to a "book, or scroll, of God." The evidence is as follows.

1. MOSES MENTIONED A BOOK OF GOD

In the Book of Exodus, it records that the Lord because angry with the nation of Israel for its creation of a golden calf to worship. In an exchange with Moses, we read the following.

> So Moses returned to the LORD, and he said, "Alas, this people has committed a very serious sin, and they have made for themselves gods of gold. But now, if you will forgive their sin, but if not, blot me out from your book that you have written." And the LORD said to Moses, "Whoever has sinned against me—that person I will blot out of my book." So now go, lead the people to the place I have spoken to you about. Indeed, my angel will go before you. But on the day that I visit, then I will visit their sin on them" (Exodus 32:31-34 NET).

Moses asked for his name to be blotted out of the Lord's book. However, the Lord refused. Instead, He said that He was going to blot the names of those that had sinned out of "His Book."

The idea seems to be that they would die for their sinful deeds. In other words, it speaks of physical death. Thus, in this context, blotting out, or erasing, the name of a person, refers to physical death and nothing more. The next verse seems to confirm that premature physical death is in mind.

> And the Lord sent a plague on the people because they had made the calf the one Aaron made (Exodus 32:35 NET).

We find a similar reference in Deuteronomy.

> The Lord will never be willing to forgive them; his wrath and zeal will burn against them. All the curses written in this book will fall on them, and the Lord will blot out their names from under heaven (Deuteronomy 29:20 NIV).

In this context, the "blotting out of a name" seems to be equal to physical death.

We should note that some commentators see these passages as references to the eternal destiny of the people; it is not merely speaking of their physical death. Therefore, "blotting out their names" speaks of everlasting separation from God. In other words, eternal punishment

2. THE PSALMIST WROTE OF GOD'S BOOK

The psalmist also wrote about the existence of God's Book. He assumed that God was recording everything about the lives of people upon the earth. In particular, his own life. We read the following words from him.

> You keep track of all my sorrows. You have collected all my tears in your bottle. You have recorded each one in your book (Psalm 56:8 NLT).

The idea seems to be is that God is keeping a record in heaven of all things that are happening on the earth among the living. He is keeping score.

3. THE PSALMIST WANTED THE NAMES OF HIS ENEMIES ERASED FROM THE BOOK OF LIFE

Later in the Psalms, the phrase, the "Book of Life" is first mentioned by name. The psalmist asked the Lord to erase the names of evil people from the Book of Life.

> Erase their names from the Book of Life; don't let them be counted among the righteous (Psalm 69:28 NLT).

In this context, the Book of Life, or the "Scroll of Life," likely represented the names of people that were living at that time. In other words, it was scroll containing the names of the citizens of a community. When a person died, their name was removed from the list.

So this requested curse of the psalmist was a way of asking that his enemies die. When a person died, their name was removed from the Scroll or the Book.

The psalmist, therefore, is asking for the death of these people. Again, the emphasis is on physical death. It does not have anything to do with their eternal destiny. The blessings that the righteous receive, in this context, are only for this life.

As is true with our first example, there are commentators who believe this is a request for their eternal punishment. In other words, that they never be listed among the righteous either in this life, or in the next.

4. ISAIAH WROTE OF THOSE RECORDED AMONG THE LIVING

Isaiah wrote about certain people as follows.

> Those who are left in Zion, who remain in Jerusalem, will be called holy, all who are recorded among the living in Jerusalem (Isaiah 4:3 NIV).

There is a record of those who are living, and those who are not.

5. THOSE FROM ISRAEL WHOSE NAMES ARE WRITTEN IN THE BOOK ARE DELIVERED (DANIEL 12:1)

Daniel wrote of a time of deliverance, or rescue, from a time of trouble that would happen to the people of Israel.

> At that time Michael, the great prince who protects your people, will arise. There will be a time of distress such as has not happened from the beginning of nations until then. But at that time your people—everyone whose name is found written in the book —will be delivered (Daniel 12:1 NIV).

This seems to be the one clear example in the Old Testament that refers to eternal salvation, not just temporary deliverance. The Lord promised to rescue the Jews living at that time. Is it a promise of national deliverance from human enemies or rather is it a promise that they will be delivered from the punishment of hell, the lake of fire? Simply put, is it a physical deliverance or a spiritual deliverance?

Whatever conclusion one makes, it is another reference of "the book" that the Lord has.

Therefore, God's Book, or the Book of Life, as seen from the perspective of the Old Testament writers, speaks of rewards and punishment in this life. With the possible exception of a statement in Daniel, it does not seem to have any reference to eternal rewards or to eternal punishment. There is also a book that records all of our deeds.

In sum, God is recording everything that we do here on earth as well as separating the righteous from the unrighteous. He illustrates this with the figure of speech of "a book."

THE BOOK OF LIFE IN THE NEW TESTAMENT

The New Testament expands on the Old Testament teaching about the Book of Life. Instead of mainly referring to earthly matters, the Book is now clearly talking about heavenly matters; the citizenship of believers in heaven.

1. BELIEVERS HAVE THEIR NAMES WRITTEN IN HEAVEN

Jesus said that the names of believers "stand written in heaven." We read of this in Luke's gospel. He said to His disciples.

> Look, I have given you authority to tread on snakes and scorpions and on the full force of the enemy, and nothing will hurt you. Nevertheless, do not rejoice that the spirits submit to you, but rejoice that your names stand written in heaven (Luke 10:19,20 NET).

While no specific Book is mentioned, the idea is certainly there in His statement. Those who have believed in Jesus have their names written in heaven. In other words, they can be confident that they belong to Him.

We read the same thing in Hebrews.

> You have come to the assembly of God's firstborn children, whose names are written in heaven. You have come to God himself, who is the judge over all things. You have come to the spirits of the righteous ones in heaven who have now been made perfect (Hebrews 12:23 NLT).

Therefore, Scripture speaks of the names of believers written in heaven.

2. PAUL MENTIONS THE NAMES OF CERTAIN PEOPLE WHO ARE IN THE BOOK OF LIFE

In his letter to the Philippians, Paul mentions some specific people who have their names written in the Book of Life.

> I appeal to Euodia and to Syntyche to agree in the Lord. Yes, I say also to you, true companion, help them. They have struggled together in the gospel ministry along with me and Clement and my other coworkers, whose names are in the book of life (Philippians 4:2-3 NET).

Being written in the "book of life" indicates they are true believers.

3. BELIEVERS' NAMES ARE NOT ERASED FROM THE BOOK OF LIFE

In the Book of Revelation, it speaks of certain people whose names will never be erased, or blotted out, of the Book of Life.

> Everyone who wins the victory will wear white clothes. Their names will not be erased from the book of life, and I will tell my Father and his angels that they are my followers (Revelation 3:5 CEV).

Those who have trusted Jesus Christ will not be blotted out, or erased, out of the Book of Life. Their destiny is eternally secured because of what Jesus Christ has done for them.

THE NAME OF EVERYONE LIVING?

There are some Bible teachers who have taught that the Book of Life originally contained the names of everyone living. When unbelievers died, God would remove, or blot out, their names from the book. Thus, when all is said and done, the book will only contains the names of believers. However, there is no evidence for this whatsoever.

4. THE LAMB'S BOOK OF LIFE IS MENTIONED IN REVELATION

There are also references to the "Lamb's Book of Life" in the Book of Revelation. We are told that the ones who worshipped the beast did not ever have their names written in this Book of Life. We read the following.

> And all the people who belong to this world worshiped the beast. They are the ones whose names were not written in the Book of Life, which belongs to the Lamb who was killed before the world was made (Revelation 13:8 NLT).

According to the New English Translation, as well as a number of other English versions, this Book was written before the world began. It reads.

And all those who live on the earth will worship the beast, everyone whose name has not been written since the foundation of the world in the book of life belonging to the Lamb who was killed (Revelation 13:8 NET).

Consequently, there is some dispute as to whether the phrase "since the foundation of the world" is referring to Jesus the Lamb that was killed, or referring to the Book that contains the name of the righteous.

Later in Revelation, it is clear that the Book of Life is the subject.

The beast, which you saw, once was, now is not, and yet will come up out of the Abyss and go to its destruction. The inhabitants of the earth whose names have not been written in the book of life from the creation of the world will be astonished when they see the beast, because it once was, now is not, and yet will come (Revelation 17:8 NIV).

The names of unbelievers have never been written in the Book of Life.

THE NAMES OF BELIEVERS ARE NOT SAID TO HAVE BEEN WRITTEN BEFORE THE WORLD WAS CREATED

A common misconception is to assume that believers names have been written in the Book of Life from the very foundation of the world. But this is not what these two passages in the Book of Revelation say.

Indeed, all they say is that the names of unbelievers have "not" been written in the Book of Life; it says nothing about the names of believers having been written before the world was created. Therefore, it is debatable as to whether we can infer that believers names were already written in the Book before the world was formed.

At the end of the Book of Revelation, we again read of the Lamb's Book of Life. It says the following.

But nothing ritually unclean will ever enter into it, nor anyone who does what is detestable or practices falsehood, but only those whose names are written in the Lamb's book of life (Revelation 21:27 NET).

The Lamb's Book of Life has only the names of believers; the names of unbelievers are not contained in this book. These are the only two passages where the term "Lamb" is mentioned with the "Book of Life."

5. JOHN ALSO WROTE ABOUT THE BOOK OF LIFE AT THE FINAL JUDGMENT

According to the Apostle John, the Book of Life is opened at the final judgment, also known as the Great White Throne Judgment. We read of this awesome scene.

Then I saw a great white throne and him who was seated on it. Earth and sky fled from his presence, and there was no place for them. And I saw the dead, great and small, standing before the throne, and books were opened. Another book was opened, which is the book of life. The dead were judged according to what they had done as recorded in the books. The sea gave up the dead that were in it, and death and Hades gave up the dead that were in them, and each person was judged according to what he had done. Then death and Hades were thrown into the lake of fire. The lake of fire is the second death. If anyone's name was not found written in the book of life, he was thrown into the lake of fire (Revelation 20:11-15 NIV).

Notice that more than one book was opened. There are books containing the names of the lost as well as their deeds. Their names were not found in the Book of Life. Those whose names were not found in this Book will be sent away for eternal punishment. The ones whose names were written in the Book will enter God's kingdom.

To sum up, in the Old Testament the "Books" that God keeps seem to mainly refer only to the living. However, in the New Testament the term, "Book of Life" and the "Lamb's Book of Life" refer to the names which are written in heaven. In other words, it refers to believers and their eternal destiny.

WHAT DOES IT MEAN: HE WON'T ERASE THEIR NAMES?

There is a passage that we have just mentioned in the Book of Revelation which speaks of believers not having their names erased or blotted out of the Book of Life.

> All who are victorious will be clothed in white. I will never erase their names from the Book of Life, but I will announce before my Father and his angels that they are mine (Revelation 3:5 NLT).

What does the Lord mean, "I will never erase their names from the Book of Life?" Does this mean other people can have their names erased from the Book of Life?

In other words, once a Christian has his or her name written in the Book of Life can it later be erased? Simply put, can a believer lose their salvation?

THREAT OR PROMISE?

To begin with, the key to understanding this verse is realizing it is a PROMISE not a threat. It is a common error to see it as a threat but when viewed as a promise it has nothing to do with one losing their salvation.

In fact, it is one of the three promises made to the overcomers in this verse. The promises include: believers will be clothed in white, their names are secure in heaven, written in the Book of Life, and the Lord will announce the names of those written in the presence of God the Father and the righteous angels. These are indeed great promises!

Next, understanding the historical background will seemingly give us the answer to this question as to why Jesus said He will "not blot out their names from the Book of Life."

A LIKELY ANSWER: THE CONTEMPORARY BACKGROUND

At end of the first century, things were getting increasingly difficult for the Jewish believers in Jesus Christ. The Jewish leaders were concerned about the continual advancement that the Christian faith was making among their own people. Indeed, many Jewish people had converted to faith in Jesus as their Messiah.

At the same time, there were some Jewish Christians who continued to associate with the synagogue. It came to the place where the Jews did not want the Christians to be identified with the synagogue any longer.

It seems that this reached a crisis point around A.D. 90 with a document produced by the Jews called the "Curse of the Minim." Minim is the plural of the Hebrew word min meaning "kinds."

The curse of the Minim was introduced by certain Jews into the "Eighteen Benedictions." It provided a way of detecting Christians in their synagogues and then getting rid of them. The curse against these Christians in the synagogues read as follows.

May the Nazarenes and the Minim suddenly perish and may they be blotted out of the Book of Life and not enrolled with the righteous.

Note that these people were placed under a curse by certain Jews. Two things were hoped for. First, that these Christians would soon die. Second, their names would be "blotted out of the synagogue registry of the faithful." This was also known as the "Book of Life."

In effect, what this curse desired was that all Jews, who put their faith in Jesus, would immediately die and then have their names blotted out of the Book of Life. In other words, their eternal destiny would not be with the God of the Old Testament, the God of Abraham, Isaac, and Jacob. Instead, they would be treated as unbelievers in the God of Scripture.

Thus, in Revelation 3:5, these Christians, who were threatened with physical and spiritual death, were assured by Jesus that they would NOT be blotted out of the Book of Life; no matter what the curse threatened. Indeed, in the strongest of words the Lord affirmed that they belonged to Him.

THESE JEWS ARE OF THE SYNAGOGUE OF SATAN

This threat would explain why, on two occasions, in Smyrna and Philadelphia, we find the Lord telling the believers that He knows about certain people who are calling themselves Jews but are not. In fact, the Lord says they belong to a "synagogue of Satan." We read His words to the church in Philadelphia.

> I know the distress you are suffering and your poverty (but you are rich). I also know the slander against you by those who call themselves Jews and really are not, but are a synagogue of Satan (Revelation 2:9 NET).

The church in Smyrna, which this passage about "blotting out" was written, was also warned about these people.

> Behold, I will make those of the synagogue of Satan who say that they are Jews and are not, but lie—behold, I will make them come and bow down before your feet, and they will learn that I have loved you (Revelation 3:9 ESV).

By saying this, the Lord states that their houses of worship, their synagogues, were no longer functioning as houses of the Lord. Indeed, they were the unbelievers in the God of the Bible, it was not the Christians!

THIS HAS NOTHING TO DO WITH LOSS OF SALVATION

Consequently, we should not infer from this statement in Revelation 3:5 that some believers will lose their salvation because this is NOT the subject under consideration. Indeed, the Bible teaches that once a person believes in Jesus Christ they are eternally secure. Jesus said.

> Very truly I tell you, whoever hears my word and believes him who sent me has eternal life and will not be judged but has crossed over from death to life (John 5:24 NIV).

Jesus said that those who believe in Him already have eternal life. Indeed, they have already "crossed over" from death to life. Eternal life is theirs now!

Elsewhere we read this in the Gospel of John.

> And this is the will of him who sent me, that I should lose nothing of all that he has given me, but raise it up on the last day. For this is the will of my Father, that everyone who looks on the Son and believes in him should have eternal life, and I will raise him up on the last day (John 6:39-40 ESV).

Everyone who believes has eternal life.

Jesus, in the strongest of language possible, also made it clear that those who are His shall never perish.

> I give them eternal life, and they shall never perish; no one will snatch them out of my hand. My Father, who has given them to me, is greater than all; no one can snatch them out of my Father's hand (John 10:28-29 NIV).

Thus, the purpose of the promise in Revelation 3:5 is to provide certainty and assurance to those people who have trusted Jesus Christ. It is not to threaten people with the possibility that there name would be blotted out. Again, this is a promise from the Lord, not a threat.

"NOT BLOTTING OUT" IS A FIGURE OF SPEECH LITOTES (LIE TO TEASE)

We also need to understand the figure of speech that is used in this verse. The statement of "not blotting out" the names is as an example of litotes. Litotes is a figure of speech where a negative statement is made to emphasize the exact opposite.

For example, when we say that someone is "not a bad singer," we mean that particular person is a "good singer." If we say that we are "not unhappy" about something it means that we "are happy." This is a common way of expressing something positive about someone or some thing by using the negative.

BIBLICAL EXAMPLES OF LITOTES

We find a number examples of this in Scripture. Jesus said the following about those who speak against, or blaspheme, the Holy Spirit.

> And whoever speaks a word against the Son of Man will be forgiven, but whoever speaks against the Holy Spirit will not be forgiven, either in this age or in the age to come (Matthew 12:32 ESV).

In other words, these unbelievers will NEVER be forgiven. It does not mean that there is forgiveness in the age to come if someone decides to repent at that time. Indeed, it is emphasizing the punishment for blaspheming the Holy Spirit extends to the age to come.

Paul spoke of his hometown of Tarsus as follows.

> Paul replied, "I am a Jew, from Tarsus in Cilicia, a citizen of no obscure city (Acts 21:39 ESV).

"No obscure city" means that Tarsus is "a very special city."

Therefore, in this verse, "not blotting out" is a way of emphasizing the following: because they are true Christians their names are securely written in heaven forever. Indeed, there is no chance whatsoever that their names could be erased.

In fact, the Greek phrase in this verse is the strongest way possible of saying something can never happen. In other words, Jesus is guaranteeing that there is no possible way that the names of believers will be blotted out. They are secure forever!

And when we understand the figure of speech that is used here, we find that it does not mean the reverse is true; that some people can have their name erased or blotted out of the Book of Life. The Bible never teaches that this sort of thing can happen.

THE THREAT DID NOT COME FROM THE LORD

To sum up, any threat of being erased from the Book of Life came from the unbelieving Jews and their curse; NOT from the Lord!

In fact, as we mentioned, this verse, Revelation 3:5, contains three specific promises. First, the believers would be dressed in white, second, their names are forever secure in God's Book, and finally, the Lord Himself will acknowledge the believers before His Father and the angels in heaven.

The third promise, that Jesus Christ will acknowledge all those who have believed as belonging to Him, is something that He taught in His public ministry. We read the following in Matthew.

> Everyone who acknowledges me publicly here on earth, I will also acknowledge before my Father in heaven (Matthew 10:32 NLT).

In another place, the Lord said.

> I tell you the truth, everyone who acknowledges me publicly here on earth, the Son of Man will also acknowledge in the presence of God's angels (Luke 12:8 NLT).

In sum, everyone who has believed in Jesus Christ is eternally secure in Him and will one day be acknowledged before God the Father as belonging to the family of the risen Lord.

SUMMARY TO APPENDIX 3
WHAT IS THE BOOK OF LIFE? IS IT THE SAME AS THE LAMB'S BOOK OF LIFE? CAN BELIEVERS HAVE THEIR NAME ERASED FROM THIS BOOK?

The Bible speaks of a number of books that belong to God. They are described as Gods' Book, the Book of Life, names written in heaven, as well as the Lamb's Book of Life. These descriptions seem to be referring to several different books. The evidence is as follows.

In the Old Testament, the Book of Life, or God's Books, seems to refer to a record of the deeds of those living at a particular time. When the person died, their names were erased from the Book; whether literally or symbolically. It only has to do with this life, not their eternal destiny. The only seeming exception is a book mentioned in Daniel.

However, in the New Testament, there is another type of book in view; one that speaks of heavenly citizenship. It only contains the names of those who have trusted God and His promises. In other words, is speaks of the saved. These are the "names written in heaven."

At the Great White Throne Judgment, the Final Judgment, those whose names are not found written in this particular Book are forever banished from God's presence.

Therefore, there are seemingly two types of books that are in view. The Old Testament "Book of Life" records the deeds of the living while the New Testament "Book of Life," or the "Lambs Book of Life" records the names of those who are citizens of heaven.

Obviously we want our names to be found written in this "Book of Life." We can guarantee that will be so if we receive Jesus Christ as our Savior. Once we trust Him, our names are forever written in this book.

Yet there is a passage in the Book of Revelation which speaks of ones name not being erased from the Book of Life. Does this mean it is possible to have your name erased once it has been entered into the book that contains the name of believers?

The answer is no. We saw that understanding the background of this verse helps to answer the question. Around A.D. 90 there was a document written by certain Jews called "The Curse of the Minim." In it, it stated that anyone who confesses Jesus as the Christ is to be removed from the synagogue rolls; blotted out of the Book of Life.

In responding to this threat, Jesus told the church of Sardis that they do not have to worry. Indeed, there is no way possible that their name would be blotted out of the Book of Life. In the strongest of terms, we find Jesus assuring the believers that they have eternal life.

Consequently, there is nothing in Revelation 3:5 that threatens believers that somehow their names may be erased from the Book of Life after believing. In fact, the verse is a promise, not a threat. Indeed, it is a promise that those who believe in the Lord are eternally secure.

APPENDIX 4

A Verse By Verse Look
At Revelation 21 and 22
(The New Jerusalem, The Holy City)

The last two chapters of the Bible give us a description of the future home of believers, the New Jerusalem, the Holy City. In fact, these chapters provide information about heaven that is not revealed anywhere else in the Scripture.

We will discover that our eternal state is an actual place. The descriptions in these chapters include a city that has buildings, trees, fruit, and water. It also tells us that heaven is a place where we will serve the Lord. In other words, believers will not merely be sitting around for all eternity doing nothing.

Therefore, it is important that we do our best to understand exactly what Scripture tells us about our heavenly home. In this extended section, we will take a verse by verse look at what the Bible has to say about the place that the Lord has prepared for us.

In these chapters, we find John describing the new heaven and new earth from 21:1-22:6. In the concluding verses, 22:7-21, there is a challenge to the readers to live a godly life in the light of eternity.

As we go through these chapters, we will answer many questions about the eternal realm. The goal is to give an explanation, as best as we can, about the coming new world which the Lord will create. Please note that the translation of the verses in these two chapters is the authors.

BACKGROUND

In the previous chapters, John records the fall of the harlot, Babylon the great, in 17:1-19:10. Next, he wrote of the return of Jesus Christ to the earth as King of Kings and Lord of Lords (19:11-21). Following His return, the Lord reigns upon the earth for a thousand years (20:1-6).

At the end of the thousand years, the Lord puts down one final rebellion (20:7-10).

In 20:11-15, John then described the Great White Throne Judgment. It tells of the destiny of the lost. All unbelievers, the ones whose names are not written in the Book of Life, will be thrown into the lake of fire. They are forever banished from God's holy presence.

In contrast to their tragic destiny, the prophet now moves on to the eternal state of believers. John will describe what our world will be like after the Millennium, the thousand year reign of Jesus Christ upon the earth.

There is some question among Bible students as to whether chapters 21 and 22 deal with the eternal state alone or whether they alternate back and forth between the Millennium and eternity. As we will see, the chronological progression in the Book of Revelation clearly places the New Jerusalem in the eternal realm. It is not in the Millennium; the intermediate earthly kingdom that occurs after the Second Coming of Christ but before the eternal state begins.

Instead, we are about to consider in these chapters what takes place after the end of the thousand-year rule of Christ upon the earth.

WHY WILL GOD DESTROY THE PRESENT UNIVERSE?

One of the questions which arises from this section is, "Why?" Why would the Lord destroy this universe which He originally created? The reasons can be simply stated as follows.

First, though this present earth was made for humans to live upon, sin has entered and completely corrupted every aspect of it. This corruption extends to the human race, the animal kingdom and the environment. Everything was corrupted. This corruption must be reversed. The new heaven and new earth will reverse the present sinful state of the world.

THE FULFILLMENT OF HIS PROMISES

There is another reason as to why the Lord will make a new heaven and new earth. It is to fulfill the promises which He has previously made.

DAVID WAS PROMISED A THRONE FOREVER

For example, King David was promised that one of His descendants would rule forever. The Bible records the promise.

> The Lord declares to you that the Lord himself will establish a house for you: When your days are over and you rest with your ancestors, I will raise up your offspring to succeed you, your own flesh and blood, and I will establish his kingdom. He is the one who will build a house for my Name, and I will establish the throne of his kingdom forever. I will be his father, and he will be my son . . . Your house and your kingdom will endure forever before me; your throne will be established forever (2 Samuel 7:11-14,16 NIV).

One particular descendant of David will indeed rule and reign for all eternity, the Lord Jesus.

AN EVERLASTING KINGDOM WILL BE ESTABLISHED

In Daniel, we also read the promise of God of a kingdom which shall never be destroyed.

> In the time of those kings, the God of heaven will set up a kingdom that will never be destroyed, nor will it be left to another people. It will crush all those kingdoms and bring them to an end, but it will itself endure forever (Daniel 2:44 NIV).

God's kingdom will last forever. In these chapters of Revelation, we will read of the fulfillment to that promise.

THE LORD PROMISED TO PREPARE A PLACE FOR US

Finally, we have the promise of the Lord Jesus. As He was about to leave this world He promised to prepare a place for believers.

> Don't let your hearts be troubled. Trust in God, and trust also in me. There is more than enough room in my Father's home. If this were not so, would I have told you that I am going to prepare a place for you? When everything is ready, I will come and get you, so that you will always be with me where I am (John 14:1-3 NLT).

The following chapters will reveal the place in which the Lord has prepared for us. It is our eternal home in the house of the Father.

Therefore, the new earth will see the complete fulfillment of these predictions and promises. The writer to the Hebrews made this clear.

> All these people were still living by faith when they died. They did not receive the things promised; they only saw them and welcomed them from a distance, admitting that they were foreigners and strangers on earth. People who say such things show that they are looking for a country of their own. If they had been thinking of the country they had left, they would have had opportunity to return. Instead, they were longing for a better country—a heavenly one. Therefore God is not ashamed to be called their God, for he has prepared a city for them (Hebrews 11:13–16 NIV).

The people of God have been waiting for this better country, a heavenly city. We will discover that the Living God will indeed create a new universe where only righteousness will dwell. In doing so, He will fulfill the promises made long ago. Indeed, believers will finally have that heavenly city, that better country, just as the Lord had promised.

Consequently, these chapters will reveal the final stage in the Lord's plan of the ages. The Lord God will deliver the human race from this fallen world into a new incorruptible world which He will create. In doing so, it will fulfill the original intention of the first creation, as well as fulfilling the promises of a future blessing.

REVELATION 21

REVELATION 21:1-4:
THE FORMER THINGS HAVE PASSED AWAY

Revelation 21:1 Then I saw a new heaven and a new earth. For the first heaven and the first earth had passed away [ceased to exist] and there was no more sea [the sea existed no more].

Textual Issue: Interestingly, the oldest manuscript that we have of the Book of Revelation, *Codex Alexandrinus*, has John repeating the words "I saw" in the last phrase. It says, "And I saw that there was no more sea."

John begins by declaring what he saw; a new universe! The old heaven and the old earth are now gone, replaced by all things new. It is new in the sense that it is a "new kind of universe." Indeed, there is a complete transformation of all things. In addition, we discover that the new earth has no sea in it.

This brings up a few questions: Will everything in the old universe be destroyed, including the home of God? What is the relationship between the old universe and the new one? Why is the new earth without the sea?

WILL HEAVEN, GOD'S HOME, PASS AWAY?

We should note that the phrase "the first heaven and the first earth" refers to the visible universe. John certainly did not mean the special abode of God will pass away! The Bible calls this unique place the "third heaven." Paul wrote.

> I know a man in Christ who fourteen years ago (whether in
> the body or out of the body I do not know, God knows) was
> caught up to the third heaven (2 Corinthians 12:2 NET).

As we have mentioned in a previous question, the third heaven is a description of the place where the Lord dwells in a special way.

In fact, we read that Jesus "passed through the heavens."

> Therefore since we have a great high priest who has passed
> through the heavens, Jesus the Son of God, let us hold fast
> to our confession (Hebrews 4:14 NET).

The first heaven and the second heaven describe the visible universe.

In sum, it is only the present physical universe that will pass away, or cease to exist, when the Lord makes a new heaven and earth. God's home, heaven, will continue to exist.

WHAT IS THE RELATIONSHIP BETWEEN THE OLD EARTH AND NEW EARTH?

What John saw, a new universe, had been promised earlier in Scripture. For example, Peter spoke of the present universe disappearing.

> The day of the Lord's return will surprise us like a thief. The
> heavens will disappear with a loud noise, and the heat will
> melt the whole universe. Then the earth and everything on
> it will be seen for what they are (2 Peter 3:10 CEV).

From the various passages that speak of the renewal of the heaven and the earth, it is not clear what relationship the new will have with the old. Will the old heaven and earth be merely renewed, or will it be entirely replaced. In other words, is this an example of creation out of nothing as took place in the initial creation of the heaven and earth? Or is it a thorough renovation of the present heaven and earth with God reconstructing the elements?

THERE IS SOME MYSTERY AS TO HOW THIS WILL HAPPEN

As is the case with the resurrected body of the believer, there is some mystery in this process. What is clear is that the present heaven and earth will pass away in the form that they are presently in and God will make something new for believers to enjoy with Him.

WILL IT BE IN TWO STAGES?

In this passage, the eternal state is called a new heaven and a new earth. However, this is not the same thing that Isaiah the prophet was referring to when he wrote about the "new heaven and new earth" (Isaiah 65:17–25). He was speaking of the Millennium, the thousand year reign of Jesus Christ upon the earth.

We know this because in this passage we find such things as sin and death still existing in Isaiah's description of this new world. In the eternal state, there will be no sin and no death.

Therefore, it seems possible, even likely, that the re-making of the heaven and the earth will take place in two stages. It will begin at the Second Coming of Jesus Christ. When the Lord returns to this earth, the world will be made new for His intermediate earthly kingdom, the Millennium. Then at the end of His thousand year rule, the entire universe will be made new.

WHY IS THERE NO SEA?

Interestingly, the new earth will not have any more seas. Presently, the seas cover over three-quarters of the surface of the earth.

The fact that there will be no more seas makes it clear that what John saw in this chapter was the eternal state which will occur after the Millennium. We know this because Scripture talks about the sea existing during the thousand year reign of Christ upon the earth.

For example, Zechariah the prophet described the Millennium as follows.

> He will make sure there are no chariots in Ephraim or war horses in Jerusalem. There will be no battle bows. He will announce peace to the nations. He will rule from sea to sea and from the Euphrates River to the ends of the earth (Zechariah 9:10 God's Word).

There are other passages in the Old Testament which also refer to the seas still existing during this intermediate earthly kingdom of Jesus Christ (Psalm 72:8; Jeremiah 31:9-10; Ezekiel 47:8-20; 48:28; and Zechariah 14:8).

The sea is one of seven evils listed in these two chapters that presently exist on our earth but will not exist in eternity. We will also discover that other evil things such as death, mourning, crying, pain, night, and the original curse will also no longer exist in the new universe which the Lord will create.

But why is the sea considered as an evil? Since there is no explanation in the text as to why it will no longer exist, this question has brought a number of explanations from commentators. We can make the following observations.

For one thing, the sea has always been foreboding to people. It is a source of storms and dangers. The sea was, therefore, a dark mystery. This is especially true of the Jews who were not sailors.

Not only was it mysterious, it also was a symbol of unrest. In other words, it was never at peace, never still. Therefore, it is a symbol of changefulness.

THE ABSENCE OF THE SEA SIGNIFIES SAFETY FROM ADVERSARIES

In the Book of Revelation, the sea is also a source of evil; the place where the enemies of God's people arise. First, we read about Satan, the dragon. After he was cast down to the earth he stood on the sand of the seashore.

> And the dragon stood on the sand of the seashore (Revelation 12:18 NET).

Next, we find that the first beast of Revelation 13, the Final Antichrist, arises from the sea.

> Then I saw a beast rising up out of the sea. It had seven heads and ten horns, with ten crowns on its horns. And written on each head were names that blasphemed God (Revelation 13:1 NLT).

Therefore, it is also a source of wickedness.

In fact in Isaiah, we read about this comparison of the wicked to the sea.

> But the wicked are like the tossing sea; for it cannot be quiet, and its waters toss up mire and dirt. "There is no peace," says my God, "for the wicked" (Isaiah 57:20,21 ESV).

This is another illustration of the sea being problematic, like the wicked it never remains peaceful.

The sea also separates people groups from one another. Indeed, nobody lives on the sea. Instead, it is something that has to be crossed to arrive at another destination.

In fact, it was the sea that surrounded the Apostle John on the tiny Island of Patmos when he wrote the Book of Revelation. At that location, the prophet was separated from the churches of Asia where he ministered. This type of separation will never happen again in the new heaven and new earth.

Therefore, when John wrote that there will be no more sea, it signified that all danger, evil, separation and mystery will be removed from the new creation of the Lord.

Revelation 21:2 And I saw the Holy City, the New Jerusalem, descending out of heaven having been prepared like a bride adorned for her husband.

As in verse one, we have the repetition of the words "I saw." John then describes what he saw; the Holy City coming down from heaven. Two things are immediately apparent.

First, the adjectives "new" and "holy" distinguish this city from our present world. Indeed, the New Jerusalem will supersede anything and everything that has happened before.

THE TWO JERUSALEM'S CONTRASTED

On the other hand, calling it "Jerusalem" points to a certain continuity between the two cities. Indeed, both the old and New Jerusalem are cities which are loved by God and have a special place in His dealings with the human race.

In fact, in the Bible, many great events have taken place, and will take place, in the old city of Jerusalem. The greatest of these were the death of God the Son, Jesus Christ, on the cross of Calvary and His resurrection from the dead. Therefore, Jerusalem is central to the biblical account of history as the place of our redemption. However, in contrast to the old Jerusalem, there will never be any sin or rebellion in the Holy City.

THE BRIDE IS ADORNED TO MEET THE GROOM

The prophet then compares the city to a bride who is adorned to meet the groom. From this verse, we have several issues that need to be addressed.

The first issue concerns the physical relationship of the New Jerusalem to the present earth. The comparison of the city to a bride also brings up a number of questions: Is the church, which is also compared to a bride, the New Jerusalem?

WHAT IS THE PHYSICAL RELATIONSHIP BETWEEN THE NEW JERUSALEM AND THE NEW EARTH?

There have been several explanations about the exact relationship of the New Jerusalem to the new earth. In other words, where will this city be located?

John sees the Holy City, New Jerusalem, coming down out of heaven, prepared as a bride adorned for her husband. The fact that it is never said to land upon the earth leads some to see it as hovering over the new earth.

In fact, there are many who believe that New Jerusalem could be a satellite city that remains above the new earth.

Others believe that the New Jerusalem will be within the boundaries of the new earth. Exactly where, is not stated.

The text does not specifically say the New Jerusalem will come down to the new earth, only that John saw it coming down out of heaven from God.

However, the fact that the Holy City is said to have a sturdy foundation would seem to imply that it is somewhere upon the new earth.

IS THE NEW JERUSALEM THE NEW TESTAMENT CHURCH?

There have been a number of people who claim that the description of the New Jerusalem, in the Book of Revelation, is actually a description of the New Testament church. The main reason for this belief is the use of the bride figure to describe the New Jerusalem. Since the church is also described as a bride, this has led them to conclude that the New Jerusalem is identical with the church.

However, the bride figure in Scripture describes not only the church but also Israel's relationship with God. The evidence is as follows.

THE BRIDE FIGURE DESCRIBES THE CHURCH

Earlier in the Book of Revelation, we find that the bride figure describes believers in an intimate relationship to Christ.

> Let us be glad and rejoice, and let us give honor to him. For the time has come for the wedding feast of the Lamb, and his bride has prepared herself. She has been given the finest of pure white linen to wear. For the fine linen represents the good deeds of God's holy people (Revelation 19:7,8 NLT).

In this passage, the bride, the true believers in Jesus, has prepared herself for the wedding.

The Apostle Paul made this comparison earlier in his letter to the Corinthians.

> I'm as protective of you as God is. After all, you're a virgin whom I promised in marriage to one man—Christ (2 Corinthians 11:2 God's Word).

In this illustration, the church is the bride who has been promised in marriage to Christ.

THE OLD TESTAMENT USES THE BRIDE FIGURE WITH GOD AND ISRAEL

The Old Testament also used the bride as a figure to describe Israel's relationship to God. We read in Hosea.

> I will accept you as my wife forever, and instead of a bride price I will give you justice, fairness, love, kindness, and faithfulness. Then you will truly know who I am (Hosea 2:19,20 CEV).

We find something similar in Isaiah.

> Your children will commit themselves to you, O Jerusalem, just as a young man commits himself to his bride. Then

God will rejoice over you as a bridegroom rejoices over his bride (Isaiah 62:5 NLT).

The Lord said the following to Jeremiah.

> The Lord spoke his word to me, "Go and announce to Jerusalem, This is what the Lord says: I remember the unfailing loyalty of your youth, the love you had for me as a bride. I remember how you followed me into the desert, into a land that couldn't be farmed" (Jeremiah 2:1,2 God's Word).

Does this mean that Israel, the church, and the New Jerusalem are three names of the same entity? The answer is, "No." They are always kept distinct from one another.

However, the New Jerusalem, while a literal city, also represents the people who live in it, the believers in Christ. Therefore, the same term can describe either the city or the inhabitants of the city, depending upon the context.

In addition, we will later discover that the names of the tribes of Israel are written on the gates of the New Jerusalem. This indicates that those believers from Israel will themselves have access to the city.

We will also learn that throughout these two chapters there is a distinction maintained between the church (who is the bride, the wife of the Lamb), the nation of Israel, and the Gentile nations. These three entities are always kept distinct from one another.

To sum up, while the believers in Christ and the city of the New Jerusalem are distinct from one another, the city and its inhabitants can be described by the same term, the bride.

Revelation 21:3 And I heard a loud voice coming out from the throne [out from heaven] saying, Behold! The tabernacle [dwelling place] of God is with humanity, and he will dwell with them,

**and they themselves shall be his people, and God himself shall be
with them [and he shall be their God].**

Textual Issues: Before we look at this verse, we must first note several
textual issues.

Some manuscripts read "out of heaven" instead of "out from the
throne."

In another variant, the word "people" is found in the singular in some
Greek manuscripts while it is found in the plural in others.

The phrase "and he shall be their God" is not found in some Greek
manuscripts of this verse.

In our translation we noted the emphasis in the Greek text: "they
themselves" . . . "God himself." In other words, it is emphatic that
"they themselves are going to be his people" and that "God himself
will be with them."

THIS MESSAGE IS IMPORTANT!

As we examine this verse, two things immediately tell us that this message is important. First, we have a loud voice coming from the throne.
Add to this, the use of the Greek word translated "behold."

Each of these indicate that a solemn message is about to be given. In
other words, they are "attention getters."

John hears a voice but the voice is not identified. It could be an angelic
voice or the voice of God Himself. This is the twentieth, and the last
time, in the Book of Revelation where John hears a loud voice. In this
instance, John hears a loud or great voice which makes the announce-
ment that God is now dwelling with redeemed humanity!

THE TABERNACLE OF GOD WILL TABERNACLE WITH THE PEOPLE

There is a play on words in the Greek. The words translated "tabernacle" and "dwell" come from the same root word. Thus, it could be

translated "the tabernacle of God is with humanity and he will tabernacle with them."

The point is that there is no longer any need for a building, a structure, a physical tabernacle for humans to approach. The tabernacle is the Lord Himself!

John had earlier emphasized this tabernacle theme. First, he spoke of Jesus as being in the beginning with God.

> In the beginning was the Word, and the Word was with God, and the Word was fully God (John 1:1 NET).

Next we learned that the One who was in the beginning, pitched His tent, or "tabernacled" among us when He came to earth the first time.

> Now the Word became flesh and took up residence among us. We saw his glory-the glory of the one and only, full of grace and truth, who came from the Father (John 1:14 NET).

The phrase "took up residence" is the Greek word for "tabernacle." The same Greek word is used here in the Book of Revelation. Jesus, as God the Son, tabernacled among the human race. In other words, He lived among us. However, in the New Jerusalem, Jesus will "tabernacle" forever with us.

THE SHEKINAH GLORY DWELLS FOREVER WITH BELIEVERS

In addition, the Hebrew word for tabernacle *Mishkan* is related to the word, "Shekinah." Shekinah speaks of the glory of God among the people. We read about this promise in Ezekiel.

> My dwelling place will be with them; I will be their God, and they will be my people. Then, when my sanctuary is among them forever, the nations will know that I, the Lord, sanctify Israel (Ezekiel 37:27,28 NET).

The Lord had originally created in the Garden of Eden a place where God could dwell with humanity in a special way. Now this will be an eternal reality. God will forever live in an intimate relationship with His people, those who have believed in Him.

In fact, we will find that this is the main point of John's description of the New Jerusalem. God's personal presence will be with redeemed humanity! This truth is stated in four or five different ways in this verse (depending upon whether the variant reading is considered part of the text).

> The tabernacle of God is with humanity . . . He will dwell with them ... they shall be his people . . . God himself shall be with them . . . [He shall be their God].

We will find this emphasis again in 21:7 where we have the promise to those who overcome. God will be their God and the believers will be His children.

In addition, in Revelation 21:11 we have another indication of God's continuous presence in the Holy City.

This is again emphasized in 22:3-4. These verses tell us of the presence of the throne of God and of the Lamb in the city. Each and every believer will have direct and immediate access to Him. The fact that it is mentioned a number of times in these chapters indicates its importance.

THE HOLY CITY IS NOT LIMITED TO THOSE FROM ISRAEL

Add to this, we find the plural form of the word "people" found in some Greek manuscripts here. If this is the original reading of the text, then it is another indication that other groups, apart from the nation of Israel, will have their part in the Holy City, the New Jerusalem.

In Scripture, the normal designation for the nation of Israel is the singular. They are usually referred to as the "people" of God. If the plural reading is original here, then it indicates other peoples will also have their habitation there.

This would fulfill what God promised Abraham over four thousand years ago.

> I will bless those who bless you, and whoever curses you I will curse; and all peoples on earth will be blessed through you (Genesis 12:3 NIV).

Paul emphasized this truth to the Galatians.

> Understand, then, that those who have faith are children of Abraham. Scripture foresaw that God would justify the Gentiles by faith, and announced the gospel in advance to Abraham: "All nations will be blessed through you" (Galatians 3:8 NIV).

We now find the ultimate fulfillment in the promise of the New Jerusalem. Indeed, it will be a place for both believing Jews and Gentiles.

In sum, this is the great truth of the Holy City. All those who have lived upon the earth, and have believed in the God of the Bible, will one day have direct and immediate access to the Lord in the New Jerusalem.

Revelation 21:4 And he [God] shall wipe away every tear from their eyes, and death shall no longer exist-neither shall there be mourning, neither crying, neither pain. For the former things have passed away [ceased to exist].

While the previous verse gives us the positive benefits of the New Jerusalem, this verse tells us what will not be there. John lists a number of evils that will be done away with.

THERE WILL BE NO TEARS

We need to understand that the expression, "God will wipe away every tear from their eyes," does not mean that there will be tears in heaven. In other words, it is not saying that every time someone cries in heaven God will immediately wipe the tears away. To the contrary, it is a way of stating that there will never be any more tears!

JOHN'S TEARS WILL BE WIPED AWAY

Earlier in the Book of Revelation, the prophet John wept bitterly when he thought that there was nobody who would be worthy to open the seven-sealed scroll.

> Then I began to weep bitterly because no one was found worthy to open the scroll and read it (Revelation 5:4 NLT).

It seemed to John that there was no answer to the problem of evil upon the earth. However, because of what the Lamb of God has done on our behalf, the tears of John, as well as those of the rest of us, will forever be wiped away!

In addition to the removal of all tears, neither will there be death, nor sorrow, nor crying. For God's people, these evils will be forever ended.

Earlier, Paul had written about the eventual defeat of death.

> Then, when our dying bodies have been transformed into bodies that will never die, this Scripture will be fulfilled: "Death is swallowed up in victory. O death, where is your victory? O death, where is your sting?" (1 Corinthians 15:54,55 NLT).

John states the reason for the end of these evils, namely, the old order of things, the first heaven and earth, will have completely passed away. The old order will be replaced by the new.

Therefore, the curse upon the human race, the animal kingdom and our physical world will be reversed. All these past curses will be gone forever. This is great news!

THE TEARS ARE WIPED AWAY AFTER GOD'S JUDGMENTS

We should note that the removal of tears will take place after all the judgments are completed. This includes the judgment seat of Christ where the believers will be evaluated for how faithful they have been to the Lord after their conversion.

WE CAN SUFFER LOSS

It should be remembered that believers can suffer the loss of reward when this day arrives. Paul wrote the following about the time believers will be evaluated by the Lord.

> If his work is burned up, he will suffer the loss. However, he will be saved, though it will be like going through a fire (1 Corinthians 3:15 God's Word).

We also discover that believers can be ashamed at the coming of Christ.

> Now, dear children, live in Christ. Then, when he appears we will have confidence, and when he comes we won't turn from him in shame (1 John 2:28 God's Word).

Some believers will be ashamed for squandering the gifts the Lord has given them. May we not be one of those people!

REVELATION 21:5-8:

ALL THINGS HAVE BEEN MADE NEW

In these next four verses, we will find God saying three things. The first is a statement telling us what He is doing (verse 5). The second, also in verse 5, is a command to John to write these things down. In the third statement, contained in verses 6-8, the Lord tells us who He is, as well as what He promises to do to both the righteous and the unrighteous.

Revelation 21:5 And the one sitting upon the throne said, "Behold," I am making all things new. And he said, "Write [it down]." Because these words are faithful and true.

John stops describing the New Jerusalem. He will now record God's spoken Word which is delivered from His throne.

Again, we find this "attention getting" word "behold" is used. As we have mentioned, it is very important because it signals something vital is about to be said or take place. And this use of the term is noteworthy because it is one of the few occasions in the Book of Revelation where God Himself speaks.

And what we have here is one of the greatest verses in the entire Bible! All things will be made new. The curse that corrupted all things in the Garden of Eden has been finally reversed! The Lord God will bring about an entirely new creation. People will have new bodies, the animal kingdom will be made new, and we will have an entirely new environment. The results of sin will be forever gone.

After making this statement, we have the Lord's command for John to write these things down. Perhaps John was so overwhelmed when he heard the actual voice of God that he forgot to write down the words. We are not told.

However, the reason for writing them down is revealed to us: The words of God are faithful and true!

We find that this is a recurring theme throughout the Bible. The God of the Bible cannot lie. Indeed, at all times, He speaks the truth. Therefore, we can always trust His promises.

Revelation 21:6 And he said to me, It is complete [They are accomplished]. I myself am the Alpha and the Omega, the Beginning and the End. To the one who is thirsty I myself shall give from the spring of the water of life freely [free of charge].

The Lord continues to speak and announces the completion of all things.

This includes the judgments of the Great Tribulation which was noted earlier in the Book of Revelation.

> Then the seventh angel poured out his bowl into the air. And a mighty shout came from the throne in the Temple, saying, "It is finished (Revelation 16:17 NLT).

The same Greek word, translated "it is complete," or "it is finished" is used here as well as in Revelation 16:17. The only difference is that the plural form of the word is used here. It could be translated something like, "they are done" or "they are accomplished."

Some English translations reflect this such as the Revised Version (1885), American Standard Version of 1901 and the New American Bible, Revised Edition. They read as follows.

> And he said unto me, They are come to pass (Revelation 17:16 Revised Version 1885).

> And he said unto me, They are come to pass (American Standard Version 1901).

> He said to me, "They are accomplished (New American Bible Revised Edition).

The plural most likely refers to all the events that had to take place have now been accomplished. In other words, all things temporal have now ended. We are now forever in the eternal state. This truth would certainly be reassuring for the believer.

The Lord then emphasizes His identity. In fact, the "I" is emphatic here in the Greek in each part of this verse. We attempted to bring out the emphasis by translating it, "I, myself."

The Lord is the Alpha and Omega. These are the first and last letters of the Greek alphabet. He is also the Beginning and the End, the Creator as well as the Reason for the creation. Indeed, He is the Originator as well as the Completer of all things.

Previously, the Lord stated this about Himself at the very beginning of the Book of Revelation.

> "I am the Alpha and the Omega—the beginning and the end," says the Lord God. "I am the one who is, who always was, and who is still to come—the Almighty One (Revelation 1:8 NLT).

This will also be repeated at the end of the book.

> I am the Alpha and the Omega, the First and the Last, the Beginning and the End (Revelation 22:13 NLT).

On these occasions in the Book of Revelation where the Lord makes the statement the "I" is always emphatic! It is He, nobody else!

This echoes what the Lord had said centuries earlier. Isaiah the prophet wrote.

> This is what the Lord says Israel's King and Redeemer, the Lord Almighty: I am the first and I am the last; apart from me there is no God (Isaiah 44:6 NIV).

The One who began all things is the One who finishes all things.

HE MEETS OUR DEEPEST SPIRITUAL NEEDS

In this verse, His promise to quench our thirst symbolizes His ability to meet our deepest spiritual needs. We read about this in Isaiah.

Come, everyone who is thirsty, come to the waters . . .
Pay attention and come to Me; listen, so that you will live
(Isaiah 55:1,3 HCSB).

The idea of God quenching the spiritual thirst of people was also reiterated by Jesus. The Lord said the following to the woman at the well in Samaria.

If you knew the gift of God, and who is saying to you, 'Give Me a drink,' you would ask Him, and He would give you living water . . . Everyone who drinks from this water will get thirsty again. But whoever drinks from the water that I will give him will never get thirsty again — ever! In fact, the water I will give him will become a well of water springing up within him for eternal life (John 4:10,13-14 HCSB).

Physical thirst is a need that each of us have. We also have a spiritual thirst that needs satisfying. Only the Lord, the God of the Bible, can meet our spiritual needs.

We should not miss the fact that the Lord gives us this water of life "freely" or "without cost." In other words, He is happy to bless us. Therefore, our spiritual thirst can always be met through His endless supply of "living water."

THE CUP OF JESUS COMPARED TO THE CUP OF THE PROSTITUTE

The cup that Jesus offers to believers is in direct contrast to the cup from which the great prostitute drank. This irony was recorded earlier in the Book of Revelation.

Now the woman was dressed in purple and scarlet clothing, and adorned with gold, precious stones, and pearls. She held in her hand a golden cup filled with detestable things and unclean things from her sexual immorality (Revelation 17:4 NET).

In the next chapter of Revelation, we read how the drinking of the contents of her unclean cup have caused the nations to fall.

> For all the nations have fallen from the wine of her immoral passion, and the kings of the earth have committed sexual immorality with her, and the merchants of the earth have gotten rich from the power of her sensual behavior (Revelation 18:3 NET).

Her symbolic cup was filled with detestable things compared to that of the Lord Jesus. His cup contained the water of life which quenches our spiritual thirst.

We must also emphasize that the offer from the Lord, to come and drink from His "living water," is still available for those who do not know Christ.

Revelation 21:7 The one who overcomes shall inherit these things and I shall be his God and he himself shall be my son [child].

A Note On Translation: In this verse, the words translated "he himself" are emphatic in the Greek. In other words, the Lord is emphasizing that those who believe will be His children.

We have another issue here with the male gender used. The last phrase says, "he will be my son." Of course, this promise does not only refer to males.

The problem is with the English language. We do not have a third person singular pronoun that can refer to both males and females. We say either "he" or "she."

This has led a number of English translations to make the words plural. They do this to indicate that both genders, male and female, are heirs to this promise.

For example, we read the following in the Contemporary English Version.

I will be their God, and they will be my people (CEV).

Other translations such the NLT, The Revised English Bible, the New Revised Standard Version, The New Jerusalem Bible, and the translation God's Word, also make it a plural.

The proper way to render verses, such as this one, has become a matter of debate among Bible-believers. While all would agree that both genders are included in the promise, not all believe that such verses should be translated by substituting the plural for the singular. There is no easy solution for this.

SPECIFIC PROMISES ARE GIVEN

In his letters to the seven churches, in Revelation 2 and 3, the Lord gave specific promises to the overcomers. We are now told that these overcomers, the believers in Jesus Christ, will inherit the blessings of this new creation of the Lord.

Inheriting emphasizes the privilege of obtaining something because of the work of another in contrast to our own work. Indeed, we are co-heirs with Jesus because of what He has done for each of us. Paul wrote.

> For his Spirit joins with our spirit to affirm that we are God's children. And since we are his children, we are his heirs. In fact, together with Christ we are heirs of God's glory. But if we are to share his glory, we must also share his suffering (Romans 8:16,17 NLT).

The believers are given special honor in that they are recognized as children of God. In our world, children have a unique relationship with their earthly father. The same holds true for the children of the Lord and their Heavenly Father.

Revelation 21:8 To the cowardly and unbelievers, the detestable, the murderers, the sexually immoral, the idol worshippers, those

who practice magic spells, and all the liars, their part will be in the lake that burns with fire and sulfur, which is the second death.

Textual Note: Some manuscripts have "and sinners" after unbelievers.

But not all are overcomers. We now hear of the opposite fate for those who are not believers. General categories of people who are not followers of the Lord are listed here. The sins mentioned are those that typically characterize unbelievers in contrast to the overcomers. These people will be assigned to the lake of fire, the second death, as their final destiny.

COWARDICE

Interestingly, we find cowardice mentioned first. This is not referring to natural fearfulness, which we all have. Instead, it seems to be speaking of those who choose their self interests rather than the Lord. Previously John recorded the threats to humanity by this coming world ruler, the Final Antichrist (Revelation 13). He is also known as "the beast."

We read that this beast will threaten people with death if they do not worship him. The cowardly will decide to worship him and his image rather than the God of the Bible.

On the other hand, we are told that those who belong to the Lord are not given a spirit of timidity or cowardice.

> For God has not given us a spirit of fearfulness, but one of
> power, love, and sound judgment (2 Timothy 1:7 HCSB).

Many people, who trust Christ, during this difficult period of tribulation and judgment, will pay for their faith in Him with their lives. The Lord will give them the strength to die for Him. Not so, with the cowardly who would rather worship the beast and deny Christ.

UNBELIEVERS (UNFAITHFUL)

Some understand this word to mean "unfaithful" or "not to be trusted" rather than non-Christians; those who do not believe in the Lord. Some English translations reflect this.

> But as for the cowardly, the faithless, the detestable, murderers, the sexually immoral, sorcerers, idolaters, and all liars, their portion will be in the lake that burns with fire and sulfur, which is the second death (ESV).

Whether speaking of unbelievers in general, or those who are merely faithless, the idea seems to cover those who do not put their trust in the Lord.

DETESTABLE, ABOMINABLE

This word is a general term. Here it likely has the idea of any person, whether Jew or Gentile, who has been stained with the various abominations of the heathen. In other words, instead of obeying the Law of God, they followed the detestable practices of the Gentiles.

As we search the Scripture, we often the Lord speaking of the "abominable" practices of the heathen. In fact, earlier in the Book of Revelation we see this sort of thing in the description of the woman on the scarlet beast.

> So the angel took me in the Spirit into the wilderness. There I saw a woman sitting on a scarlet beast that had seven heads and ten horns, and blasphemies against God were written all over it. The woman wore purple and scarlet clothing and beautiful jewelry made of gold and precious gems and pearls. In her hand she held a gold goblet full of obscenities and the impurities of her immorality (Revelation 17:3,4 NLT).

This description is illustrative of the vile practices of the heathen.

MURDERERS

The fact that murderers are third on the list seems to mean that these sins are not listed from the greater evil to the lesser. There may also be a special reference here to those who purposely murder believers. However, this term condemns all types of homicide.

SEXUALLY IMMORAL

The sexually immoral constitute those who commit any sexual sin. These are listed in various places in Scripture. In this context, it may be specifically addressed to those who practice various sexual sins in their worshipping of idols.

THOSE WHO PRACTICE MAGIC SPELLS

The Greek word here is *pharmakeia*. As can readily be seen, our English word "pharmacy" is derived from it. The use of practicing magic spells often involves the usage of drugs.

IDOLATERS

Idolatry, idol worship, was a particularly bad sin. In fact, it is the second of the Ten Commandments. The Lord said.

> You must not make for yourself an idol of any kind or an image of anything in the heavens or on the earth or in the sea. You must not bow down to them or worship them, for I, the Lord your God, am a jealous God who will not tolerate your affection for any other gods (Exodus 20:4 NLT).

Idolatry is roundly condemned throughout Scripture.

ALL LIARS

Finally, we end with liars. Jesus said the devil was both a murderer and a liar.

You are of your father the devil, and your will is to do your father's desires. He was a murderer from the beginning, and does not stand in the truth, because there is no truth in him. When he lies, he speaks out of his own character, for he is a liar and the father of lies (John 8:44 ESV).

Again, this list is representative of the sins of unbelievers.

Tragically, believers at times will commit these sins. Yet, they characterize those who are lost. Paul wrote.

Or do you not know that wrongdoers will not inherit the kingdom of God? Do not be deceived: Neither the sexually immoral nor idolaters nor adulterers nor men who have sex with men nor thieves nor the greedy nor drunkards nor slanderers nor swindlers will inherit the kingdom of God. And that is what some of you were. But you were washed, you were sanctified, you were justified in the name of the Lord Jesus Christ and by the Spirit of our God (1 Corinthians 6:9-11 NIV).

It is clear that the unbelievers are in view in this verse since we are told that their destiny will be in the lake of fire, hell.

THE LOCATION OF HELL

We discover that the lake of fire continues to exist after the first heaven and the first earth pass away. This should forever demonstrate that hell is not in the center of the earth as so many people think.

In the last book in our series on the afterlife, which deals with the subject of hell, we give a detailed answer about its location. We do know this: wherever the lake of fire does exist, it does not exist as part of the old earth and it will have a separate existence from the new heaven and the new earth.

THE SECOND DEATH

It is important that we understand what is meant by the "second death." The first death is physical death which is the general rule for humanity. We all die.

The second death is spiritual death or eternal death which means everlasting separation from the Lord. The only remedy to the second death is the new birth; trusting Jesus Christ as Savior. Those who believe in Him will not experience the second death.

These first eight verses in Revelation 21 could be summed up by the words that Paul wrote to the Corinthians.

> Therefore, if anyone is in Christ, he is a new creation.
> The old has passed away; behold, the new has come
> (2 Corinthians 5:17 ESV).

THE NEW JERUSALEM FURTHER EXPLAINED 21:9-27

Earlier in the Book of Revelation the focus on Babylon the Great shifted from the woman to "the great city, Babylon" (Revelation 18:10). That evil city was eventually destroyed because of great sin.

In a similar manner, the focus now shifts from another woman, the bride of Jesus Christ, the church, to "the Holy City," the New Jerusalem. In contrast to destroyed Babylon, this city will last forever!

Revelation 21:9 Then one of the seven angels who had the seven bowls full of the seven last plagues came and said to me, "Come, I will show you the bride, the wife of the Lamb."

One of the seven angels who was involved in the bowl judgments re-appears on the scene. This unnamed angel will now give John a more detailed understanding of the New Jerusalem.

Earlier in the Book of Revelation, we find that one of the angels with the seven bowls of judgment served as John's guide in this part of his vision.

One of the seven angels who had the seven bowls came and said to me, "Come, I will show you the punishment of the great prostitute, who sits by many waters" (Revelation 17:1 NIV).

We should not miss the fact that one of these particular angels helped John understand the two cities. First, it was the mystery of the city of Babylon. Now, in sharp contrast to that evil city, we have the Holy City, the New Jerusalem.

The word translated "come" is not an invitation here. Rather John is summoned or commanded to come with the angel.

This messenger of the Lord refers to the Holy City as "the bride, the wife of the Lamb." This is usually understood to mean that the Holy City is the residence of the bride, the New Testament church.

The "bride," the wife of the Lamb, is equated with the New Jerusalem. From the description that follows it also seems clear that the New Jerusalem is a city. As we mentioned previously, while the term mainly refers to the actual city it may also refer to the inhabitants of that city.

At this time, the marriage of the Lamb is something that has already taken place. The New Testament believers are called "the wife of the Lamb."

THE EMPHASIS ON THE LAMB

Jesus is now referred to as "the Lamb." In fact, we will find this particular designation of Him seven times in this section of the Book of Revelation (9, 14, 22, 23, 27; 22:1,3). This title is emphasized as we are now given an explanation of the eternal realm.

Interestingly, when John the Baptist introduced Jesus to his disciples, this is how he described Him.

The next day he saw Jesus coming toward him, and said, "Behold, the Lamb of God, who takes away the sin of the world" (John 1:29 ESV).

When we see this word "behold" used before a new character is introduced, we know that this person is going to be a "main character" in the story. In this verse, it also indicates His mission; the Lamb of God has come to die for the sins of the world.

Revelation 21:10 And he carried me away by the spirit to a mountain that was great and high, and he showed me the Holy City, Jerusalem, coming down from God out of heaven.

John is now transported in a vision to a high mountain where he can see the Holy City. Interestingly, the word "new" is not found here as a description of Jerusalem.

The transportation of John, though in the spirit, reminds us of an event in the life of Christ. Indeed, Jesus Himself was taken to a high mountain during His temptation by the devil.

> Again, the devil took him to a very high mountain, and showed him all the kingdoms of the world and their grandeur (Matthew 4:8 NET).

The Lord was showed the kingdoms of this sinful world system. In contrast, John is now shown the Holy City.

In another contrast, John was in the wilderness, the desert, when he saw Babylon.

> So the angel took me in the Spirit into the wilderness. There I saw a woman sitting on a scarlet beast . . . A mysterious name was written on her forehead: "Babylon the Great, Mother of All Prostitutes and Obscenities in the World (Revelation 17:3,5 NLT).

Now he sees the Holy City from the vantage point of a high mountain.

Again we are told that this city comes down out of heaven. Whether it comes all the way down to the new earth is a matter of debate.

Revelation 21:11 having the glory of God, its brilliance was like a precious stone, like jasper, clear as crystal.

The description of the Holy City is that of a light-giver. It does not reflect light like the moon, neither does it generate light in the same way as the sun. Instead, light originates from the city. In other words, it is the source of God's light.

Here it is compared to a jasper stone. In the ancient world, the jasper stone was a designation for any opaque precious stone. The stone could come in various colors including green, a reddish color, brown, blue, yellow, and white. The term was not limited to what is today called jasper.

The fact that the stone is transparent and gleaming has caused a number of commentators to believe it is referring to a diamond. While we cannot be certain, the description certainly does fit. If this is true, then we have a diamond in a gold mounting! In other words, the city is a wedding ring.

Whatever type of precious stone is in view, we do know that it looked magnificent!

Revelation 21:12 It had a great high wall with twelve gates, and twelve angels at the gates and the names of the twelve tribes of the children of Israel were inscribed on the gates.

We are specifically told about a high wall that surrounded the Holy City. The wall would speak of security but certainly it was not there for defense because there was nobody to defend against. The enemies of the Lord, whether human or angelic, have been forever banished from His presence. In addition, we later find that the gates are never shut (21:25).

> There is also threefold repetition of the number twelve; twelve gates, twelve angels, twelve tribes. The twelve tribes of Israel on the gates would immediately remind those of Ezekiel's description of the millennial temple (Ezekiel 48:30-35).

One angel is stationed at each of the twelve gates. We are not told why they are positioned there. As we mentioned, it could not be for protection because there is nobody outside the city who could cause harm.

The twelve tribes of Israel have their part in the New Jerusalem. The fact that their names are inscribed on the wall emphasizes this truth.

IS DAN ONE OF THE TWELVE TRIBES?

This brings up the question of the tribe of Dan. For some unexplained reason, the tribe of Dan is not mentioned in chapter seven along with the other tribes of Israel. However, it is likely here in the Holy City.

Chronologically, the events of Revelation 7 take place before the Millennium which, as we have mentioned, takes place before the eternal realm. For whatever reason Dan is not mentioned among the twelve tribes in chapter seven but the tribe is restored in the Millennium.

In Ezekiel 48:32, the gates of Jerusalem in the Millennium are also named after the twelve tribes and we find Dan among the tribes.

> On the east wall, also 1½ miles long, the gates will be named for Joseph, Benjamin, and Dan (Ezekiel 48:32 NLT).

However, the names of the twelve tribes, which inscribed on the wall of the Holy City, are not named for us here. Therefore, we cannot be certain if Dan is one of the twelve listed.

Revelation 21:13 on the east side, three gates, and on the north side three gates, and on the south side three gates, and on the west side three gates.

The description of the gates is consistent with the dimensions of the city with an equal number of gates on each of the four side. The city is a cube.

East, north, south and west is an unusual order of listing the gates. However, it is the same order that we find in Ezekiel 42:16-19.

As to why this particular order of the direction of the compass is listed we are not told. As can be imagined, this has not stopped commentators for speculating on the answer.

Revelation 21:14 And the wall of the city has twelve foundations and the names of the twelve apostles of the Lamb are upon them.

The number twelve again is prominent. The twelve foundations of the walls will bear the names of the twelve apostles of the Lamb. This may be a reference to the fact that they laid the foundation of the church after Christ ascended into heaven. Paul wrote.

> You are like a building with the apostles and prophets as the foundation and with Christ as the most important stone (Ephesians 2:20 CEV).

While the apostles and prophets were the foundation, the building would be nothing without Christ. He is the most important stone.

EXCURSUS: WAS PAUL THE TWELFTH APOSTLE?

It is often contended that Saul of Tarsus, who became the Apostle Paul, was meant to be the twelfth apostle, not Matthias whom the Eleven chose. While the eleven disciples chose Matthias to be the apostle that replaced Judas, Jesus chose Saul of Tarsus. Is this what the Bible teaches?

THE CASE FOR PAUL BEING THE TWELFTH APOSTLE

Those who argue that Paul was the twelfth apostle do so as follows.

JESUS CHOSE THE TWELVE APOSTLES

The Bible makes it clear that Jesus originally chose the twelve apostles. It was His selection alone. He did not consult His disciples or anyone else. Therefore, the replacement of one of them would again be the choice of Jesus alone, since they were His unique group of men.

JESUS CHOSE PAUL

Jesus did choose the twelfth apostle; Saul of Tarsus. The New Testament emphasizes that Saul, who became Paul, was the direct choice of Jesus to be His apostle. After Saul's conversion the Lord said the following about him to Ananias.

> But the Lord said to him, "Go, for he is a chosen instrument of mine to carry my name before the Gentiles and kings and the children of Israel (Acts 9:15 ESV).

The Lord Jesus specifically chose Paul.

JESUS DID NOT CHOOSE MATTHIAS

In contrast to choosing Paul, Jesus did not choose Matthias. He was chosen by the Eleven Disciples after Jesus had ascended into heaven. Since Jesus had been on earth for forty days after His resurrection and before His ascension, He could have easily designated another person to take the place of Judas. Yet He did not. His choice, Saul of Tarsus, had not yet been converted.

THE HOLY SPIRIT HAD NOT YET COME TO THE DISCIPLES WHEN THEY CHOSE MATTHIAS

The disciples were specifically told to wait in the city of Jerusalem for the power of the Holy Spirit to come upon them. We read of this in the first chapter of the Book of Acts. It says.

But when the Holy Spirit has come upon you, you will receive power and will tell people about me everywhere—in Jerusalem, throughout Judea, in Samaria, and to the ends of the earth (Acts 1:8 NLT).

These disciples were supposed to be waiting for the promise of the Holy Spirit. Instead of waiting, they decided to choose a person to complete the number of apostles to "twelve." The Holy Spirit had not yet arrived in His fullness, yet they went ahead and made the foolish choice of a replacement for Judas.

There is something else. The fact that they cast lots to replace Judas shows how the entire episode was not Spirit-led. This is in contrast to Jesus' personal choice of the Twelve while He was here on earth, and then His selection of Saul of Tarsus after His ascension into heaven.

PAUL'S PROMINENCE IN THE BOOK OF ACTS SHOWS HE WAS JESUS' CHOICE

We find the Apostle Paul is a prominent figure in the Book of Acts. In fact, he is the central figure in the last half of the Book. It is obvious that Paul was God's choice to have a crucial role in the spreading of the gospel of Jesus Christ.

MATTHIAS WAS NEVER HEARD FROM AGAIN

Matthias, in contrast to Paul, was never heard of again. After his selection to be the twelfth apostle, he is never mentioned again in Scripture.

The evidence is thus clear. The twelve apostles were all specially chosen and commissioned by Jesus. Jesus chose Paul as an apostle. He did not choose Matthias. The power of the Holy Spirit had not yet come to the apostles when they chose Matthias to replace Judas. History makes it clear that Paul was God's choice. Indeed, he was one of the two central figures in the Book of Acts and early Christian history while Matthias was never heard of again.

THE CASE AGAINST PAUL BEING ONE OF THE TWELVE

While the arguments for placing Paul as the twelfth disciple may seem impressive, the clear evidence from Scripture is that Matthias, not Paul, was indeed the disciple who took Judas' place. We can make the following observations.

THE FIRST CHAPTER OF ACTS DESCRIBES THE APOSTLES' AUTHORITATIVE SELECTION

For one thing, the first chapter of the Book of Acts explains how Matthias took the place of Judas as the twelfth Apostle. Contrary to what some have alleged, there is nothing whatsoever in the account to suggest that the choosing of Matthias was not according to the leading of the Lord.

THEY ASKED JESUS TO MAKE THE CHOICE

To begin with, the apostles did not choose without the help of Jesus. Indeed, they asked the Lord, and the Lord answered them. The Bible explains it as follows.

> And they prayed and said, "You, O Lord, who know the hearts of all, show which of these two You have chosen "to take part in this ministry and apostleship from which Judas by transgression fell, that he might go to his own place" (Acts 1:24,25 NKJV).

Thus, they did not decide this matter for themselves; they asked Jesus to decide.

In addition, the casting of the lot was a biblical practice that was ordained by God. We should not assume that this was less than what God intended.

THEY WERE WAITING FOR THE POWER TO WITNESS – NOT WISDOM TO MAKE DECISIONS

What the disciples were waiting for was the power of the Holy Spirit to witness for Jesus Christ. Indeed, they were waiting not for the Holy

Spirit or guidance from the Holy Spirit. The Holy Spirit was already guiding them.

JESUS HAD ALREADY GIVEN THE DISCIPLES HIS AUTHORITY

Once Jesus ascended into heaven His unique authority was given to His specially chosen apostles. In other words, once He left this world they were acting on His behalf.

PAUL WAS CHOSEN FOR ANOTHER APOSTOLIC MINISTRY

Paul was indeed chosen by Jesus Christ but it was not to be one of the Twelve. Jesus chose him to be the apostle to the Gentiles, the non-Jews. He had a unique and powerful ministry but it was not as one of the Twelve.

MATTHIAS IS NUMBERED WITH THE TWELVE BEFORE PAUL'S CONVERSION

It is clear that the New Testament sees Matthias as the twelfth apostle. In fact, he was numbered with the Twelve before the conversion of Saul.

We find that on the Day of Pentecost, Matthias was considered to be one of the Twelve. We are told that Peter stood up with "the Eleven."

> But Peter stood up with the eleven, raised his voice, and addressed them: "You men of Judea and all you who live in Jerusalem, know this and listen carefully to what I say (Acts 2:14 NET).

The Eleven would include Matthias.

Later, it speaks of the Twelve as a group. We read about this in the Book of Acts.

> So the twelve called the whole group of the disciples together and said, "It is not right for us to neglect the word of God to wait on tables (Acts 6:2 NET).

This makes it clear that the Bible assumes that Matthias was indeed the man who was chosen to replace Judas Iscariot.

EARLIER THEY WERE CALLED THE ELEVEN

Earlier, after the death of Judas but before the choosing of Matthias, Luke, the author of Luke/Acts, referred to the inner circle of Jesus' disciples as "the Eleven."

> When they came back from the tomb, they told all these things to the Eleven and to all the others (Luke 24:9 NIV).

Later on the same day he repeats this title.

> They got up and returned at once to Jerusalem. There they found the Eleven and those with them, assembled together (Luke 24:33 NIV).

Then after Matthias is chosen, we find that Luke refers to the group as "the Twelve." Writing under the divine inspiration of the Holy Spirit Luke certified the disciple's choice of Matthias.

> And they cast lots for them, and the lot fell on Matthias, and he was numbered with the eleven apostles (Acts 1:26 ESV).

Matthias was numbered with "the Eleven" before the conversion of Saul of Tarsus. This did not change after Saul's conversion. We never find Paul numbered as one of the Twelve.

PAUL DISTINGUISHED HIMSELF FROM THE TWELVE

Furthermore, while Paul claimed to be an apostle, he distinguishes himself from the Twelve. He wrote to the Corinthians.

> He appeared to Cephas, and then to the Twelve . . . and last of all he appeared to me also, as to one abnormally born (1 Corinthians 15:5,8 NIV).

In speaking of the appearances of Jesus Christ after His resurrection from the dead Paul differentiates himself from the Twelve. It is obvious that he did not consider himself part of this unique group.

MOST OF THE TWELVE APOSTLES WERE NOT HEARD OF IN ACTS

The fact that Matthias is not specifically named after the first chapter of the Book of Acts is not an argument against him being one of the twelve. Most of the twelve disciples are not specifically named in the Book of Acts. In fact, of the Twelve, Peter and John and James are the only ones specifically named in the Book of Acts.

We conclude that Saul of Tarsus, who became the apostle Paul, was neither one of the original twelve disciples, nor was he the one chosen to replace Judas.

Therefore, we expect to find the name Matthias, not Paul, inscribed on one of the foundations of the Holy City.

Revelation 21:15 And the one speaking with me had a measuring rod of gold, in order that he might measure the city, its gates and its wall.

Next we find that a golden measuring rod is used to measure the Holy City. Earlier in Revelation, we are told that the earthly temple in Jerusalem was also measured.

> Then a measuring rod like a staff was given to me, and I was told, "Get up and measure the temple of God, and the altar, and the ones who worship there. But do not measure the outer courtyard of the temple; leave it out, because it has been given to the Gentiles, and they will trample on the holy city for forty-two months (Revelation 11:1-2 NET).

The contrast is stark. The temple in the old Jerusalem of the previous earth was measured with a regular measuring rod. Now it is the New

Jerusalem, the Holy City, that is measured. In this instance, it is measured with a golden measuring rod!

Revelation 21:16 And the city was laid out as a square, its length was the same as its width. And he measured the city with his measuring rod, it was 12,000 stadia [1,400 miles]. Its length, width and height are equal.

Like the Holy of Holies in the tabernacle in the wilderness, and then later in the temple in Jerusalem, the Holy City will also be laid out as a square; actually a perfect cube since all sides were equal.

The Greek word translated "square" is only found here in the New Testament. It has the idea of a building with four sides and four right angles. Some translations render the word "foursquare."

> The city lies foursquare, its length the same as its width . . .
> (Revelation 21:16 ESV).

This term is rather archaic.

Using this gold measuring rod, this particular angel discovered that the city was approximately twelve thousand stadia. One stade, the singular term for the plural stadia, was about 607 feet or 75 meters. This make the entire city approximately 1400-1500 miles (or 2,200 kilometers) in length, width, and height.

This cube-shaped heavenly city is not only greater in size than the old city of Jerusalem, it will actually extend far beyond the boundaries of the land that was originally promised to Abraham.

Revelation 21:17 And he measured its wall, 144 cubits, according to human measurement which is also the angel's.

The number 144 again is prominent in the Book of Revelation.

The Greek expression says, "according to human measurement, that is, of an angel" means that the angel mentioned in verses 9 and 15 used the same units of measure employed by humans when he measured the city. In other words, it was not some special angelic way of measuring the wall.

In this verse the Greek text describes the walls in cubits. It says the size is "144 cubits." This translates into about 216 feet, 72 yards or 65 meters in our modern standards of measurement.

Some English translations, as we did above, like to use the words "cubits" in describing the walls.

> Then he measured its wall, 144 cubits according to human measurement, which the angel used (Revelation 21:17 HCSB).

The size of a cubit varied throughout history; usually from 18-24 inches.

Other translations, like the Contemporary English Version, render the cubits into feet when it translates this verse.

> Then the angel measured the wall, and by our measurements it was about two hundred sixteen feet high (Revelation 21:17 CEV).

HEIGHT OR THICKNESS?

Note that the CEV believes it is the "height" of the wall that is 216 feet. However, there are other translations which believe it is the "thickness" of the walls, and not its height, which is referenced here.

For example, the New Living Translation reads as follows.

> Then he measured the walls and found them to be 216 feet thick (according to the human standard used by the angel) (Revelation 21:17 NLT).

The Greek text merely says "its wall." It does not state whether it is the thickness of the wall or its height which is in view.

Therefore, we find that a number of translations, such as ours above, merely says, "he measured its wall" without trying to determine if it was the height or thickness that is being described. In other words, they leave the ambiguity in the translation.

In sum, like the exact dimensions of the Holy City, we also have some ambiguity here with respect to the walls.

Revelation 21:18 The material of the wall was jasper and the city was pure gold like clear [transparent] glass.

The Greek word translated "material" here is rare. This is the only time it is found in the New Testament.

The wall of the city was made out of jasper. It was not merely "like jasper" or will have some jasper built into it. As we noted, this could refer to a number of possible jewels and colors. A good case can be made for it being a diamond.

Earlier in Revelation, jasper had been used as a symbol of God.

> The one sitting on the throne was as brilliant as gemstones—like jasper and carnelian. And the glow of an emerald circled his throne like a rainbow (Revelation 4:3 NLT).

HOW CAN GOLD BE LIKE CLEAR GLASS?

This description presents a problem because gold is not clear; it is opaque. In what sense is gold like clear glass? There have been a number of suggestions as to what John meant.

It is possible that John is referring to the appearance of the city. In other words, the gold shone like clear glass.

There is another possibility; John is comparing the value of gold to glass. The idea is that these materials were extremely valuable. Indeed, in the ancient world, glass was very valuable and therefore extremely costly.

In fact, earlier in Revelation, we find that glass was something found in the throne of God.

> And in front of the throne was something like a sea of glass, like crystal (Revelation 4:6 NET).

This point seems to be that the Holy City was built of the most costly materials known to humanity.

In sum, the description of the Holy City gives the feeling of indescribable brilliance. While it made be hard, if not impossible, for us to visualize such a city, the idea certainly comes across. Indeed, its beauty is beyond our wildest imagination!

Revelation 21:19 The foundations of the walls of the city were adorned with every king of precious stone. The first was jasper, the second sapphire, the third was chalcedony, the fourth emerald, the fifth onyx, the sixth carnelian, the seventh chrysolite, the eighth beryl, the ninth topaz, the tenth chrysoprase, the eleventh jacinth, the twelfth amethyst.

Twelve different stones are mentioned as foundations of the walls. It is impossible to identify all these gems with any type of precision. Some are seemingly identifiable but others are either difficult or impossible for us to properly identify. What we can say with certainty is that its magnificence is overwhelming!

We will briefly summarize what each stone is thought to have looked like.

JASPER

As we mentioned, we are not certain of the identity of this stone. It could very well be a diamond. It is described as crystal clear, which would reflect light and color. It was obviously very beautiful and very valuable because it is mentioned often in Revelation.

SAPPHIRE

Today when we speak of sapphire, we are referring to a blue transparent stone. It is also known as "lapis lazuli." This stone occurs in Exodus 24:10 as being under God's feet.

> There they saw the God of Israel. Under his feet there seemed to be a surface of brilliant blue lapis lazuli, as clear as the sky itself (Exodus 24:10 NLT).

However, the Roman writer Pliny describes it as opaque with gold specks.

CHALCEDONY

Again, what the modern term means is not necessarily what the ancients described as chalcedony. Today it is a variety of quartz. Whether this is what John referred to here is a matter of debate.

EMERALD

This was apparently a green stone like our present-day description of an emerald.

ONYX

This is usually associated with a variety of agate. In fact, some translations use the word agate in describing this stone.

CARNELIAN

This particular stone was mentioned earlier in Revelation.

> The one who was sitting there sparkled like precious stones of jasper and carnelian (Revelation 4:3 CEV).

The Greek word is *sardion*. It was named for the town of Sardis where it was discovered. The stone is fiery red.

CHRYSOLITE

This seems to be a gold stone.

BERYL

This is a precious stone, sea-green in color.

TOPAZ

Yellow rock crystal is often associated with Topaz.

CHRYSOPRASE

This is thought to be a variety of quartz.

JACINTH

There is no consensus about what this stone looked like. Some take it to be blue while others assume it was red in color.

AMETHYST

Finally, amethyst is assumed to be a purple transparent quartz crystal.

We should note, that the twelve precious stones which adorned the foundation, are similar, if not exactly the same, as those stones on the breastplate of the high priest. In fact, a number of Bible commentators believe they are exactly the same.

Consequently, the twelve stones seemingly represent the twelve tribes of Israel. In addition, it adds to the idea that the Holy City, like the Holy of Holies in the tabernacle and then later in the temple, is place where people meet God.

WERE THE STONES CORRELATED WITH THE SIGNS OF THE ZODIAC?

In dealing with the various stones found in this verse, we need to clear up a popular misconception. Some ancient writers, such as Josephus and Pliny, as well as a few modern ones, have claimed that the stones found here correlate with the signs of the zodiac; though John has them in the exact opposite order as to how the sun passes through the constellations.

By doing this, many see John as repudiating the pagan concept that the zodiac had some influence over the behavior of humanity.

While this view has gained popularity, recent scholarship has refuted it. Indeed, the basis for this theory has been shown to be flawed. In other words, there is no real evidence for any correlation between the order in which these stones are listed and the signs of the zodiac.

Instead of the reverse of the zodiac, the stones mentioned here are seemingly those found in the breastplate of the high priest.

Revelation 21:21 And the twelve gates were twelve pearls, each one of the gates was made from one pearl. And the main street of the city was pure gold, like transparent glass.

This is the description of the "pearly gates." The twelve gates are each made of an individual pearl.

This would immediate remind us of Jesus' parable of the "pearl of great price" where the Lord compared the kingdom of heaven to the discovery of a pearl.

> The kingdom of heaven is like what happens when a shop owner is looking for fine pearls. After finding a very valuable one, the owner goes and sells everything in order to buy that pearl (Matthew 13:45, 46 CEV).

In this parable, Jesus is the shop owner, the merchant man, who obtains the pearl. We are that pearl. The Lord paid the ultimate price for it, His death on the cross of Calvary. Peter wrote.

For you know that you were redeemed from your empty way of life inherited from the fathers, not with perishable things like silver or gold, but with the precious blood of Christ, like that of a lamb without defect or blemish (1 Peter 1:18-19 HCSB).

Therefore, these twelve gates would serve as a continual reminder of the sacrifice of Christ "who bought us with a price." Indeed, it was the price of His own life.

We are also told that the street of the city was made of pure gold. The pure gold was like transparent glass. In other words, there was no flaw whatsoever in it.

Revelation 21:22 And I saw no temple in it, for the Lord God, the Almighty, and the Lamb are its temple.

Certain things are missing from the Holy City. From the very beginning of life here upon the earth, there has always been a place where humans could meet God, a tabernacle or a temple. In the Garden of Eden, before humanity sinned, there was no need for such a place because God was personally interacting with Adam and Eve.

In the same way, there will be no temple in the Holy City. Indeed, God the Father, and the Lamb of God, the Lord Jesus, are dwelling with us in the New Jerusalem. Therefore, God will not be confined to one area in the Holy City such as in a temple. Instead His presence will be everywhere.

We should also note that John lists a number of titles here; Lord, God and Almighty. While each of these titles have been used previously in the Book of Revelation, the cumulative effect of using all three adds to the majesty of God.

Add to this, we have the mention of the Lamb, the central character in the Book of Revelation. Indeed, this revelation is from Jesus and it is also about Jesus.

In fact, the very first sentence of the Book frames it nicely for us.

The revelation of Jesus Christ (Revelation 1:1 NET).

It is from Him, and it is about Him.

Revelation 21:23 And the city had no need of the sun neither of the moon in order that it might illuminate it. For the glory of God gives it light and its light is the Lamb.

Not only is a temple unnecessary in the New Jerusalem, we will neither find the sun or the moon. The Lord Himself will provide the light. This includes both God the Father and God the Son. Here God the Father and the Lamb, the Lord Jesus, are equated. In other words, they are placed on the same level.

THE GOLDEN LAMPSTAND

One further thing should be mentioned. In the tabernacle in the wilderness, there was a golden lampstand. It was a wonderful picture of the person and ministry of Christ. In the Holy City, Christ Himself is the golden lampstand! He is the light that illumines this place of worship.

Revelation 21:24 And the nations will walk by its light, and the kings of the earth will bring their glory and honor into it.

The believers from the nations of the world, as well as those from Israel, will enter the Holy City. They will be like the High Priest of old who, once a year on the Day of Atonement, entered the Holy of Holies in the tabernacle and then later the temple. Instead of the nations bringing the blood of the sacrifice, the Lamb Himself, who was that sacrifice, will be there in person to meet them. What a fabulous picture we have here!

It is not clear whether people from the nations of the world dwell in the Holy City or merely come there to worship. The fact that they come there to see the Lamb may indicate that they live elsewhere.

Revelation 21:25 And its gates will never ever be closed during the day (for there will be no night there).

The Greek expression here emphasizes that there is no possible way that the gates will ever be closed. This is why we translated it "never ever" in an attempt to bring out the emphasis.

In the world to come, there will be no need to close the gates because there will be no night. Indeed, it is a land of fadeless day. This illustrates that in the Holy City there is perfect security and freedom of access.

This is in contrast to the old city of Jerusalem, which like all ancient cities, closed its gates by night. Night was associated with all sorts of evils. This not only included thieves, but also the practice of magic spells and other demonic activity. These will all be things of the past for there is nothing to fear in the New Jerusalem

In fact, all those who will walk through the gates of the Holy City will be peaceful. There will be no aggressors, no attacking armies, only peace, prosperity, and security.

Revelation 21:26 And the glory and honor of the nations will be brought into it.

In a previous verse, we were told the kings bring glory and honor to the city. Now we are informed that the nations will likewise bring their glory and honor. This reflects an ancient practice. In biblical times, the kings and nations would bring their wealth and glory to the city of the greatest king of all. The psalmist wrote.

> The kings of the earth are bringing tribute to your Temple in Jerusalem (Psalm 68:29 NLT).

In the Holy City, everyone will now honor the "King of kings and Lord of Lords!"

Revelation 21:27 And nothing unclean shall never ever enter into it, nor anyone doing any thing detestable or practice falsehood, but only those whose names have been written in the Book of Life of the Lamb.

In the Holy City only believers will dwell with God. There is no need for a temple because the entire city is a temple.

THE EARTHLY TEMPLE HAD BEEN DEFILED

In the Old Testament, we are told that abominations were sometimes brought to the temple, the house of the Lord. The prophet Ezekiel was allowed to see the abominations that were taking place.

> "Go in," God said, "and see what horrible and evil things the people are doing." Inside, I saw that the walls were covered with pictures of reptiles and disgusting, unclean animals, as well as with idols that the Israelites were worshiping. Seventy Israelite leaders were standing there, including Jaazaniah son of Shaphan. Each of these leaders was holding an incense burner, and the smell of incense filled the room. God said, "Ezekiel, do you see what horrible things Israel's leaders are doing in secret? They have filled their rooms with idols" (Ezekiel 8:9-12 CEV).

This will never happen again! In fact, there will be no unbelievers entering the Holy City. Like the outcasts in the ancient world, who lived outside the city walls, the same is true for the New Jerusalem.

WE HAVE BEEN MADE CLEAN

In our present sinful nature none of us is clean. Indeed, we have all sinned and have come short of God's perfect standard. However, if we have trusted Jesus Christ as our Savior our names are written in His Book; the Book of Life of the Lamb.

Therefore, we are made clean through His sacrifice and consequently we are allowed entrance into the Holy City.

THERE WILL BE THOSE WHO WILL NEVER ENTER

This passage also makes something else clear. Indeed, there will be those who will never be allowed admittance to the New Jerusalem. This, among many other passages in Scripture, should once-and-for-all refute the idea that everyone who has ever lived will have access to God's presence in eternity. Tragically, countless people will not be there. As Scripture repeatedly states, this will their own choice. Rejecting God's provision for salvation in this life will cause them to spend eternity away from His glorious presence.

REVELATION CHAPTER 22

Revelation 22:1 Then he showed me the river of the water of life, clear as crystal, flowing from the throne of God and the Lamb.

Textual Issue: Some manuscripts have the word "pure" before the word river.

The personage who showed John this next scene is not identified. It seems to be an angel who is in view here.

He shows John some specifics of the city. In the eternal state, we find that the people of God will live at the source of a life-giving river. The water is described as clear as crystal. We also discover that the source of this stream will be the very presence of God Himself.

EDEN

In God's original creation, a river flowed from Eden.

> A river went out from Eden to water the garden. From there it divided and became the source of four rivers (Genesis 3:10 HCSB).

THE MILLENNIAL TEMPLE

In the millennial temple, we also find life-giving water emanating from it.

> Then he brought me back to the entrance of the temple and there was water flowing from under the threshold of the temple toward the east, for the temple faced east (Ezekiel 47:1 HCSB).

Now in the New Jerusalem we find an eternal source of living water flowing from the throne of God.

Revelation 22:2 [the water was flowing down] through the middle of the main street of the city. On each side of the river, was the tree of life. It was bearing twelve kinds of fruit, yielding its fruit every month. And the leaves of the tree are for the healing of the nations.

A pure river of the water of life flows from the throne of God and of the Lamb through the middle of the street in the New Jerusalem. On either side of the river grows the tree of life bearing its twelve kinds of fruit. This suggests God's ceaseless provision for every season.

There are a number of questions that arise from this verse.

WAS THERE ONE TREE OF LIFE OR MANY TREES?

This tree of life was on either side of the river. Interestingly, a number of Bible commentators take the reference to the "tree" as referring to many trees. Even though the Greek word is in the singular, they see this as a generic reference.

In other words, they assume that John really saw many trees, not merely one tree. Some Bible translations reflect this. For example, we read the following.

> Then it flowed down the middle of the city's main street. On each side of the river are trees that grow a different kind of fruit each month of the year (Revelation 22:2 CEV).

However, it is possible that John saw the river dividing and the water flowing on both sides of the one tree. It seems that a singular tree is in view here.

WHAT WAS THIS TREE OF LIFE?

The idea of a tree of life takes us all the way back to the beginning. The Bible says that created the tree of life and placed it in the midst of the Garden.

> The Lord God made all sorts of trees grow up from the ground—trees that were beautiful and that produced delicious fruit. In the middle of the garden he placed the tree of life . . . (Genesis 2:9 NLT).

When Adam and Eve disobeyed God and brought sin into the world, they lost all their access to the tree of life. The Bible says the following.

> Then the Lord God said, "Look, the human beings have become like us, knowing both good and evil. What if they reach out, take fruit from the tree of life, and eat it? Then they will live forever!" So the Lord God banished them from the Garden of Eden, and he sent Adam out to cultivate the ground from which he had been made. After sending them out, the Lord God stationed mighty cherubim to the east of the Garden of Eden. And he placed a flaming sword that flashed back and forth to guard the way to the tree of life (Genesis 3:22-24 NLT).

Now we discover that in the eternal city, the New Jerusalem, the residents will once again have access to a tree of life. And, since there will never be any more sin, this tree will be able to be eaten from for all eternity.

Instead of producing its fruit seasonally, this tree will perpetually produce its fruit. In fact, it will produce a new crop each month of the year. Therefore, the new earth will constantly be fruitful. This is another illustration of God's blessings in the world to come.

Since there will be no moon and no night, there will not be a lunar calendar to mark time. Evidently there will be some other type of method that will define the different months for the inhabitants. We are simply not told how there can be days and months without the cycle of the sun and the moon.

WILL IT BE NECESSARY TO EAT FROM THE TREE OF LIFE?

We noted that eating from the original tree of life in Eden could perpetuate life forever. Some Bible students think that this may also be the function of this tree of life in the New Jerusalem as well. In other words, in some unknown sense, it may exist to maintain the immortality of the inhabitants. However, this is only conjecture since nothing specific is said of the necessity of eating from this tree to remain immortal.

IN WHAT SENSE IS THE TREE FOR HEALING?

Since there will be no death in the new world, in what sense are the leaves of the tree for the healing of the nations?

Some Bible students suggest the "healing tree" is referring back to the Millennium. But this does not fit the fact the we are dealing with eternity, not a temporary kingdom upon the earth.

It is contended that the leaves, in some unexplained sense, promote wellbeing. They will provide healing from the conditions of the old creation. In fact, some understand the word 'healing' to mean "health-giving." Whether they promote wellbeing literally or symbolically is not clear.

WHO ARE THE NATIONS?

In the eternal state, we find that nations still exist. They are groups of people which are viewed according to their old creation divisions.

There will be a literal Millennium that will take place on the earth before the eternal state begins. From this thousand year period, there will be countless number of children born to those who initially enter.

These children will have the same ethnicity as their parents. Therefore, the simple answer to this question seems to be that the nations are the offspring who have trusted Christ during the Great Tribulation period. These people, who were born during the Millennium, have also put their trust in Christ.

Revelation 22:3 There will no longer be any curse. The throne of God and the Lamb will be in the city. His servants will worship Him.

Again we have the emphasis that the "curse" has been removed. The curse in view is the curse that God pronounced on the old creation at the Fall. In contrast to the fallen world in which we now live, God the Father and God the Son will be dwelling in the midst of the people.

Some Bible-students contend there will no longer be a curse because the tree of life will heal or redeem the nations.

What we do know is that God will have intimate fellowship with His people because this curse has now been lifted. Among other things, believers will occupy themselves serving God and the Lamb in the new earth.

The Greek word translated as "serve" seems to mean priestly service. Indeed, the other uses of this term in the book of Revelation has this idea.

> He lets us rule as kings and serve God his Father as priests (Revelation 1:6 CEV).

We later read of the song the redeemed will sing in heaven.

> Then they sang a new song, "You are worthy to receive the scroll and open its seals, because you were killed. And with

your own blood you bought for God people from every tribe, language, nation, and race. You let them become kings and serve God as priests, and they will rule on earth" (Revelation 5:9,10 CEV).

This answers one of the questions often asked about heaven, "What will we do there?"

WE HAVE ANOTHER INDICATION OF THE TRINITY

Though we will worship the Father and the Lamb, two distinct personages, they are both referred to as "Him." This is consistent with the rest of Scripture. While distinct from one another, God the Father and God the Son, along with God the Holy Spirit, are one being, one essence.

Revelation 22:4 And they shall see his face, and His name will be on their foreheads.

There are two question that this verse brings to us. In what sense shall we see the face of God who has no physical form? Also, will the name of God actually be written on our foreheads?

IN WHAT SENSE WILL WE SEE GOD'S FACE?

Those who have trusted in the promises of God are assured that they will be with Him for all eternity. In addition, believers will live in His holy presence. In fact, Jesus promised that they would "see God."

> Blessed are the pure in heart, for they will see God (Matthew 5:8 NIV).

For those who have been redeemed by Jesus, they will be changed. Indeed, everyone will be pure in heart, righteous, and holy.

WE SEE IMPERFECTLY NOW

Our ability to view God's glory is limited now. Some day, our imperfect view of God will change.

Dear friends, now we are children of God, and what we will be has not yet been made known. But we know that when Christ appears, we shall be like him, for we shall see him as he is (1 John 3:2 NIV).

While we are told that we will see God in the eternal realm the Bible does not tell us whether we will see all three members of the trinity, only two of them, or only one of them.

WHAT DOES IT MEAN, GOD'S NAME WILL BE WRITTEN ON OUR FOREHEADS?

We also discover from this verse that God's name will be written on the foreheads of those who will be with Him for all eternity. The mark is a sign of ownership. Indeed, we belong to Him and consequently we will reflect His glory forever.

PREVIOUS REFERENCES TO THE MARK OF GOD IN REVELATION

Three previous times in the Book of Revelation we find a reference to the mark of God upon believers.

> The one who is victorious I will make a pillar in the temple of my God. Never again will they leave it. I will write on them the name of my God and the name of the city of my God, the new Jerusalem, which is coming down out of heaven from my God; and I will also write on them my new name (Revelation 3:12 NIV).

In this context, a number of things are promised to the victorious ones. Symbolically, they will be made a pillar in God's temple. This is speaking of His holy presence. These believers are also guaranteed that they will never leave God's presence. This is another indication that they are eternally secure in Jesus Christ. In addition, the Lord will write His name upon them as well as the name of the Holy City, the New Jerusalem which will come down from heaven.

In the next instance, we find that the judgment on the earth is temporarily halted until the Lord places His protective seal, or mark, upon the foreheads of a certain group of people.

> Wait! Don't harm the land or the sea or the trees until we have placed the seal of God on the foreheads of his servants (Revelation 7:3 NLT).

This group of servants who were sealed are the 144,000. Later, this same group, who have been protected from the judgments, is seen standing with the Lord.

> Then I saw the Lamb standing on Mount Zion, and with him were 144,000 who had his name and his Father's name written on their foreheads (Revelation 14:1 NLT).

They have the name of the Lamb, the Lord Jesus, as well as the name of God the Father, on their foreheads.

In each instance, we find that the mark of God was a sign of identification, ownership and privilege. In addition, it indicated God's protection from all harm.

THE MARK OF THE BEAST PARODIES GOD'S MARK

We should also mention that earlier in the Book of Revelation we find that the second beast, the false prophet, will cause everyone upon the earth to take the mark of the first beast.

> He also caused everyone (small and great, rich and poor, free and slave) to obtain a mark on their right hand or on their forehead. Thus no one was allowed to buy or sell things unless he bore the mark of the beast—that is, his name or his number (Revelation 13:16,17 NET).

These marked people will belong to Satan in a similar manner as those marked by God will belong to God.

Revelation 22:5 There will be no more night, and they will not need any light from a lamp or light from the sun, because the Lord God will shine on them. They will rule [as kings] forever and ever.

The day/night cycle will no longer exist. The sun, which many pagans have historically worshipped, will no longer exist. The light of God will shine on them. In addition, we are told that the believers will rule with Him forever.

Several questions arise from this verse. For one thing, who will rule as kings?

WILL WE BE KINGS AND PRIEST OR A KINGDOM OF PRIESTS?
(REVELATION 1:6)

There is a question as to whether the Scripture says believers will rule as kings and priests or rather we will be like a kingdom, who are priests to God. The reason for this is that the Greek manuscripts have two different readings in Revelation 1:6 that addresses this issue.

KINGDOM OF PRIESTS

One possible reading in Revelation 1:6 is "kingdom of priests" or "he has appointed us as a kingdom, priests to God." A number of translations render it this way.

and has made us to be a kingdom and priests to serve his God and Father (Revelation 1:6 NIV).

and made us a kingdom, priests to his God and Father (Revelation 1:6 ESV).

and has appointed us as a kingdom, as priests serving his God and Father (Revelation 1:6 NET).

He has made us a Kingdom of priests for God his Father (Revelation 1:6 NLT).

Most modern English translations have this reading. If this is the correct reading, then the idea of believers ruling as kings seems to be eliminated.

Consequently, we will be a kingdom of believers who serve as priests to God.

KINGS AND PRIESTS

Those who contend that "kings and priests" is the correct reading consider this to be one of the great promises we have in Scripture. Indeed, believers will eventually rule as both kings and priests in the kingdom of God. In other words, we will all be kings. A few English translations reflect this.

> Christ loves us, and by his blood he set us free from our sins. He lets us rule as kings and serve God his Father as priests . . . (Revelation 1:5,6 CEV).

> and has made us kings and priests to His God and Father (Revelation 1:6 NKJV).

Therefore, if this is the correct reading of the text, believers will serve the Lord as priests as well as rule with him as kings. In other words, we will be servant kings.

The fact that this verse says that believers will "rule" forever seems to indicate that believers will indeed rule as "kings." In fact, the Greek word for rule can be translated "rule as a king."

EPILOGUE 22:6-22:21

Revelation 22:6 And he said to me, "These words are faithful and true. And the Lord, the God of the spirits of the prophets sent His messenger to show His servants that it is necessary for these things to take place soon.

We again have the emphasis that the words of the Lord are faithful and true.

WHAT ARE THE SPIRITS OF THE PROPHETS?

There is a unique phrase here. He is the God of "the spirits of the prophets." What does this phrase mean? Most likely, He is speaking of all of the previous prophets, both male and female. The Lord has been the One who has divinely inspired them.

EMPHASIS AGAIN ON SOON

Again, the Lord sends His messenger, or angel, to emphasize that these events will take place soon.

Revelation 22:7 (Behold! I am coming soon. Blessed is the one who obeys the words of the prophecy of this book).

This statement is parenthetical. The Lord Jesus Himself is now speaking.

The word which is translated "soon" or "quickly" suggests the idea that Christ could come at any moment. In other words, the Lord coming for His saints, at the rapture of the church, could appear suddenly without any visible signs preceding it.

This blessing recorded at the end of the Book repeats what was said at the very beginning.

> Blessed is the one who reads aloud the words of this prophecy, and blessed are those who hear, and who keep what is written in it, for the time is near (Revelation 1:3 ESV).

Lest we forget, the Book of Revelation is a prophecy. Those who heed the words of this prophetic book will receive one of the seven blessings that are mentioned in the Book (see 1:3; 14:13; 16:15; 19:9; 20:6; 22:7 and 22:14).

This is an important biblical truth. When we study the Book of Revelation it should not merely be to satisfy our curiosity. Instead, it should change the way in which we live our lives.

Revelation 22:8 I, John, am the one who is hearing and seeing all these things. And when I heard and saw them, I fell down [threw myself down] to worship at the feet of the angel who showed them to me.

This first statement is emphatic in the original Greek. John emphasizes that he actually heard and saw the things which he recorded. In other words, he is giving us eyewitness testimony.

In First John, we see the same sort of emphasis. John emphasized that he is writing down what he heard and saw.

> . . . Our ears have heard, our own eyes have seen, and our hands touched this Word. The one who gives life appeared! We saw it happen, and we are witnesses to what we have seen. Now we are telling you about this eternal life that was with the Father and appeared to us. We are telling you what we have seen and heard, so that you may share in this life with us . . . (1 John 1:1-3 CEV).

This is firsthand evidence, primary source testimony, from an eyewitness. John was in a position to testify about the earthly life of Jesus, as well as what the Lord allowed him to experience as documented in the Book of Revelation. Why? It is because he was an eyewitness to these events.

As can be imagined, John is overwhelmed by all that he saw. This caused him to throw himself down in a position of worship at the feet of the angelic being who had showed him these things.

Revelation 22:9 But he said to me, "No, see that you do not do this. For I am a fellow servant of God, just like you and your brothers

the prophets, as well as all who obey what is written in this book. You give worship only to God!"

The angel immediately corrects John. Worship of angels is forbidden! In fact, worship of any object, whether it be human, angelic, or something material, is strictly forbidden by the Lord. Interestingly, this is the second time this happened to John as recorded in the Book of Revelation.

> Then I fell down at his feet to worship him, but he said to me, "You must not do that! I am a fellow servant with you and your brothers who hold to the testimony of Jesus. Worship God." For the testimony of Jesus is the spirit of prophecy (Revelation 19:10 ESV).

John didn't seem to learn the lesson the first time.

Interestingly, the angel compares himself to humans including John, the other prophets, and those who obey the words of the Book of Revelation. While angels are a different order of being than humans, this passage, among others, makes it clear that we are all created beings. In other words, there is no linking the angels to God in the sense of an uncreated being. God is the Creator, all other beings have been created by Him.

Revelation 22:10 Then he said to me, "Do not seal up the words of the prophecy of this book. For the time is near.

Notice the emphasis: do NOT seal up these words for the time is at hand. This is in contrast to what the Lord told Daniel at the end of his book.

> But you, Daniel, close up these words and seal the book until the time of the end. Many will dash about, and knowledge will increase (Daniel 12:4 NET).

Daniel was told to seal up the book until the time of the end, John was specifically told not to do it. This is one of many indications that the Book of Revelation can be understood.

Again, the emphasis that the time is near. However, nowhere in Scripture do we find a set date for Jesus' return. In addition, we never find any definite promise that the coming of the Lord would take place within the lifetime of the Christians living in the first century.

Nevertheless, the possibility that the Lord would return at any moment was always present. Indeed, it is still present!

Revelation 22:11 The one who is doing harm let him continue to do harm. And the one who is vile, let him continue to be vile still. And the one who is righteous let him continue to live righteously. And the one who is holy let him continue to be holy."

Once more, we find the contrast of the righteous with the unrighteous. What is interesting is that there is no middle ground; a person is either righteous or unrighteous, either saved or lost.

There is a certain amount of irony in this verse with respect to the unbelievers.

Revelation 22:12 Behold! I am coming soon and My reward is with me to repay to each according to their deeds.

The word "behold" again appears in this section. This "attention-getter" is telling us that something important is about to be said.

Jesus is now speaking. When the Lord returns, each person will be repaid according to how they have lived and what they have done. This echoes what Paul told the Thessalonians.

> God is just: He will pay back trouble to those who trouble you and give relief to you who are troubled, and to us as well. This will happen when the Lord Jesus is revealed from heaven in blazing fire with his powerful angels. He will punish those

who do not know God and do not obey the gospel of our Lord Jesus. They will be punished with everlasting destruction and shut out from the presence of the Lord and from the glory of his might (2 Thessalonians 1:6-9 NIV).

The unbelievers will be repaid for their lack of belief as well as for their evil deeds.

Revelation 22:13 I am the Alpha and the Omega, the First and the Last, the Beginning and the End.

The Lord again asserts His divine authority; repeating His identity. We saw these claims in 1:8, and 21:16.

Revelation 22:14 Blessed are those who wash their robes [who keep His commands]. Their authority will be over the tree of life and they shall enter through the gates of the city.

Textual Issue: There is a variant reading in the Greek text here. The verse may read, "Blessed are those who keep His commands" or "Blessed are those who wash their robes."

Whatever reading one accepts, it emphasizes the importance of keeping His commandments. This is not advocating salvation by works.

The phrase, "Their authority will be over the tree of life" means that they can have access to the tree of life.

Those who have believed will be allowed to eat of the tree of life as well as to gain entrance into the Holy City.

Revelation 22:15 Outside are the dogs and the sorcerers and the sexually immoral, the murderers, the idol worshippers and every one who loves and practices falsehood.

Again there is the contrast between those inside the Holy City and those outside. The unbelievers are given a number of evil labels that sums up their character.

WHO ARE THE DOGS?

In Scripture, "dogs" can be a reference to the following: male prostitutes, Gentiles who are ceremonially unclean, and Judaizers. We read the following in Deuteronomy.

> You must not bring the earnings of a female prostitute or of a male prostitute into the house of the Lord your God to pay any vow, because the Lord your God detests them both (Deuteronomy 23:18 NIV).

The Hebrew word translated "male prostitute" is actually "of a dog." It was a slang term for the male prostitute.

Jesus used the term dogs to refer to Gentiles who, to the Jews, were ceremonially unclean.

> He answered, "It isn't right to take the children's bread and throw it to their dogs" (Matthew 15:26 HCSB).

In this instance, the Lord used a form of the word for dogs that referred to little dogs or household pets.

Finally, Paul uses the term "dogs" to refer to the Judaizers.

> Beware of dogs! Beware of those who do evil things. Beware of those who insist on circumcision (Philippians 3:2 God's Word).

In this context in Revelation, it most likely refers to unbelievers in general.

SORCERERS AND LIARS

The sorcerers are those who practice "magic arts." In other words, they are involved in the occult. John had singled them out elsewhere.

> Little children, guard yourselves from idols (1 John 5:21 NET).

He also targeted the liars.

> Who is the liar but the person who denies that Jesus is the
> Christ? This one is the antichrist: the person who denies the
> Father and the Son. Everyone who denies the Son does not
> have the Father either. The person who confesses the Son
> has the Father also (1 John 2:22,23 NET).

Revelation 22:16 "I, Jesus, I have sent my messenger to give you this message for the churches. I am Root and the Offspring of David. I am the bright Morning Star."

This statement of Jesus is emphatic in the original Greek. The Lord "Himself" has sent His angel with this message to the churches.

DAVID'S OFFSPRING

The Lord speaks of Himself as the "Root and the Offspring of David." Interestingly, we see both His humanity and deity emphasized.

Indeed, as to Jesus' deity, He is David's Creator. On the other hand, as to the Lord's humanity, He is an Israelite, a descendant of David, David's Son.

Jesus is, therefore, the rightful heir of the Davidic throne.

THE TWO APPEARANCES OF CHRIST

The bright morning star appears in the sky before the sun rises. As this bright Morning Star, Jesus Christ will return first to bring the church, the true believers in Christ, back to the Father's house. This event is known as the "rapture of the church."

Later, the Lord will return to the earth as the Sun of Righteousness with healing in His wings. We find this recorded by the prophet Malachi.

> The Sun of Righteousness will rise with healing in his wings
> for you people who fear my name (Malachi 4:2 God's Word).

The Son is also the sun!

Revelation 22:17 And the Spirit and the bride say, "Come." Let anyone who hears this say, "Come." Let anyone who is thirsty come. Let anyone who desires drink from the water of life free of charge.

This is the only time in the Bible we see the Spirit and the bride linked in this way.

There are two basic ways of understanding this verse.

First, it may be a gospel appeal where we find the Holy Spirit, the bride, and the hearer urging the thirsty to come to Jesus Christ for salvation. This threefold witness testifies of the need to come to Jesus for spiritual life.

Some view the first use of the word "come' as a prayer for the return of Christ to the earth. The final two uses of the word are direct invitations to unbeliever to come to Christ for the water of life. This is a reference to the salvation of their soul. In doing so, they will then be ready for His return.

For us, the important thing to note is that the invitation to come to Jesus Christ is still being offered to a lost world!

Revelation 22:18 And I myself declare to everyone who hears the words of prophecy written in this book: If anyone adds anything to what is written here, God will add to that person the plagues described in this book.

This warning is emphatic in the Greek!

The warning given here is similar to what we read elsewhere in Scripture.

> Do not add to what I command you and do not subtract from it, but keep the commands of the Lord your God that I give you (Deuteronomy 4:2 NIV).

The Lord has given His Word to the human race. It should never be tampered with!

WHAT IT DOES NOT MEAN?

Some have mistakenly assumed that this is a warning to copyists not to change the text of Scripture. While this certainly should not be done by those copying the sacred text, this is not what is in view here.

The Lord is warning those who attempt to add to what God has already revealed to the human race. The Book of Revelation completes the revelation of God to humanity. Nothing more needs to be said.

Revelation 22:19 And if anyone removes any of the words from this book of prophecy, God will remove that person's share in the tree of life and in the Holy City that are described in this book.

We have a similar warning as found in the previous verse. Nobody has the right to take away from what the Lord has revealed to humanity. God has spoken and we must obey His Word. Nothing needs to be added but certainly none of us should attempt to change or take away what the Bible so clearly teaches. The penalty for purposely doing so is everlasting separation from the Lord.

Textual Issue: There is an interesting variant reading in the text here. Is it the "tree of life" or the "book of life" that the Lord will remove their share from? The King James Version reads as follows.

> And if any man shall take away from the words of the book of this prophecy, God shall take away his part out of the book of life, and out of the holy city, and from the things which are written in this book (KJV).

The New King James Bible reads something similar.

> and if anyone takes away from the words of the book of this prophecy, God shall take away his part from the Book

of Life, from the holy city, and from the things which are written in this book (NKJV).

In contrast, the NIV, like almost every modern English translation, reads as follows.

And if anyone takes words away from this scroll of prophecy, God will take away from that person any share in the tree of life and in the Holy City, which are described in this scroll (NIV).

So which is right? Is it Book of Life or tree of life?

Simply stated, the reading "book of life" has no Greek manuscript support here! The "tree of life" is the correct reading.

If this is so, then how did this incorrect reading get into the text?

This came about when the Dutch Greek scholar Erasmus was putting together the first printed text of the Greek New Testament. Unfortunately, the last six verses were missing in Erasmus' Greek copies of the Book of Revelation. Undaunted, he translated these verses back into Greek from the Latin Vulgate. As a result of this he created seventeen textual variants which are not found in any Greek manuscripts! The one we are looking at is the most notorious of the bunch. It was Erasmus' Greek text that was the basis for the Greek text behind the King James Version. This is how this reading entered into English translations.

How did this other reading originate in the Latin? The best answer seems to be a transposition of two letters in the Latin manuscripts. The form of the word for "tree" in Latin in this passage is the word lingo. The Latin word for "book" is **libro**. Note that there is only a two-letter difference. This two-letter difference seems to account for an accidental alteration in some Latin manuscripts of Revelation.

In addition, each of these phrases, "book of life" as well as "tree of life" are expressions found in the Book of Revelation. Consequently, this is probably why it was unnoticed by Erasmus as well as those who translated the King James Version.

The sad thing about all of this is that the reading "book of life" hides a wonderful biblical truth. Indeed, humanity will be once again be able to eat from "the tree of life." Recall the original reason for the banishment of Adam and Eve from the Garden. They were not allowed to eat from the tree of life lest they live forever in a sinful situation.

Now we find that in God's eternal program, the banishment of humans from the tree of life at the beginning now comes full circle. Indeed, what was lost at the beginning is now restored to the believers at the very end. And it is restored forever!

Revelation 22:20 The one who is testifying to all these things says, "Yes, I am coming soon!" Amen! Come, Lord Jesus!

Again the Lord emphasizes the fact of His return.

John echoes the heartfelt cry of every believer, "Come, Lord Jesus!"

Revelation 22:21 May the grace of the Lord Jesus be with all of you.

These final words of benediction are addressed to believers. Indeed, we cannot receive the grace of God unless we have first received the mercy of God. Mercy is not getting the penalty that we deserve for our sins. In other words, it is not justice. If we received justice, then we would suffer for our own sins.

Grace is getting something we do not deserve. It is God's unmerited favor. God's riches are given to us when we place our faith in Jesus Christ.

In light of the final words of the Book or Revelation, may the reader experience the riches of God's grace as we live out our lives in a world that so desperately needs Jesus Christ.

About The Author

Don Stewart is a graduate of Biola University and Talbot Theological Seminary (with the highest honors).

Don is a best-selling and award-winning author having authored, or co-authored, over seventy books. This includes the best-selling *Answers to Tough Questions*, with Josh McDowell, as well as the award-winning book *Family Handbook of Christian Knowledge: The Bible*. His various writings have been translated into over thirty different languages and have sold over a million copies.

Don has traveled around the world proclaiming and defending the historic Christian faith. He has also taught both Hebrew and Greek at the undergraduate level and Greek at the graduate level.

**OUR NEXT BOOK IN THE AFTERLIFE SERIES:
VOLUME 5**

Hell

This last book in our series deals with the difficult topic of hell. We will answer such questions as:

Is there really a place called hell?

Who goes there?

Why do people have to go to hell?

And how can a person avoid going to hell?

We will look at these, as well as other related questions about the final state of the wicked, as we wrap up our series on the afterlife.

While this is the longest book in our series, we realize that much more could be said about this subject. Indeed, there are many questions concerning this topic that can be further developed. If necessary, in the future, we will go into additional detail on this most difficult of subjects.

Made in the USA
San Bernardino, CA
24 January 2020